W9-CYZ-910

THE GRAIL MOVEMENT
AND AMERICAN CATHOLICISM, 1940-1975

NOTRE DAME STUDIES IN AMERICAN CATHOLICISM

Sponsored by the
Charles and Margaret Hall Cushwa Center
for the Study of American Catholicism

The Grail Movement and American Catholicism, 1940-1975

ALDEN V. BROWN

University of Notre Dame Press
Notre Dame, Indiana

Library of Congress Cataloging-in-Publication Data

Brown, Alden V.
  The Grail movement and American Catholicism,
1940-1975.

  (Notre Dame studies in American Catholicism)
  Bibliography: p.
  Includes index.
  1. Grail movement (Catholic)—History.   2. Catholic
Church—United States—History—20th century.
I. Title. II. Series.
BX809.G72B76 1989   267'.442   87-40615
ISBN 0-268-01015-3

Contents

Acknowledgments

I want to express my sincere and great thanks to the women of the Grail for facilitating this study: the community at Loveland, Ohio, which provided me with working and living space, help with the Grail's papers, and much friendly support during my initial three months stay and several return visits; and scores of other members visiting Grailville who volunteered their time to recount their experiences and share their perspectives on the movement.

Special thanks are due to Eileen Schaeffler, Mary Cecilia Kane, and Dorothy Rasenberger who reviewed the manuscript in its initial stage. Their interest in deepening the Grail's self-understanding was admirable and their criticisms were extremely helpful.

I am also greatly indebted to Dr. Lydwine van Kersbergen, the leader of the Grail in the United States from 1940 to 1962, for her generosity in granting an extended interview in Holland in the summer of 1980. The vision of Jacques van Ginneken and that of Dr. van Kersbergen herself came alive during those days. Appreciation is also due the many other Grail members I met in Holland, especially those who provided hospitality at de Tiltenberg, the Grail's first training center, in Vogelensang.

Other persons associated with the Grail were also most helpful. Mr. Daniel Kane, who with his wife, Mary Cecilia, has lived next door to Grailville since 1946 and was actively involved with the movement even before that time, offered rich insights into the Grail as well as other early Catholic Action groups. Special mention must also be made of two long-time priest friends of the Grail, Monsignor James Coffey of Bay Shore, New York, and Monsignor George Fogarty of Flushing, New York.

This study began as a doctoral dissertation at Union Theological Seminary in New York, under the direction of Professor Robert T. Handy, now emeritus. The praises of Dr. Handy have been sung by a large chorus of students and colleagues. I happily add my voice. I cannot imagine being blessed with a more honest, able, and friendly mentor.

At a later stage, my manuscript was read by Philip Gleason of the University of Notre Dame. Professor Gleason, I think, is the most acute student of American Catholicism we have. His comments were invaluable.

Finally, a word of thanks for friends and family — especially my father and my late mother, and my wife Maureen, who has helped me to write better and to live better.

Introduction

At this writing the term "lay apostolate" has not been heard in the American Catholic Church for more than fifteen years. Its predecessor, "Catholic Action," needless to say, has also faded into the mists of the pre-Vatican II Church. Though the term and many of the organizations which embodied it are now in eclipse, they ought not be forgotten. For the lay apostolate was a serious, if flawed, attempt to foster the engagement of the Church with the modern world in a more constructive way than had previously been known, that is, through the prism of a deeply felt and theologically informed Catholic faith. It also played a significant role in the late stages of the evolution of American Catholicism from immigrant community to full participant, for better or worse, in American society.[1]

This book tells the story of the Grail movement, which entered the arena of American Catholic Action in 1940. For the better part of three decades the Grail provided a significant number of laywomen (and some men as well) with an attractive alternative to the conventional Catholicism of their time.

The attractiveness and power of the Grail resided principally, I think, in two areas: 1) its sense of the need for and the value of a distinct and autonomous role for the laywomen in the Church; and 2) the breadth (though not necessarily the depth) of its vision in regard to the Church's engagement with the modern world.

From its inception as the Society of the Women of Nazareth in Holland in the early 1920s, the Grail worked at creating a community of *free* women—free, that is, to nurture and exercise apostolic holiness without the restrictions of the cloistered or semicloistered religious life; and free, as far as possible, from clerical (male) control. This proved no easy task, of course. There was always someone to ask, "Why are these women not nuns?" or, "What is the canonical standing of this group?" For the most part, however, the Grail succeeded in maintaining its autonomy and in attracting women delighted to discover an avenue which might lead them to a deeper and more active Catholic life but not to the convent.

Besides this relative autonomy for women in the Church the Grail offered a broad range of opportunities for developing the "womanly virtues" which the movement held indispensable for the renewal of modern society. Unlike most other lay groups, the Grail consistently refused to confine itself to one or another apostolic work. Its founder, the Dutch Jesuit Jacques van Ginneken, said the Grail's goal was to be "the conversion of the world," and the so-called Catholic Revival which, as will be seen, also played a large role in shaping the Grail's outlook, hoped for "a new Christendom"; the modern secular spirit could not be permitted to undo the work of faith in ordinary life or in those areas properly called cultural. The Grail therefore called women, who were by nature "the keepers of the gracious customs and fundamental standards of the race," to a variety of tasks. It welcomed and trained artists, social workers, farmers, nurses, teachers, and secretaries, and sent them out as lay apostles in their own countries and in many foreign lands.

The pressure of history, of which Vatican II was a significant part, eventually moved the Grail to question the form and practical consequences of these major elements of its life. One may see immediately that the roster of apostolic vocations just given does not include theologians, businesswomen, or politicians. Most of the 1960s, in fact, were taken up with an agonizing re-evaluation of the Grail's structure and goals—a re-evaluation which included a nearly complete abandonment of the movement's prevailing views on the nature and role of women. Today's Grail nevertheless works at three interrelated priorities which still bear a clear resemblance to the formulations of the past: Woman, Search for God, and Liberation; or in another version: living faith, full potential of women, and work for transformation of the world into a universal society of justice, love, and peace.

There are at present some two hundred American Grail members. They belong to "an international movement of women rooted in Christian faith" which is active in approximately twenty countries around the world. The Grail uses the expression "rooted in Christian faith" because, although most of its members are Roman Catholics, the movement is now "open to the participation of women of other traditions and welcomes association with all people who are engaged in spiritual search and the struggle for human liberation."[2]

The history of the Grail in other parts of the globe remains for the most part outside the scope of this book. However, the origins and early growth of the movement in Europe are essential to an understanding of the spirit it brought to the American scene. Chapter 1 therefore examines them in some detail. Here one meets the intense and all embracing vision of Jacques van Ginneken and an enthusiastic youth movement which in time ran afoul of the equal but opposite enthusiasms of the Third Reich. The remaining chapters trace the Grail's story in America: its initial place in the lay apostolate, its rapid expansion in the 1950s, its tumultuous "coming of age" in the 1960s, and its recent resolve to go on with the task of refining and transforming its original inspiration. An Afterword ventures an angle of interpretation on the Grail's fortunes and those of the Catholic Revival/lay apostolate era in general.

1

The Rich Roman Life

The Second Vatican Council (1962-1965) declared that the Church carries on its fundamental mission of bringing the world into relationship with Christ through *all* its members: the Christian vocation is by its very nature a vocation to the apostolate. Lay people, therefore, sharing in the priestly, prophetic, and royal office of Christ, have a proper and active role to play in the Church's life and work.[1]

It had not always been so. The affirmations of Vatican II in fact followed upon a long struggle over the place of the layperson in Roman Catholicism. The Church in the Middle Ages and the Reformation created a largely negative and constricted image of the laity. Pope Boniface VIII, for example, faced with the "extortionist" emperors, kings, and princes of Europe, declared in 1296 that "antiquity shows us that the laity has always been exceedingly hostile to the clergy."[2] And the sixteenth-century Reformers' insistence on "the priesthood of all believers" caused popes and theologians to speak of the laity with scant theological reference; Robert Bellarmine, typically, "did not say one word about the laity's part in directly forwarding the work of God's kingdom or of its place in the Church as a spiritual organism."[3]

In the nineteenth century, however, the laity slowly began to come into their own. With most of Europe's Catholic monarchies in decline and power shifting into more democratic, secular, and frequently anticlerical hands, some proposed that Catholic citizens—rather than prelates—might be the Church's most effective instruments for influencing the social order.

The initial response of the papacy to this line of thinking

was not encouraging. Gregory XVI (1831–1846) and Pius IX (1846–1878) were not concerned to squelch the lay voice as such; indeed Pius XI was well pleased with the likes of Louis Veuillot, whose newspaper, *L'Univers*, supported him unswervingly. But these popes would have no truck with the growing number of laymen, and their clerical supporters, who went so far as to advocate an actual rapprochement with liberal democracy. The Church, the pontiffs maintained, should hold fast to its temporal authority, attempt to protect its freedom by direct, clerically exercised diplomatic ties, and, in general, wait upon the new Europe to come to terms with the papacy's spiritual power. To make their points unmistakably clear, Gregory XVI and Pius IX took concrete actions. Rejecting the concept of "a free Church in a free state," the former condemned the Abbé Felicité de Lammenais, who called for an alliance of the Holy See with "the People" rather than with governments; and Pius IX, hard on the heels of the liberally oriented congresses of laity and clergy at Munich (1860) and Malines (1864), issued his celebrated "Syllabus of Errors," which rejected the proposition that "the Roman Pontiff can and ought to reconcile and harmonize himself with progress, liberalism, and with modern civilization." The definition of papal infallibility at the First Vatican Council (1870) was but the capstone of the papacy's position.[4]

The liberal Catholics of the mid-nineteenth century nevertheless laid a groundwork for the future. Their call for freedom of scholarly inquiry endured, and so did their notion that the laity could and should take an active role in the Church's mission. One of their theological essays, at least, John Henry Newman's *On Consulting the Faithful in Matters of Doctrine*, became a rallying point for later generations.

The pontificate of Leo XIII (1878–1903) made room at last for the significant development of lay initiative. Leo's support of France's Third Republic was accompanied by a call for a "militant Christian citizenship," and his concern for the plight of the working class (expressed most vividly in the encyclical *Rerum Novarum*) moved him to encourage associations of Catholic workingmen. Leo's teaching, especially in regard to the right of private property, was ringed round with warnings about divergence from the views of the hierarchy. But engagement, rather

than Pius IX's noncooperation, was its clear message to the
Church. In this new atmosphere lay activity increased considerably and began to diversify. Some Catholics entered the political
arena, as in Germany where they constituted the majority of the
Center party; others, like Albert de Mun, founder of the Association Catholique de la Jeunesse Française (ACJF) in 1886, organized outside politics but with the patent intention of apply-
ing Catholic principles to social problems.[5]

The reign of Leo's successor, Pius X (1903–1914), was a
mixed blessing for lay involvement in Church and society. It has
been argued that Pius X was the "true begetter" of the modern
lay movement, but this judgment does not stand up to the facts
in any positive sense.[6] It is true that this pope called for "select
Catholic troops" to fight anti-Christian civilization and restore
Jesus Christ to the family, the schools, and all of society. But
Pius X exercised his rule in much the same manner as Pius IX—
that is, he encouraged lay action only when it suited his pur-
poses. While tolerating Charles Maurras' right-wing Action
Française, for example, he condemned Marc Sangnier, whose
Le Sillon moved beyond de Mun's ACJF to become a force on
France's political left. Pius X removed all doubt about his think-
ing in the encyclical *Pascendi Dominici Gregis*, which condemned
Modernism. There he called the attention of his fellow bishops
to "the appearance of that pernicious doctrine which would make
the laity a factor in the progress of the Church."[7]

And yet the strictures of Pius X were critical for the advancement of the lay apostolate. Because of them movements were
conceived which sought to avoid political and theological confrontation with the Vatican without, however, surrendering the
role of the layperson in either the Church or society. The baptismal dignity of the individual Catholic, and his membership
in the Church as the Mystical Body of Christ, became their primary focus. From this sense of personal and corporate identity,
it was hoped, a deep and unassailable commitment to society
would flow. This more "religious" approach, which was born
of prudence but also rested on the sincere conviction that social
renewal could only arise from spiritual wellsprings, became the
norm for the Catholic lay apostolate in the twentieth century.

Such movements began to appear during the brief reign of

Benedict XV (1914–1922). Best known among them, perhaps, was the Jeunesse Syndicaliste, later the Jeunesse Ouvrière Chrétienne (JOC). Founded by the Belgian abbé Joseph Cardijn, the JOC introduced the idea, considered revolutionary by some, that laypersons—workingmen—be trained as apostles to their peers.[8]

Less known in its early years was the Society of the Women of Nazareth—to be known in time as the Grail movement. Like the JOC it flourished worldwide, and it exemplified even more clearly the new trend toward the spiritual training of laypersons for the task of re-Christianizing Western society. Jacques van Ginneken, its founder, did not fail to notice the social ills of his time—especially the situation of new arrivals from the countryside in the cities of Holland. But he was above all a director of souls.

Born a brewer's son in Oudenbosch, the Netherlands, in 1877, Jacques van Ginneken belonged to a small circle of Dutch Catholics who believed that the time was ripe for an aggressive, apostolically minded Catholicism. He was surely one of this group's most determined and enthusiastic members, for he insisted that World War I itself could be understood not only as a punishment for Europe's sins but as a "great blessing" for both Church and society. In the ensuing "elbow of time," as he called it, the West might come to grips with its profound spiritual confusion (which had caused the war) and allow itself to be regenerated by means of the Catholic faith. Van Ginneken was decidedly hopeful because he believed, moreover, that he could discern "a spiritual current passing through the modern world which leads to Catholicism."[9]

If the Church were to seize upon the "unlimited possibilities" of the "elbow of time," however, it would itself have to experience a change of heart. Catholics were needed, van Ginneken said, "who give themselves to God in the midst of the world—who precisely there, lead a life radically different from what the world expects, people who bring the Cross of Christ back among humanity."[10] But he could find few such people around him. Dutch Catholics had survived a wave of Calvinist resentment following the restoration of their hierarchy in 1853, and they had made great strides in the realm of civil freedom in the prewar years: Catholic labor unions had flourished and state subsidy was won for Catholic schools. But these advances (which culminated in the election of a Catholic prime minister after universal suffrage was adopted in 1918) had come at a price, it seemed to van Ginneken. Catholics had acquiesced in the organization of Dutch society along strictly confessional lines. Like the Reformed and liberal (secular) segments of the population, they maintained their own school system, political and workers' organizations, newspapers, and youth groups. Within the confines of this subculture, Dutch Catholics were preoccupied with protecting their hard-won rights and their faith. They perpetuated, van Ginneken said, a "fear Catholicism."[11]

Catholics, then, were to enlarge their horizons. But how? Van Ginneken exhibited no interest in political solutions or in efforts to foster interconfessional cooperation (which the Dutch bishops discouraged anyway). He proposed instead a vigorous missionary ideal—in his words, nothing less than "the conversion of the world." Catholics were first to be re-educated in the truly catholic, universalist dimensions of their tradition. Then non-Catholics, some of whom might be converted to the Church, would recognize Catholicism's true and palpable love of the whole world and catch its spirit. Social renewal and unity would follow, resting on secure spiritual foundations.

Van Ginneken carried something of this outlook from his youth, it seems. After earning a doctorate in Dutch language and literature at the University of Leiden, and after his ordination as a Jesuit priest in 1910, he looked forward to putting it into practice. An especially strong stimulus to do so came from the lay author and publisher, Gerard Brom, whose lecture of September 24, 1913, van Ginneken later called a milestone in the development of a more aggressive and irenic Dutch Catholicism. The young Jesuit was especially taken with Brom's statement that it would be suicide for the Church not to accept the laity as apostles and "fully accredited representatives of Catholic culture."[12] By March 1919, when Brom assembled a Committee for the Conversion of the Netherlands, van Ginneken (who presided at the meeting) had already launched his first missionary project, his Conferences on Catholicism for Non-Catholics.

In these conferences—they took the form of eight-day retreats or "reunions"—van Ginneken set himself the large task of
demonstrating that the Catholic Church was neither unfamiliar
with nor unsympathetic to contemporary religious longings.
Even though these feelings led many to occultism, spiritism, or
theosophy, they could find a home in Catholicism. Speaking in
the first person (as he did frequently, struggling to overcome
his own Dutch Catholic reticence), van Ginneken said that in
his conferences he always sought to do justice

> . . . to the most diverse orientations and variations with a view
> to allowing an all-encompassing spaciousness and a catholic,
> worldwide breadth: I tried to pursue Jesus, the unattainable, who
> became ALL for ALL, with a stammering prayer to be allowed to
> do MUCH for MANY.[13]

The meeting of the Committee for the Conversion of the
Netherlands (which adopted as its motto, "Work or Leave") apparently inspired van Ginneken to proceed directly toward his
primary goal, the encouraging of Catholics to learn and take up
the vocation of apostle. For within the next two years, he established four communities of laypeople: the Society of the Women
of Bethany, the Order of the Crusaders of St. John, the Knights
of St. Willibrord, and the Society of the Women of Nazareth.

Three of these groups failed to sustain van Ginneken's
dreams. The Society of the Women of Bethany, situated at Bloemendaal, near Haarlem, delivered catechetical instruction to the
children of urban working-class families. Within the society a
number of contemplatives trained other women for their work
in the city and welcomed them back for periods of spiritual re-
freshment. A dispute arose, however, between Bloemendaal's
parish priest, who emphasized the contemplative, and van Ginneken, who was clearly more interested in a modern synthesis
of contemplation and action. As a result van Ginneken was removed by his Jesuit superiors in 1924 and the Women of Bethany
later became a religious community of the conventional type.
The Order of the Crusaders of St. John, a community of laymen,
founded a number of apprentice schools for adolescent boys in
Rijswick, near the Hague. Van Ginneken's association with this
group also came to an end after a short period, for reasons which

are not really clear. And the Knights of St. Willibrord, a community of married men and women who were to evangelize Holland's better families, survived only for a brief time.[14]

The Society of the Women of Nazareth, however, became van Ginneken's great success. He remained its teacher and guide until his death in 1945, by which time it had evolved, almost definitively, into the Grail movement.[15]

Established intentionally on the Feast of All Saints, November 1, 1921, the Society of the Women of Nazareth was to engage in work parallel to that of the Crusaders of St. John: assisting teenage girls to overcome the dangers of their working environment and move ahead into the professions open to them. But at the outset the society consisted of just four members and was forced, therefore, to set its apostolic ambitions aside for a time. With a young Belgian, Margaret van Gilse, as leader, the first four young women took up residence at Amersfoort and opened a small sewing center in order to support themselves. After a short while they moved on to Overvoorde, a country house on a wooded property in Rijswick where Jacques van Ginneken had begun to hold his conferences for non-Catholics. There they thought about the future and spent their free time serving as "guardian angels" for those who came to listen to their mentor.[16]

The next several years brought the Women of Nazareth a variety of difficulties: the proximity of the Crusaders of St. John (they lived on the same wooded land) gave rise to some uncharitable local comment; word that the Women of Nazareth wore a distinctive garb inside but not outside their house reached the ears of Monsignor A. J. Callier, the bishop of the diocese of Haarlem, and the prelate asked that the situation be clarified by means of a written rule; Father van Ginneken, who was appointed to a professorship at the newly established Catholic university at Nijmegen in 1923, was absent for a year's time and another priest came to take his place; financial problems dictated another move, to de Voorde, a smaller house on the Rijswick grounds; and finally, the society failed to grow appreciably—after five years it had only six members.

Suddenly, however, things took a turn for the better. In what was referred to by their fellow undergraduates as "the kidnapping of the Sabine women," four of van Ginneken's students at Nijmegen interrupted their studies and withdrew to de Voorde. A retreat of initiation was held, four of the first six young women made formal dedications to the society, and plans were formulated for a number of apostolic ventures. In May 1927 Bishop Callier was sufficiently impressed with the society to give his approval *"sine fine"* to its constitution (which van Ginneken, taking the *Spiritual Exercises* of St. Ignatius Loyola as his model, had hastily drawn up in response to the bishop's earlier request).

The Women of Nazareth soon began to work at their several projects. The goal of the former Nijmegen women was especially ambitious: the establishment of a university for women in the Dutch East Indies. Inspired by van Ginneken's ideas about the compatibility of Catholicism and all human aspirations, they intended to base their school's curriculum on Oriental history and thought and therefore set about acquainting themselves with the languages and culture of Indonesia. At the same time, other members of the society studied local conditions at first hand, taking positions in Holland's chocolate factories and forming clubs of young workingwomen.

In April 1928 the death of Bishop Callier led to the most serious problem the Women of Nazareth had faced so far. Callier's successor, Monsignor J. D. J. Aengenent, a sociologist preoccupied with the de-Christianization of his largely urban diocese, insisted that the society devote itself exclusively to a formal youth movement for Catholic girls and young women. He told the Women of Nazareth that their missions were to be at home; they would have to abandon their plans for the Far East, their work with van Ginneken's retreats, their factory jobs, and the clubs they had established.

The Women of Nazareth were taken aback, to say the least, by the bishop's terms, but Jacques van Ginneken counseled them to comply. Obedience to authority, the Jesuit said, would surely yield unforeseen benefits. And so, on March 1, 1929, the demanded youth movement, called the Grail (after the Eucharistic cup of medieval legend), was begun.[17]

The Women of Nazareth soon realized that far from being diverted from their basic aims, they had been presented with an undreamed of opportunity to advance the cause of the apostolate of the laity. The statutes of the youth movement, first of all, made it clear that the Grail was not to be merely another social work agency; it was to "organize all Catholic adolescent girls, not only to protect them from dangers, but primarily to train them to be fervent Catholic women who are an example in everything."[18] This formula meshed neatly with Jacques van Ginneken's announced goal of "the conversion of the world," and from this moment the training of laywomen for participation in the Church's mission became the central work of his disciples. Secondly, after little more than a year's time Bishop Aengenent decreed that the Grail was to be the *only* Catholic young women's movement in the diocese of Haarlem, "directed according to the aims of the Grail under the leadership of the Women of Nazareth."[19] Aengenent's policy, which undercut the control of the local clergy, was short-lived. But at the time it was a significant endorsement of something else the Women of Nazareth had been taught by van Ginneken: that they were to function as a movement of women under the immediate direction of women themselves.

With strong episcopal sanction the Grail spread rapidly. By 1931 it had twenty-three urban centers, seventeen outposts in rural areas, six hundred and forty leaders, and eight thousand members. The movement was coordinated from de Tiltenberg, the Women of Nazareth's training center located in Vogelenzang, a small town south of Amsterdam.

A complex organizational structure was rapidly developed for the Grail, with each location, function, and degree of involvement marked off by a distinctive uniform or badge. The movement was also distinguished by its bold contemporary style. Its centers were furnished "in a modern way with daring use of colors," and its members recognized each other with the enthusiastic greeting, "Excelsior, Alleluia, Forward!" This style was shocking to some whose roots in Dutch Catholic sobriety ran deep, but it was consciously designed to appeal to those who might be ready to answer the challenge of modern life with a proud and self-confident Catholicism, especially the young.[20]

The Grail attracted its greatest public attention with a series of massive dramatic presentations. At Easter 1931 in Amsterdam's Olympic Stadium, thirty-two thousand people saw three thousand actors, girls drawn from all over Holland, in "The Royal

Road of the Cross," a pageant based on the twelfth chapter of *The Imitation of Christ*. The "Pinksterzegen" (Pentecost play) was performed in the same place in 1932 by ten thousand girls. Based on the hymn "Veni Sancte Spiritus," it featured fifteen speaking choruses and reached its climax in the promise of all those participating to win the world for Christ through love and sacrifice.

Most observers were impressed with these and the Grail's many other public demonstrations of faith, which included processions on ember days and the Feast of All Saints and "campaigns" carried out under such slogans as "Spreading Joy and Goodness," "Charming, Chic, and Catholic," and "Who Shall Find a Valiant Woman?" The followers of Joseph Cardijn demurred, considering the mass dramas "schools of vanity" which diverted attention from the actual suffering of working people. But their complaint was swept aside. It was a time for youth movements — the Boy Scouts and Girl Guides in Britain, for example, and closer to home, the Young Socialists; and it was time for a new spirit which transcended (and yet promised) concrete results. The Grail soon emerged as the quintessential expression of "the rich Roman life" of Dutch Catholicism.[21] They gave color to the times, these "Grail girls in ther vivid, rainbow-assorted uniforms fluttering in the breeze . . . [with] their high-spirited enthusiasm devoid of self-consciousness or fear. . . ."[22]

The Grail soon found itself invited to other countries. It opened a house in Berlin in 1931, and in January 1932, before an audience of eighteen thousand in the city's Sportspalast, presented an Advent drama, the "Gralspiele Rorate." Eight hundred Dutch and four hundred German girls took part. England was next. The Women of Nazareth, known there as the Ladies of the Grail, established a headquarters in Sloane Street, Hyde Park, London, in 1933, and in October of that year five hundred English Grail members performed the morality play *Everyman* in the Royal Albert Hall.

By the early 1930s an apostolic role for the laity had begun to win a real measure of acceptance, under the rubric "Catholic Action." Pope Pius XI (1922–1939) had become its principal champion, encouraging the laity in his very first encyclical, *Ubi Arcano*, bestowing his blessing on Cardijn's Jeunesse Ouvrière Chrétienne in 1925, and in 1928 supplying Catholic Action with its classic definition: "nothing less than the participation of the laity in the apostolate of the hierarchy."[23] The pope's favorable attitude, however, did not settle the issue of the laity; his definition in fact gave rise to several new questions. Where the political interests of the Church were involved (as in Italy where the papacy encouraged the laity first to support and later to oppose the Mussolini regime), Catholic Action clearly required a "mandate" and close supervision.[24] But what of other "action by Catholics," the publication of an independent journal like *Commonweal* in the United States, for example?[25] And what of such groups as the Grail, which pursued obviously spiritual goals but worked in close cooperation with the bishop of Haarlem? Many laypeople in the 1930s grappled with the question of their status, either on the basis of personal scruples or as a result of hierarchical probing. In the Grail's case it was the latter. Suspicions which surfaced in Rome in 1934 prompted the movement to accept affiliation with the youth section of the International Catholic Women's Leagues and the official title, "Feminine Youth Movement for Catholic Action, the Grail." But, as frequently happened following a gesture of loyalty, no real changes in course were demanded. With the continued support of Haarlem's bishops (Monsignor J. Huibers, Monsignor Aengenent's successor, even arranged an audience with Pius XI in 1936), the Grail continued to grow. In 1935 it boasted 15,000 members, and in 1940 claimed more than 21,000.[26]

In 1932, as the Grail's impact in Holland and Germany became apparent, Jacques van Ginneken was prevailed upon to supply a fuller statement of his vision of the lay apostolate and of the movement he had inspired. He obliged with thirty-two lectures called "The Grail as a Young Woman's Movement" and a further thirty-two conferences known afterward as "Retreat by Father van Ginneken." These addresses contain the essence of the Grail's spirit. Most striking among them, perhaps, are those which convey the considerable study and reflection van Ginneken devoted to the historical role of women in the Church.[27]

Van Ginneken expressed guarded approval of the Grail's mass dramas. They were compatible, he said, with his own strong conviction that the Church should "use everything as a beautiful means to achieve the greater glory of God, . . . as much the things of a circus as of a carbaret [and] as of a large theater." But there was danger in them as well. Obviously, they might deteriorate into "show-off Catholicism." More importantly, they might cause the Grail to forget that it was never to be satisfied with any particular apostolic project. Its fundamental vocation, van Ginneken said, was to champion and exemplify the idea of the lay apostolate, specifically that of laywomen. For this task the Grail needed a sense of history and a solid spiritual foundation. A great deal of "prosaic daily plodding" lay ahead. So did ever new challenges, to which the movement must always be ready to adapt itself.[28]

The apostolate of women was so crucial for van Ginneken because he believed that Western society had developed in a destructively masculine fashion. The brief appearance of "feminine potential" in Jesus and the early Church had been overlooked by succeeding generations. A certain revival of matrilineal culture in the chivalric tradition of the Middle Ages had been stifled by the Reformation, which van Ginneken considered basically masculine. The French Revolution had been a "masculine outburst," and its offspring, liberalism and socialism, pursuing "a spiritless quest merely for bread and better working conditions," were no different. The modern women's movement itself, initially at least, had adopted a masculine stance.[29] The Grail must see to it that the West benefited at last from "the possibilities of women." What was the movement's mission? It was

> to counterbalance in the world all masculine hardness, all the angles of the masculine character, all cruelty, all the results of alcoholism and prostitution and sin and capitalism, which are ultra-masculine, and to Christianize that with a womanly charity. Well, what is that [but] the conversion of the world?[30]

Van Ginneken (who spent most of his early life in an all-female household) attempted to specify the potential of women as it complements but also surpasses the strengths of man. Woman possesses, he said, a unique "emotionality" marked by a "single-mindedness, a high and terrible refinement of concentration." This is not to be understood as "power," as with man; woman's emotional character issues not in control but in daring. Man, finding himself "with three feelings at once," is paralyzed; but woman dares, and when she does

> . . . she is altogether daring. When she is anxious she is filled with anxiety. If a woman is in love, nothing exists but the object of her love. . . . No one less than the fine French Bishop Fénelon said that woman is a born extremist, a born Bolshevik—it means the same thing, and so, a maximalist.[31]

Feminine daring was critical, for Ginneken, to loosening the bonds of modern oppression, even on a natural plane. But it was also the key, he said, to the heroic Christian faith required to exploit the possibilities of the "elbow of time." It prepared women for a profound encounter with the daring of Jesus himself:

> In the very extremeness of His character as God and man, Jesus was a magnificent subject for the subtle emotionality of all gifted women. The women understood Jesus much sooner than the men. The men began to doubt and waver in their faith as soon as anything happened that seemed wrong in their way of thinking. The women saw all that at once. They were afraid, of course, but they saw the greatness of Jesus in [His crucifixion]. Jesus' greatness suffered nothing in the eyes of Mary Magdalene and His Mother.[32]

Catholicism especially needed to recover its lost sense of feminine daring. For if it did not, the women of the modern world would be engaged either by the women's movement outside the Church or by Bolshevism itself, which despite its irreligion van Ginneken considered a "beautiful synthesis of masculine and feminine, matriarchy and patriarchy."[33]

Van Ginneken also provided role models for his disciples. In the course of "The Grail as a Young Woman's Movement" he related the stories of women in the scriptures, the Netherlands' thirteenth-century saint, Lydwina of Schiedam, Joan of Arc, and the Sisters of the Common Life. It was the Englishwoman Mary Ward (1583–1646), however, who seemed to him

nearest the ideal for modern times. Ward had founded the Institute of Mary for the education of young girls, and intended
that it function without a permanent cloister. She wanted her
followers to be in close touch with the world and they were not,
therefore, to wear the usual religious habit. Ward was also determined not to be controlled by the clergy or by an order of
male religious. Taking the Society of Jesus as her guide, she envisioned, according to van Ginneken, "a centralized, a beautiful
order with many houses" headed by one mother general directly
under the authority of the pope. Van Ginneken conceded that
Ward had erred in her too literal imitation of the Jesuits. (In
this, he said, "She has been a woman. She had not made a sufficiently good synthesis.") She had even invited the ill-treatment
eventually dealt her by Roman authority. (She was imprisoned
for a time and her community was suppressed.) But except for
the direct relationship with Rome, the Grail would do well to
adopt Mary Ward's basic concepts. Her personal virtues, van
Ginneken hastened to add, should also serve as Grail models:
"Mary's bright happy face," with which she fascinated everyone
and "got them on her side," and her penitential practices.[34]

Van Ginneken told the Grail that its task was to be a
"quasi-religious nucleus of the lay apostolate."[35] Its leaders,
those who would commit their lives totally in the Society of the
Women of Nazareth, were not necessarily to be full-time contemplatives (as formerly in the Women of Bethany), and they
were certainly not to be religious women in the sense delineated
by canon law. Unlike nuns, they would take no *vows* of poverty,
chastity, and obedience. They would, however, make *promises*
to the same effects and their obligations to the Grail, to the
apostolate, and to God would be "exactly the same" except for
the fact that

> you remain real lay people and you are free to wear an ordinary
> costume, you are free not to have an enclosure, you are free
> and have the right to dress as lay people whilst no one can
> say "you are not wearing your own costume; you are a religious
> in disguise."[36]

This, in general, was the course the Grail followed. Although a simple, uniform dress (glimpsed earlier) was worn inside de Tiltenberg until World War II, the term "novitiate" often

applied to the training center, and the title "Mother" used in reference to the movement's chief officer (to whom the promise of obedience was made), the Grail understood itself clearly as a community of laywomen.

In order to insure further its lay identity and to safeguard its freedom of action, Jacques van Ginneken also recommended that the Grail avoid ecclesiastical (and therefore also canonical) entanglement. Connection with the hierarchy of the Church was to be preserved solely by means of obedience to the personal directives of the bishop of the local diocese and, at a distance, to the teachings of the popes. The Grail also followed this course, maintaining a friendly, somewhat informal, relationship with bishops and recruiting sympathetic priests to help rather than govern the movement. (Van Ginneken himself, it should be noted, consistently avoided the role of ruler or legislator.) This gave the Grail, in effect, the status of a "pious union" under the 1917 Code of Canon Law. In future years, when pressed, it accepted this designation. But, except for its English branch, it resisted the category of "secular institute" which Pope Pius XII formalized in 1947 and which would have involved supervision by the Vatican's Sacred Congregation for Religious.[37]

Van Ginneken obviously did not mean "quasi-religious" to imply any compromise in the spiritual life of the Grail. He wished, in fact, to foster a combination of "the strictest spirituality and the freest women in the world."[38] Grail members were to achieve freedom to transform the world precisely through a joyful personal acceptance of the Cross of Christ. This involved the determined practice of self-denial:

> But let us understand once again the deep connection: No Grail movement without heroic daily mortification. No outward radiance without severe interior mortification. And, if you want to be great, to become greater for Jesus' sake, well then, become great in your mortification.[39]

Van Ginneken did not wish this spiritual discipline to be understood, however, in conventional, that is, individualistic terms. It was rather to be accepted as a means of gaining the strength to step out into the vast world which must be claimed for Christ. In a series of unique descriptive definitions, van Ginneken explained that

Mortification is: the going beyond the mark of yesterday. Mortification is: ploughing fallow soul-land and converting it into fruitful acres. Mortification is: reclaiming spiritual moorland. Mortification is: breaking the bonds of the commonplace to be free to do extraordinary things. Mortification is: greatly extending the bounds of tradition so as to greatly increase its treasures.[40]

Nevertheless, mortification was to be practiced most immediately and most carefully in obedience to authority within the Grail. "The Catholic Church may still have many shortcomings," van Ginneken observed, "but her fidelity to obedience and to the Cross gives a great and sure guarantee for the Last Judgment Day: the Catholic Church will stand 'en bloc' among the sheep." The sheep will have obeyed the Good Shepherd, but they will also have obeyed "the dog who sometimes takes the place of the shepherd":

> The shepherd sends him after the strayed sheep and the dog bites them and so calls them to order and into the right path. . . . Our leaders are there for the scoldings, which are sometimes more painful than the bite of a dog; but understand that it is necessary, because we have original sin in us. . . . That is why it is so good for you to obey your international President, but also the others, e.g., the one who is leader in a smaller house or who is over you in the kitchen.[41]

Van Ginneken may seem to have retreated here to less adventuresome ground, but he insisted at the same time that obedience was never to become an end in itself. Although he urged his charges not to "let any day of your life go by again without your having done ten good mortifications," he declared that "strict rules of sacrifice" should never be drawn up for the Grail. The "radical surrender" necessary to the apostle consisted rather in "making ever new sacrifices and in suddenly accepting those which are least expected," especially those which demanded moves to new countries and completely new circumstances.[42]

Fears were occasionally expressed that the total self-giving called for by van Ginneken might lead to a certain uniformity of personality among his lay apostles. In the mass dramas, it was noted, no role was played by an individual actor; actors, writers, and composers all remained anonymous. Van Ginneken, who was also an early experimenter in psychological testing and lectured on "personality culture," professed, however, to be in search of an antidote to the seemingly anarchic individualism of the masculine, capitalist West. He was after "a harmony of extremes," which he frequently spoke of as a dialectic realized perfectly in Jesus, between the Lion of Judah and the Lamb of God. Using his own character once again as an illustration, he confessed that he was himself striving to integrate the most divergent human qualities:

> timid meekness next to undaunted courage; realization of my own unworthiness next to the sense of strength conquered through God's grace; absolute slavery and absolute royal liberty; Lion and Lamb.[43]

The Grail member was not, therefore, merely to fall into lockstep. She was to embrace this dialectic in the interest of drawing out the talents peculiar to her. She was to meditate often on the motto (taken from John Henry Newman) which van Ginneken repeatedly urged upon her, "Lord, let me grow to be that for which you have destined me."

Jacques van Ginneken thus bestowed upon the Grail and the Women of Nazareth (who remained at the heart of the larger movement) a range of ideals and practical instructions which they were to take with the utmost seriousness. The radiant Catholic faith, spiritual daring, and steadfast obedience which van Ginneken proposed ought, he said, to give rise both to "a smoothly running organization and a flexibility which only women can achieve."[44] It was not, it seemed, so much a matter of what the Grail should do—it could do nearly anything—as a matter of what the movement was: a community of laywomen whose every effort in behalf of "the conversion of the world" was rooted in the humility and yet the strength of Christ.

Throughout the 1930s the Grail continued to flourish in Holland, England, and Germany. In 1936 five of its members were sent to establish a headquarters in Sydney, Australia, and two years later a beginning was made in Edinburgh, Scotland.

The approach of war, however, began to cast a dark shadow over the movement in Europe. In Berlin the Grail youth movement made bold to parade in the streets opposite the Hitler Youth, and when war finally came its property was promptly confiscated and its members dispersed. A similar fate befell the Grail in Holland following the Nazi invasion of May 1940. Dutch Grail women were forced to destroy their membership lists and operate as best they could in covert fashion, and Jacques van Ginneken went into hiding.[45] The scene of the Grail's greatest growth and development now shifted dramatically to a territory as yet little known to the movement, North America. Van Ginneken had looked forward to such a move, since with many of his contemporaries, he had come to understand the conflict taking place within the "elbow of time" as a three-way rivalry between "America and her capitalism, Soviet Russia and her communism, and last not least, Christ." America was in special need of redemption, actually, for it lacked the matriarchal strain with which Bolshevism was endowed. "Sooner or later," van Ginneken had told the Grail, "we shall tackle such a large country as North America, and suddenly start a hundred houses at a time."[46]

The initial reality fell ninety-nine houses short of the dream, but energy continued to flow from Jacques van Ginneken's vision and from the exhilarating European experiences of the 1930s. It was not long before the Grail began to make its mark in the New World.

2

In the Heartland of
Catholic Action

Catholic Action developed quite slowly in twentieth-century America. Bishop John Ireland of St. Paul, speaking at the Catholic Lay Congress held in Baltimore in 1889, observed that the laity were too dependent on their priests, that lay action was needed in the Church, and even that "laymen in this age have a special vocation." But his sentiments and those of other "liberals" of the time went unheeded in the several decades following. Church leaders spent much of their efforts battling each other over the manner and pace of Catholic adaptation to American mores and courting the support of Rome for their various positions (the "Americanism" controversy). And the Church generally devoted itself to caring for the waves of immigrants who continued to arrive until after World War I. Furthermore, the laity in America, while perhaps overly deferential, were not severely alienated from the hierarchy, as in Europe. Less need for the evangelization of Catholics was perceived, therefore, and no Cardijns or van Ginnekens appeared on the American scene.[1]

The National Catholic Welfare Conference (NCWC), which took permanent form in 1923, created a Department of Lay Organizations which became the home of the National Council of Catholic Men and the National Council of Catholic Women. These councils constituted a step forward for the laity, especially as the latter gave women a greater opportunity to be heard on the problems of Church and society. But they concerned themselves primarily with education along classroom and discussion-group lines and with the coordination of local chapters.[2] Like the established fraternal and charitable organizations such as the St. Vincent de Paul Society and the Knights of Columbus, the councils also remained bereft of theological inspiration. The same must be said of the most militant advocate of Catholic social involvement in the 1920s, John A. Ryan, director of the NCWC's Social Action Department and author of the Bishops' Program of Social Reconstruction (1919). For Ryan, theology seemed merely an adjunct to social ethics rooted in Catholic natural law theory. Such an approach led not to renewed spiritual vigor and a sense of the Church but to the political arena and close identification with the reform program of Franklin Delano Roosevelt.[3]

In general, the 1920s were not conducive to the growth of a Catholic sense of mission. Postwar prosperity blunted the impulse to social reform, and the resurgence of anti-Catholicism (the Ku Klux Klan early in the decade and anti-Al Smith sentiment in the 1928 presidential election) inclined the American Church to triumphalism at times (the 1926 Eucharistic Congress in Chicago) and angry resignation at others.

The onset of the Great Depression, however, and the arrival of new resources from Europe, combined to effect a significant shift within American Catholic Action circles toward a more consciously Catholic and apostolic spirit. The most important product of the Depression in the American Church, certainly, was the Catholic Worker movement. Dorothy Day, a convert in 1928, continued to search for a way to integrate her new-found faith and the social passion she retained from her secular, radical youth and in 1933 began to learn such a way from the itinerant French peasant Peter Maurin, with whom she founded the Worker. For Maurin, who introduced Day to the ancient and modern classics of the Christian tradition, it was time "to blow the lid off so the Catholic Church may again become the dominant social dynamic force."[4] This meant, above all, putting into practice the doctrine of the Church as the Mystical Body of Christ, a notion which emphasized both the baptismal dignity of the individual and the Church as the model of a truly organic, unified, and just society. The Catholic Worker, with its "lay orientation, its interest in the whole spectrum of Catholic life and thought, and its atmosphere of radicalism combined with loyalty to the Church" became for many the prototype of a new brand of American Catholicism.[5]

Peter Maurin looked beyond mere adjustments in America's capitalist social order (government could probably not achieve them anyway) to radical change flowing from the spiritual riches of Catholic life. His approach was seconded and developed by others as the 1930s progressed, notably the Benedictine priest Don Virgil Michel and Catholic University professor Paul Hanley Furfey. Michel, who founded the liturgical journal *Orate Fratres* in 1926, began in 1933 to concentrate his thinking on a new synthesis of worship, the Church as the Mystical Body of Christ, and social reconstruction. For him, active participation in the liturgy, which had been recommended by Pope Pius X but largely neglected in America, was the key to this synthesis. A Catholic laity active in communal worship would surely be inspired to take responsibility for the Christianization of its surroundings. Furfey, as impatient as Maurin with attempts to solve social problems by "purely human" methods, contributed the notion of "theological sociology" to the cause. It aimed, he said, to apply the revealed doctrines of Christianity, especially voluntary poverty, directly to the ills of the social order.[6]

A crucial factor in the development of this new style of Catholic activism, one sometimes overlooked, was the increasing influence of European Catholic literature. The most discussed document of the 1930s (and the most variously interpreted) was Pope Pius XI's encyclical *Quadragesimo Anno* (On the Reconstruction of the Social Order). But the wide range of works which constituted the Catholic Revival in Britain and on the Continent created a deeper and more lasting effect. Thanks primarily to Frank Sheed and Maisie Ward who opened a New York branch of their London publishing house in 1933, the Revival's impressive array of novelists, poets, historians, theologians, and philosophers — among them Hilaire Belloc, G. K. Chesterton, Robert Hugh Benson (a favorite of Jacques van Ginneken's), and Christopher Dawson; Léon Bloy, Charles Péguy, Paul Claudel, and Jacques Maritain; Karl Adam, Gertrud von Le Fort, and Romano Guardini — became the close companions of the minority of more searching American Catholics over the next three decades. All these authors sought in one way or another to reassert the great Catholic themes of sin, faith, redemption, and the Church over against the failed liberalism and materialism which they believed responsible for having brought Western civilization to its knees.

The more theoretically inclined among them, Dawson and Maritain especially, argued the need for a "new Christendom" which Catholicism alone, with its ability to preserve (in Dawson's phrase) "the tradition of sacred culture," could guarantee. The Catholic Revival presented itself, in a way, as a form of Catholic Action. Its real root, Frank Sheed said in retrospect, was "the return of theology to the layman."[7]

Sanctity, then, nourished by a vivid sense of belonging to the Mystical Body of Christ experienced most directly in the liturgy, was the new and powerful element added to American Catholic social concern in the 1930s. But considerable conflict arose about how it was to be put to use—conflict, for example, within the Catholic Worker as to whether or not the movement should involve itself in the efforts of organized labor. Thus when yet another European import, Canon Cardijn's Jocism, arrived in America promising a clear method of action as well as an emphasis on holiness, it too was welcomed by many. Jocism found its most ardent champion in Reynold Hillenbrand, rector of the archdiocese of Chicago's St. Mary of the Lake Seminary. Already a determined advocate of papal social teaching and an admirer of the ideals of the Catholic Worker (except for its avowed "anarchism"), Hillenbrand was converted in the late 1930s to the conviction that Jocism would finally supply both the depth and effective organization that American Catholic Action had so far lacked. Jocist "cells," using Cardijn's method of "see, judge, and act" and organized according to sex, age, and vocation, were to be called to "a greater sanctity and into a planned attack upon forces in the environment which prevented others from striving for that same sanctity." Hillenbrand quickly consolidated the Jocist-oriented Young Christian Workers (YCW) and Young Christian Students (YCS) into the Chicago Catholic Action Federation and was soon hoping to make Cardijn's approach virtually synonymous with Catholic Action.[8]

The region of the United States where this new Catholic spirit sank its deepest roots was the Middle West, where it built upon and influenced such established groups as the National Catholic Rural Life Conference, founded by Edwin V. O'Hara in 1923, and the Catholic Youth Organization, created by Chicago's auxiliary bishop Bernard Sheil in 1930. It was to this area, and in particular to the archdiocese of Chicago, that the Grail was drawn as Europe was engulfed by World War II.

America was indeed little known to the Grail. But news of some of the developments just described began to reach Europe in the 1930s and, in turn, a few accounts of the Grail's activities in England and Holland began to circulate in the United States.[9] Upon this trickle of information, and more importantly upon the favorable impressions of a handful of visitors to Europe, the Grail was able to lay the foundation for its mission to the New World.

The first discernible Grail contact with American Catholics was a letter written by Lydwine van Kersbergen to Dorothy Day in 1936. Having heard about the Catholic Worker, van Kersbergen seized the opportunity to describe the similar spirit but distinct character of her own movement. The Grail's aim, she wrote, neatly stating the position which the youth movement experience in Europe had served to clarify and consolidate, "is not primarily the offering of a social program, or even of specified external activities," but rather, "the character training of its members, that the inherent gifts which each possesses, both natural and super-natural, may be developed and used for the apostolate." Never-theless, van Kersbergen was quick to add, the Grail was "eager to accept opportunities to work for the cause of Catholic Action in whatever manner possible." Van Kersbergen's letter marked the beginning of a relationship between the Grail and the Cath-olic Worker which remained close for many years to come.[10]

The first American visitor to Europe whose interest in the Grail proved critical for the movement's future in the United States was a young priest awaiting acceptance of his doctoral thesis at the University of Louvain in the winter of 1936–37. In-troduced to the Grail in Holland and England, James Coffey was deeply impressed with its dedication to the apostolate of the laity. He later became a trusted friend of the movement.[11]

A reader of reports on the Grail's activities in American Catholic periodicals was the second significant visitor and in fact was to become its first American member. Mary Louise Tully, her interest piqued by articles in *America* and *Commonweal*, obtained an invitation (through the good offices of Frank Sheed) to Sloane Street, London, during a trip to Europe with her parents in the summer of 1937. Though told there that "the only thing we know about Americans is that they all take lemon in their tea," Mary Louise was strongly attracted, both in England and subsequently in Holland, by "the colors of the Grail." She returned in each of the following two years, first as a "live-in guest" in England and then as a subject of spiritual training at de Tiltenberg.[12]

At about the time of Tully's initial visit, the English and Dutch Grail also received Bernard Sheil, then on a tour which included an exploratory survey of European lay apostolate groups. Sheil, too, was impressed and assured the Grail of the favorable disposition of his archbishop, George Cardinal Mundelein. Here, suddenly, was a prospect of the episcopal support the movement required to move into new territory.[13]

With the Sheil-Mundelein connection very much in mind, the Grail sent two of its members, Lydwine van Kersbergen and Alberta Lücker, as delegates to the Pax Romana Congress held in New York in the fall of 1939.[14] When news followed that England and France had declared war on Germany, Lücker, a German national, returned to Europe immediately. But van Kersbergen proceeded west, to Chicago, and succeeded in obtaining an audience with Cardinal Mundelein. Escorted by the parents of Mary Louise Tully, she was received at the cardinal's residence and given his personal assurance that he would be pleased to see the Grail established in America. Nothing was committed to writing, but this meeting subsequently served as the basis for the Grail's announcement that it had indeed come to the United States "at the invitation of His Excellency, Cardinal Mundelein."

Van Kersbergen soon returned to Holland where, as she wrote to Bishop Sheil, "I was received with the American national anthem, and everybody wanted to hear more about America." She suggested to her superior, Margaret van Gilse, that the Grail begin its new venture as soon as possible, though not on such a grand scale as Jacques van Ginneken had envisioned. The movement, she advised, should try "very quietly to get together some young American women who are willing to join our Society as Ladies of the Grail and to give their whole life [sic] to the Apostolate."[15] Van Gilse agreed, and a list of four names was drawn up.[16]

Van Kersbergen had already sought permission from Sheil to establish a Grail "novitiate" in the archdiocese of Chicago, and asked if he would "be so kind to help us getting a house, which could be used for that purpose? I think a house in the country, but as near as possible to Chicago, would be the best."[17]

Cardinal Mundelein, as it happened, died (on October 2, 1939) before he could make his own answer. But Sheil, who had been designated the Cardinal's liaison with the Grail, replied favorably by telegram:

> HAVE ACQUIRED BEAUTIFUL SITE WITH
> SEVERAL BUILDINGS NEAR CHICAGO
> WILL YOU ARRANGE TO START WORK AT
> EARLIEST CONVENIENCE.[18]

The Grail was thus free to embark on its mission to America. But because of the difficulties in Europe it now found itself able to send just two lay apostles. Van Kersbergen and Joan Overboss arrived in New York in March 1940, carrying great hopes for the future and the sum of one hundred dollars.

Both van Kersbergen and Overboss, having immersed themselves in the ideals and successes of Jacques van Ginneken's movement, were eager to put their experience and talent to work in America. Van Kersbergen, now thirty-six years old, had joined the Society of the Women of Nazareth in 1926 when its membership was tiny, and had subsequently earned a Ph.D. in Dutch literature at the University of Nijmegen. She had also spent a year at the University of London studying the Oxford movement—especially the works of John Henry Newman. Thereafter she had headed the Grail in both London and Sydney, Australia, and was in consequence quite fluent in English. Tall and imposing (and bearing a remarkable resemblance to Queen Wilhelmina of Holland, it was said), van Kersbergen was clearly *the* leader of the Grail's new enterprise. Joan Overboss, thirty, had entered the Grail in the days of the youth movement in Holland. She had not pursued higher studies and spoke little English on her

arrival in the United States. But she had led the Grail aggres-
sively in Berlin during the years of the Nazis' consolidation of
power. And, in addition to a lively and engaging personality,
Overboss possessed a mind of her own about the aims of the
Grail—as time would reveal. Together, these two women would
take on America and build a movement whose character would
give pause to Grail leaders elsewhere. For the present, however,
there were merely hopes and a fair measure of anxiety.[19]

The anxiety was generated largely by Bishop Sheil. It was
several weeks before a letter from Sheil's secretary finally reached
van Kersbergen and Overboss in New York telling them that
the bishop would soon appear there in person to "outline the
program he has planned for you in Chicago."[20] And when Sheil
did arrive, after two more weeks, and called the women to his
rooms at the Waldorf-Astoria Hotel, he stunned them by rec-
ommending that they spend some more time getting to know
"the swing of New York." Van Kersbergen and Overboss left
their meeting with the bishop wondering what, if anything, the
future was to bring.[21]

The weeks of waiting for Sheil were profitable, however,
in other respects. Van Kersbergen contacted James Coffey, by
then professor of philosophy at the Seminary of the Immaculate
Conception in Huntington, Long Island, and Coffey arranged
several receptions for her and Overboss. A priest attending one
of them immediately carried news of the Grail to his parish in
Brooklyn, where it prompted a young woman already involved
in the local beginnings of Catholic Action to call on the Grail
leaders in Manhattan. Within months, Mary Catherine Leahy
became the first American to enter Grail training in the United
States.[22]

Worried but clearly undaunted by Bishop Sheil's vagueness
to this point, van Kersbergen and Overboss soon resolved to
take what action they could: they drove boldly to Chicago, took
advantage again of the hospitality of the Tully family, and com-
mended themselves once more to the bishop. Their tenacity paid
off, for Sheil, whatever he previously had in mind, declared that
he was now ready to follow through on his original promise.
On May 19 the two Dutch women arrived at the "beautiful site
with several buildings," Doddridge Farm in Libertyville, Illinois,

just outside Chicago, one hundred and fifteen acres which Sheil
had acquired from the Episcopal Church. The bishop had had
a plan for the Grail women after all. He wanted them to conduct a summer camp at Doddridge Farm for girls from the poor
parishes of Chicago's South Side.

This was not exactly what van Kersbergen and Overboss,
who were looking forward to getting on with their "novitiate,"
had hoped to hear. Neither were they much encouraged by the
ramshackle condition of the farm. They discovered mice everywhere, as well as other unexpected visitors ("We woke to find
our shoes filled with acorns," van Kersbergen recalled later.)[23]
Furthermore, they had no sooner arrived when Sheil, the sup-
porter of "countless rebels with holy causes,"[24] announced that,
in a change of plans, Doddridge Farm would become the home
of no fewer than five hundred refugee children from Britain,
France, Belgium, and Poland. As sometimes happened with the
bishop's projects, however, this latest idea failed to materialize,
and the Grail leaders found themselves free to spend their time
setting things in order for the summer camp and, to a certain
extent, for their own headquarters.[25]

These initial trials took their toll, but van Kersbergen and
Overboss were buoyed up by their simultaneous discovery that
as far as general interest in the apostolate was concerned, they
had come to the right place at the right time. Mid-western Catholic Action revealed itself all around them. Within little more
than six months after their arrival three events held in the city
of Chicago itself gave evidence of the vitality of Catholic life in
the region: the Jocist convention, which created the Chicago
Catholic Action Federation; the first Catholic Youth Conference,
held at Bishop Sheil's CYO headquarters; and the first National
Liturgical Week, which met at Holy Name Cathedral.[26]

The Grail leaders began at once to familiarize themselves
with their new surroundings and to make themselves known
as widely as possible. They went out to address numerous high
school student bodies and Catholic women's groups, and at the
Chicago Youth Conference Lydwine van Kersbergen announced
the Grail's intention to train young women who would "join in

the great movement of Catholic Action already under way in America."²⁷ The Grail leaders also invited various groups to spend a day or a weekend at Doddridge Farm and many came, "helping to get the buildings clean while they became acquainted with our spirit." Among the first visitors were Catholic Workers from that movement's Chicago house and members of the Catholic student organizations at Northwestern University (the Sheil Club) and the University of Chicago (the Calvert Club).²⁸

The Grail's efforts to acquaint itself with American Catholicism soon reached out beyond the Chicago area. In the autumn and winter of 1940–41 van Kersbergen, Overboss, and Mary Louise Tully (who had returned home after a harrowing journey through wartime Europe) began to undertake trips through the Middle West, the East, and the South, speaking at scores of parishes, schools, and meetings of Catholic organizations. Van Kersbergen also attended the convention of the National Catholic Rural Life Conference (NCRLC) held in St. Cloud, Minnesota. This proved to be an especially critical moment for the Grail, for at the convention van Kersbergen met the vigorous executive secretary of the NCRLC, Monsignor Luigi Ligutti, and was strongly attracted to his ideas about the nurturing of Catholic life in the United States. Ligutti, who later became the Vatican's permanent observer with the United Nations Food and Agriculture Organization, was at the time promoting various projects which encouraged Catholics to move "back to the land" where they could more easily and naturally relate their faith to all the dimensions of their existence. "Long after our unbelieving cities will have completely abandoned Christ and the commandments," Ligutti had written, "the American rural dweller will bow in the simplicity of his heart in silent prayer to thank God for the bountiful gifts of mother earth."²⁹

Van Kersbergen was not without her hesitations about Ligutti's point of view. She was an urbanite herself (having been raised in The Hague), and as her correspondence with Bishop Sheil indicated, she was wary of locating too far out in the country. ("I had never seen a cow," she confessed later.) But she allowed herself to think that the Grail's training program, at least, might benefit from the discipline and wholesomeness of rural living; it might be rendered more "useful, positive, and normal." Ligutti responded to her interest by naming van Kersbergen a vice-president of the NCRLC.[30]

After a difficult winter at Doddridge Farm the Grail leaders were ready to offer their first formal program, a retreat for young women held during Holy Week 1941. With this retreat the Grail suddenly came to life in America. Most strikingly, these several days showed that the movement had absorbed the spirit of liturgical renewal as few others had so far (and to a greater degree than the Grail had in Europe). Each morning began with the recitation of the Hour of Prime, followed by a fully sung Mass. And on Tuesday, Wednesday, and Friday, Tenebrae (Vespers) was prayed "with the girls reciting the psalms in English and the priests singing the lamentations." Other parts of these days were filled up with a variety of paraliturgical services: on Holy Thursday, a Paschal Meal of roast lamb and unleavened bread; on Good Friday, the Stations of the Cross in solemn procession in the open air and the blessing of a large wooden cross on a hilltop near the entrance to the farm; and finally, on Holy Saturday, the renewal of baptismal vows by the retreatants, each holding a white candle. The participants were enthralled. "I am sure," one of them (who became a Grail member the next year) wrote, "we are going to have a hard time to keep from singing out in our parish churches." Even the most informed and ardent leaders of the liturgical movement must also have been impressed, for here was full participation in worship—something which remained unknown to the vast majority of American Catholics for two more decades—realized not in a monastery or even in a parish, but in a tiny community of laywomen.[31]

Following the retreat, the Grail's leaders paused to compose a grand summary of what they had seen and done in their first year in the United States. Written for Bishop Sheil, whom it addressed as "the Inspiration and Guide of the Youth of America," this Tocquevillesque document is perhaps the most extraordinary and yet the most characteristic statement the movement produced.[32] It certainly bears witness to the virtually boundless determination of Lydwine van Kersbergen and Joan Overboss in the face of the difficulties which had beset them thus far.

The Grail women had discovered, they said, many attractive qualities in America's young women: a spirit of generosity; spontaneity and simplicity of heart; a spirit of adventure, optimism, and confidence; and youthful energy. The American mind they had found "flexible, not hampered by tradition but rather attracted to new things." They rejoiced that education was open to all—and well beyond the age of fourteen when it came to an end for most Europeans. They had also discovered that "what social classes do exist are not sharply defined." Most importantly, they had discerned that "more than in any other country and greater than ever in the history of the Church are the chances for women in America at the moment to bring about a renewal of the womanly virtues, which the world needs so much to regain its lost balance."

There was also, of course, a negative side to the American condition, traits, and circumstances, which represented for the apostolate "obstacles to overcome rather than foundations on which to build." Americans exhibited a lack of concentration and were infected with a spirit of materialism. Their educational system was flawed in a way which caused the Grail leaders particular distress, for it was built upon the erroneous assumption that "men and women have no important differences, that they should receive the same training and take up the same jobs." The results of this system: merely verbal facility, self-centeredness, and ambition, were especially inappropriate to women. American women also lacked physical strength, the Grail leaders noted. Due to the current fad of dieting, "young girls starved themselves just at that time before marriage when they should be well-nourished." Finally, the Grail women had been disappointed to find "no collective desire to express Catholic ideals in ordinary life."

Clearly there was much work to be done. Just how much was revealed in the staggering list of objectives "to be accomplished, perhaps, in the next ten years" with which van Kersbergen and Overboss continued their report: an agricultural college for women; a school for "soaring and aviation" ("We feel certain that some day in the future Your Excellency will see a flight of aeroplanes across the sky on the way to our new centers"); a group of "city workers" who would find means of re-Christianizing the working population; an apostolate among Negroes; "departments of Catholic culture" such as press and film ("We hope that a department of film will grow out in time into a center in Hollywood"); apostolates among married people and non-Catholics; and a missionary outreach in foreign countries.

As unreachable as some of these goals must have seemed (to Sheil and others), it would not be long before the Grail was actively pursuing all of them. Amazingly, the movement realized most of its stated aims in some form or other within the next two decades.[33]

For the present, however, van Kersbergen and Overboss told Bishop Sheil that their primary goal was the development of a group of "free workers," that is, women who would devote all their time as members of the Grail to promoting, organizing, and exercising the lay apostolate. To this end, they looked forward to the establishment of their permanent "novitiate" in which these future leaders, "removed from all distractions, wearing the habit, and remote even from the program of Catholic Action activities," could spend three years of spiritual training for the tasks that lay ahead. Secondarily, the Grail wished to provide training for other laywomen "who will live and work in the world . . . seeing it as their vocation to work as apostles in their own surroundings."[34]

But even closer at hand were the further plans Sheil had in store for the Ladies of the Grail (as they were being called in the United States, as in England and Australia). The bishop soon announced that he would again send children from the poor parishes of Chicago, three groups of one hundred each, for two-week stays at Doddridge Farm. The small Grail community, which now numbered four and had accepted four others for formal training, had hoped to concentrate its efforts on a summer school for young women of college age who had expressed interest in the movement. But, as usual, it was forced to adjust to Sheil's wishes. The young women, forty-five of them, were therefore recruited as camp counselors and received their formation in the lay apostolate in whatever time the Grail could eke out for it. Faculty members from an institute being held at nearby St. Mary of the Lake Seminary helped out. Among them was the Benedictine liturgical scholar Godfrey Diekmann, who became a frequent Grail visitor.

Although it was Sheil's project, the Grail leaders did not merely go through the motions in conducting the summer camp, which was populated by eight- to ten-year-olds. They created a liturgical framework for it, much like that of the Holy Week retreat, and imbued it with a spirit of apostolic fancy which echoed the youth movement experience in Europe. The children's dormitories were called Galahad, Percival, Gawaine, and Gareth. After Mass each day came "Slaying the Dragon" (cleaning), "Palaces of Glass" (inspection), "To the Swan" (swimming), "To the Promised Land" (gardening), and "The Magic Grove" (handicrafts). Each day was observed as it appeared on the liturgical calendar but also in accordance with a theme designed to set forth an aspect of the apostolic Christian life. Thus the children were guided through "Family Day" (the Mystical Body of Christ), "Happy Day" (the Joyful Spirit of the Cross), and "Our Lady Day" (the Greatest Woman).[35]

Despite the rigors of working at two programs at once, the Grail leaders drew an optimistic and significant conclusion from their time spent with the counselor-trainees. "A group of spiritually determined people could," they asserted, "create a vital and joyous Catholic atmosphere." Furthermore, more could be accomplished with American girls by "concentrating the training in unbroken periods" in a setting "free from distractions and interruptions" than in weekly meetings held near home or work. A breach was in the making here between the Grail and Reynold Hillenbrand's Jocists, whose "in the environment" approach ("the environment" was the workplace or the city) involved just the kind of formation the Grail found wanting.[36]

In the midst of the summer camp the Grail also received its first national notice, an article in *Time* entitled "Nuns in Mufti." Unfortunately, it served mainly to complicate further the movement's already problematic relationship with Bernard Sheil. Focusing as much on the bishop himself ("Mundelein's energetic, liberal-minded right hand") as on the Grail, the article observed that in "the tasteful, flowered prints they wear for a Chicago summer, the Ladies of the Grail look more like clubwomen than nuns." Van Kersbergen, Overboss, and the others were horrified to find their lay vocation thus distorted beyond recognition. But Sheil was unperturbed. Delighted that any group under his sponsorship had attracted public attention, he cautioned the Grail against oversensitivity. Avoidance of the limelight, he said, would make them look like fifth columnists.[37]

The following fall and winter saw Grail leaders take to the road once more. At the National Liturgical Week held in St. Paul, Minnesota, in October, Joan Overboss gave a brief history of the Grail and went on to stress the relationship between the active lay apostolate and a deep spiritual life centered in liturgy. In the liturgical life of the Grail, she said (a bit awkwardly but with conviction),

> we have realized more and more the responsibility of lay people to bring our generation back to Christ, but especially to have so strong an interior life, to be so filled with Christ, that the world just couldn't be anything else.[38]

The strong link between the Grail and the liturgical movement became clearer still when Gerald Ellard, S.J., one of the original associate editors of Dom Virgil Michel's *Orate Fratres*, gave the retreat conferences during Christmas Week 1941 at Doddridge Farm. Developing the theme of "the three comings of Christ," Ellard also delivered "a brief and enlightening homily" at Mass each day. These talks were highlights of the week, but the Grail again worked to provide them with a lively and meaningful setting. As at the previous summer's camp, everything and everybody was renamed for the occasion: the farm became "Saintonville," the forty-eight participants "Les Saintons" (the little figures around the Christmas crèche), and the buildings "The Chancery" (the priests' house) and "The White Lamb" (the dining hall). Solemn Vespers were chanted antiphonally in English (while the priests recited them in Latin), and on the final evening a "mystery play" was given which illustrated Ellard's theological theme. In the play, one young woman wrote, "the familiar texts from the liturgy, cast in dramatic form, took on new and deeper significance."[39]

The enthusiasm generated by such events did not serve, however, to lessen the uncertainty of the Grail's situation in the archdiocese of Chicago. Now there was not only Bernard Sheil to contend with, but also Cardinal Mundelein's successor, Archbishop Samuel Stritch, who seems to have regarded the Grail primarily as one of his mercurial auxiliary bishop's many projects. In May 1942 Stritch reacted unfavorably to the Grail's publicity for its two-week summer course to be called "The Vineyard." "It seems to me that there are many inaccuracies in it," he wrote to Lydwine van Kersbergen, "and that in its present form it ought not to be published." The first inaccuracy was the Grail's statement that Bishop Sheil had placed Doddridge Farm at its disposal. Sheil had arranged for them to use it, but the farm, the archbishop insisted, "is a property of THE ARCHDIOCESE OF CHICAGO." Stritch also took exception to the way in which the Grail described the lay apostolate. "It would be more Catholic," he advised, to include a clause such as " 'lay apostles working in subordination to the Hierarchy.' " As far as strategy was concerned, "the program of Catholic Lay Action is not planned by them but, as the Popes say, is given by the Hierarchy." Finally, the Grail's words, "together we will celebrate the Holy Mysteries," could not be allowed to stand unqualified. "In the language of the Church," Stritch wrote, "the faithful assist at Mass, and uniting themselves to the Priest, offer Holy Mass to God, but they do not celebrate Mass, which essentially consists in Acts of exclusively priestly power."[40]

Since Catholic Action had been defined by Pope Pius XI as a participation of the laity in work which was properly that of the hierarchy, the question of "Who's in charge?" was never far below the surface, especially when laypeople took it upon themselves to speak in theological language.

An audience with the archbishop ensued which, despite an intervening conciliatory letter, van Kersbergen described as "a very difficult visit, very tense." Stritch also reacted now to the Grail's talk about "transforming the world" through lay action. "There is a tendency nowadays to see religion as something natural, to talk about the 'social programs' of the Church, but

that is all wrong," he warned; "The Church is not a social program; the Church, a Catholic means: super-natural life, union
with Christ, and from that all other activities should flow." Van
Kersbergen concluded that the archbishop "agrees with us in
principle," but that it was "definitely necessary that he start co-
operating more closely with us" in order to realize that this was
the case.[41]

Despite this tension with Stritch, van Kersbergen did not
hesitate to acquaint him with the frustrations the Grail had experienced in managing Bishop Sheil's camp. The Grail leaders,
no strangers to discipline, had established a strict code of be-
havior at Doddridge Farm: smoking and brief attire were banned
for all; and the trainees who served as camp counselors were
not to wear slacks or use makeup. Some of the young women
had resented the restrictions and decided before long that the
Grail was not for them. But the worst offenders had been a
group of "CYO boys" sent by Sheil the previous summer to
help put the farm in order. They had ignored everything they
were told, and to make matters worse their priest-supervisor had
"backed them up and [had given] a dinner for them." The priest
had also been unsympathetic to the Grail's attempt to introduce
the boys to the liturgy. Van Kersbergen boldly told Stritch that
"A spirit of compromise in our time is impossible. It is either
whole-hearted Catholicism or paganism." But the archbishop's
response was again less than encouraging and even ominous.
Having informed van Kersbergen that she would have to tolerate
the CYO boys for another year, he added the suggestion that
she begin to consider the possibility of a Grail training center
altogether separate from the activities at Doddridge Farm.[42]

The summer of 1942 was therefore taken up with four camp
sessions and, in addition, a CYO Youth Congress. The Grail's
adjustment this time was to conduct its own programs in June
and September. The first, previously mentioned, was "The Vineyard," which focused on the fundamental principals of the lay
apostolate and attracted "forty eager young women from all parts
of the country . . . for a fuller realization . . . of the ravishing
dignity of being Catholics." Among the speakers for this course
was the formidable Reynold Hillenbrand, who dwelt on themes
most congenial to the Grail. "The world has largely fallen back

into paganism," he declared, and a renewal of Catholic life based on self-denial and the active participation in the liturgy called for by Pope Pius X and his successors was urgently needed. (The popes, Hillenbrand added in characteristic fashion, ought to be listened to because they "are always way, way ahead of us.") Two other lecturers wove high praise for the Grail into their remarks. Benedict Ehmann, a seminary professor from Rochester, New York, who spoke on "The Cosmic and Sociological Effects of Being Incorporated into Christ," said that Doddridge Farm was already one of the few places in the country where one could find a true "miniature of the Church." As at Dorothy Day's houses of hospitality and Catherine de Hueck's Friendship House, "here at the Grail you are finding a foretaste of what the whole Church should be and what it certainly will be when it issues in the Kingdom of God." Vincent McAloon of the Catholic Action students' group recently established at the University of Notre Dame by Louis Putz, C.S.C., also had enthusiastic words. "Right now," he declared, "we [at Notre Dame] look upon Doddridge Farm with a holy envy and with a great lust to imitate it."[43]

As usual, however, these lectures were merely one aspect of the Grail's course. Participants in "The Vineyard" also studied, worked, feasted, and prayed together. There were dishes to be done and farm animals to be cared for. Some helped with the preparation of meals and, according to one young person's account, "to our delight we were even allowed to mix and bake bread. Never before had we understood so well what Christ meant: 'The Kingdom of God is like leaven. . . .' We determined to be modern leaven permeating the pagan masses of today." Participation in the liturgy was again extensive, and a revelation to most:

> Those to whom the Dialogue Mass was something new, found it a joyous event to chant the Offertory verse as we slowly filed up to place our own host in the Ciborium, and the idea of our offering ourselves with the priest and with Christ to God became very real.[44]

Once more, worship was moved outdoors. A newly planted vineyard on the farm was blessed with the appropriate prayer from the Roman Ritual, surrounded with an elaborate ceremony. The entire group processed from the chapel across the fields, led by a cross and a white banner bearing a large cluster of grapes in purple and "The Vineyard" in vivid red letters. After the blessing there were prayers for the great Vineyard of the Church: for its dead branches, its new ones (converts), its strong ones (the hierarchy), and finally for "the hurt and wounded branches in the winepresses of the world." With all gathered around the cross, Father Ehmann concluded the ceremony with a meditation on words from the Canticle of Canticles, "Catch me the little foxes that spoil the vines." "It is your task," he said, "to catch the little foxes of materialism and Godlessness that eat their way among the grapes, the members of the Church."[45]

The second program revealed just how powerful the influence of Luigi Ligutti on Lydwine van Kersbergen had been. Ligutti himself helped with the preparation for this "Rural Life School" and a full roster of speakers addressed themselves directly to various theories and activities of life on the land, such as decentralization and folk dancing. Even those who spoke on seemingly unrelated topics, the University of Chicago's Mortimer Adler, for example, found themselves accommodated to the occasion; Adler, it was said, "may have been surprised at our rural life interpretation of his lecture" (which dealt with materialism in education). Paraliturgical services, again aimed at integrating "liturgy and life," focused squarely on the rural context. One of them, a carefully worked out ceremony surrounding the sowing of winter rye, was recounted by a young participant in lyrical fashion:

> With bursting aprons filled with rye tied about our waists, we strode firmly over the field, scattering the seed in a wide arc before us. Hot beat of the noonday sun, intense blue of the sky above us, pungent odor of the freshly plowed earth—with a rush came the meaning of the Scripture text, "Unless the grain of wheat, falling into the ground die, itself remaineth alone; but if it die, it bringeth forth much fruit."[46]

The Rural Life School concluded with an especially happy event, the wedding of a young couple who announced that they would soon establish their new home on the land.

In the late autumn and winter of 1942 Grail leaders again went on tour, determined to spread their message about the lay apostolate and to cultivate interest in their own movement. Joan Overboss and Janet Kalven, a convert from Judaism who had been Mortimer Adler's associate in the Great Books Program at the University of Chicago, journeyed first to Peoria, Illinois, where they shared a discussion session with Dorothy Day at the convention of the National Catholic Rural Life Conference, and then to St. Meinrad, Indiana, for the third National Liturgical Week.[47] At the latter Kalven reported on her success at Doddridge Farm in teaching young children to make all the responses (in Latin) at Mass, and Overboss expounded a perhaps startling, van Ginnekenesque theme: "what I think might be called the woman's view-point in the matter of suffering." Women, Overboss said, were made in "a very special way" to bear suffering, and this idea was beginning to have an impact in America:

> Our experience as Ladies of the Grail with the young women in America is that once they discover the beauty of suffering, all this, of course, in union with Christ's suffering, their whole lives seem to change. . . . They found they were not happy at all; whereas once they really understood how everything that happens, not only the beautiful things, but also the hard things, could be made an act of praise to God, they really found happiness and peace.[48]

The Overboss-Kalven tour continued east to Pittsburgh, Philadelphia, and New York, and then back through Green Bay, Wisconsin; Columbus, Ohio; Springfield, Ohio; and Peoria again, with talks on the Grail and the lay apostolate delivered at colleges and seminaries all along the route. In many of these places groups of "Grail enthusiasts" sprang up which promoted the movement and sent recruits.[49]

Christmas Week again brought a course in the lay apostolate at Doddridge Farm, with another of the giants of the liturgical movement, Monsignor Martin Hellriegel, pastor of Holy Cross Parish in St. Louis, giving the principal talks. Developing the week's theme, "Quare fremuerunt gentes, et populi meditati sunt inania?" ("Why do the nations rage, and the people plan vain things?"—from Psalm 2), Hellriegel offered counsel which also seemed to echo the sentiments of Jacques van Ginneken.

Exhorting his listeners to become neither "pious goody-goodies" nor "harmless worldlings," he declared that "to convert the world, we need an entirely different type . . . women with intelligence and holy impertinence . . . women with vision and radical conviction, women who are determined to live on principle twenty-four hours a day." Instruction in the apostolate and daily living was drawn, as usual, from the current liturgical setting. Hellriegel explained that there are three tables in the Christian life: the Banquet Table of the Mass, the Dining Table of Everyday, and the Feasting Table in heaven. His point fell upon eager ears. "As Catholics, therefore," a young Grail member concluded, "our eating should become a sacred ceremony, both in the family and in the Christian community." And, "As a matter of fact," she added, "during the meals [of the week] we looked suspiciously like the family of the Church Triumphant feasting in eternity." As the course ended, the New Year was welcomed with yet another dramatic paraliturgical ceremony:

> We began by asking forgiveness for the sins of the past, and chanting together the solemn Confiteor. Then there was an act of thanksgiving for the spiritual gifts we had received and an act of reparation for the sins that were being committed all over the world on this evening. These were personal prayers spoken by different girls before the Tabernacle. At twelve o'clock the farm bell rang out joyously over the fields, and we spent the first minutes of the new year in praising God and singing the Gloria. After this we gave each other the Kiss of Peace, expressing our unity in Christ, and sang the "Ubi Caritas."[50]

By the spring of 1943, then, the Grail had settled firmly into the ranks of American Catholic Action. By means of "a charming imperiousness," as one observer put it, the movement had drawn a number of eminent teachers and pastors to Doddridge Farm.[51] It had elicited considerable admiration from other Catholic organizations: besides the remarks quoted earlier, one officer of the National Catholic Rural Life Conference publicly expressed the hope that "the Grail will soon be established just beyond the boundaries of every American city."[52] And the Grail had attracted several hundred young women—between the age limits it established of seventeen and twenty-five—from all over the country. Most, as anticipated, took the movement's vision of the lay apostolate back home with them, in many cases to the married life they had been preparing for. Twelve of them, however, had remained with Lydwine van Kersbergen and Joan Overboss to become permanent members of the community. Curiously, these women were not asked to make the formal promises (not vows) of poverty, chastity, and obedience which Jacques van Ginneken had prescribed for the Society of the Women of Nazareth. In fact, they were not told much, if anything, about the Women of Nazareth. Nevertheless, they understood that they had made a permanent commitment and would be leaders of the Grail in time to come.

The Grail's principal problem at this moment was its tense relationship with the archdiocese of Chicago. It was soon to issue in a painful upheaval.

In a report prepared for Archbishop Stritch in April 1943 Lydwine van Kersbergen again raised the question of the Grail's future at Doddridge Farm. She continued to hope that it could become a permanent training center for the lay apostolate with "a school for the womanly arts" and a house of formation for full-time Grail members. But van Kersbergen now had to inform the archbishop that Bernard Sheil was at it again; he had announced that soldiers, or the WAACS, or the WAVES, or the government might be taking over Doddridge Farm at any time. She had also heard that a CYO boys' camp which had lost its facilities to the government would soon be relocated on the property. The Grail's plans, it seemed, were once again to be inhibited, if not totally frustrated.[53]

By the time Stritch got around to answering van Kersbergen the story about the CYO camp was discovered to be fact, and the archbishop's reply showed him no more willing than before to intervene in Sheil's affairs. He could not give the Grail exclusive use of Doddridge Farm, he said, and a solution to the movement's difficulties could lie only in securing another suitable location where it might conduct its programs "under my authority and jurisdiction."[54]

Van Kersbergen told Stritch that his decision came "as a great blow to all of us." Within two weeks, however, she was writing again to say that she had found an alternative site for the Grail's program for the coming summer; it was Childerly, the Calvert Club's retreat center at Wheeling, Illinois. Stritch professed his pleasure at this news but added a note of warning characteristic of his dealings with the movement: the situation at Childerly must be regarded as temporary, and any future arrangement must be made "without any sort of affiliation other than with ecclesiastical authority."[55]

Putting aside its worries for the moment, and housing some of its young women at a nearby convalescent home run by the Servants of Mary, the Villa Adorata, the Grail proceeded with its program in Wheeling. It was its most ambitious one so far, consisting of three parts.

The program's first segment was entitled "The Valiant Woman, a Three-Week Course on the Role of Woman in a Christian World Reconstruction." It was clearly to be a serious business. Publicity for the course explained that the United States was presently being tested "to see if it can rise to the tremendous task which God has planned for it in this time of world-war and world-destruction," and it posed a challenging question: "Will our Catholic young women in a radiant spirit of self-sacrifice use their talents and energy to steer our country and the whole world closer to God?" The advance instructions which students received also conveyed a tone of high determination. Participants were to bring a Missal, a Bible (Old and New Testaments), and ration books; they were *not* to bring slacks or shorts. And they were to understand that "because of the full program of the training weeks, no other time for outside correspondence will be available."[56]

The second segment, called "The Vanguard," consisted of a series of two-week courses dealing with Catholic culture, rural family life, and the liturgy and plain chant. The third was "The Harvest," three weeks devoted to the principles and practice of rural living. Among those in attendance was Dorothy Day, just then beginning a kind of sabbatical from the Catholic Worker and in search of an agreeable place to think and pray. Her report on "The Harvest" provides a particularly full and sensitive portrait of the Grail's activities and their underlying spirit at this stage of the movement's development in America.

Day enjoyed the instruction in sacred singing given by the Benedictine Dom Ermin Vitry, Lydwine van Kersbergen's lecture on women and agriculture, Reynold Hillenbrand on the priesthood of the laity and the doctrine of the Mystical Body, and Luigi Ligutti on "The Moron Quail," "The Country Pastor," and "The Lilies of the Field." But she also grasped and relished the Grail's intention that these instructions be heard in a larger, integral experience of the land and the Christian spirit. "We have learned to meditate *and* bake bread," she wrote, "pray *and* extract honey; sing *and* make butter, cheese, cider, wine, and sauerkraut."

In virtually the lone mention of the subject to appear in print, Day also reported on the strong ascetical dimension of the Grail's life and training. She noticed that "when we feasted with the martyrs, someone kept a fast, just as when there was much discussion, someone kept silent—silent with the eyes as well as with the lips. Always there was someone sent to the chapel to pray 'for an hour and a half' for others. Always there were little penances distributed, to illustrate the points of meditation." Jacques van Ginneken's theology of mortification had survived and was to remain a powerful behind-the-scenes factor for many more years.[57]

For Dorothy Day neither this penitential spirit nor its rural life setting was anything new or troublesome. The Grail's version of the "Green Revolution," however, continued to make a new, deep, and perhaps not quite intended impression on others. Lydwine van Kersbergen and Joan Overboss had not exactly aimed to make the Grail a rural life movement, but it was beginning to look that way. One participant in "The Harvest," for instance, wrote that the course had begun to make her think about the self-sufficiency of life on the land in contrast to the "dependency" of city dwellers. Thereafter, "It was remarkable how many of the evils of city life flocked into my mind."[58]

Although its tenure at Childerly had proved successful, the Grail concluded finally that in light of the attitudes of its episcopal patrons it could no longer profitably remain in the archdiocese of Chicago. "The Ladies of the Grail are a homeless bunch of Desert Fathers right now," Dorothy Day observed, "but they are ready for anything in these days when whole continents are on the move."[59] Fortunately, their readiness was abetted by their friend Luigi Ligutti, who pointed them southeast, toward Cincinnati, Ohio.

3

Permanent Roots: Grailville, Loveland, Ohio

Almost without exception, the young women who joined the Grail in America in the 1940s and 1950s experienced Lydwine van Kersbergen as a powerful, authoritative figure. Besides her obviously keen intellect and ability to speak up to Church leaders, she alone was responsible for deciding who was suitable for the Grail, and later, for assigning the right person to the right apostolic task. Her judgments on these matters always seemed firm; she expressed them in unequivocal terms. Nevertheless, van Kersbergen was herself bound to Jacques van Ginneken's theology of obedience, and faced with the problem of leaving Chicago and finding a new base of operations, she would certainly have sought the direction of her superior, international leader Margaret van Gilse. The war in Europe, however, had closed this avenue, and so, in mid-1943, van Kersbergen turned to the American whom she held in the highest regard, Luigi Ligutti. Again Ligutti responded, pressing his rural life ideals on van Kersbergen and offering specific advice. The Grail should seek out a real farm, he said (Doddridge had been "a place where a carrot could not grow"),[1] and it should approach Archbishop John T. McNicholas of Cincinnati as a likely patron. Still not completely comfortable with the Grail's close identification with the "back to the land" movement, van Kersbergen nevertheless left her charges behind at a convent in Techny, Illinois, and set off immediately for Ohio. There she found the help she needed, and more.

McNicholas, one of the more influential and intellectually inclined of American prelates, was also reputed to be something of an authoritarian.[2] In the Grail's case, however, he proved to be a genial and even permissive benefactor. After meeting with van Kersbergen, McNicholas took several actions on the Grail's behalf: he arranged for van Kersbergen to inspect several sites on which her new headquarters might be established; he invited her community to take up residence at Crusade Castle in Cincinnati, the home of the Catholic Student Mission Crusade; and he asked the Grail to conduct an institute on the lay apostolate at the College of Our Lady of Cincinnati. The archbishop also took the trouble to write to his pastors and school officials urging them to send young women to the lay apostolate institute; the Ladies of the Grail, his letter said, did not wear a distinctive religious habit, but they lived "a normal, healthy, self-sacrificing life for the welfare of the Church."[3] In the six years which remained to McNicholas, Grail leaders treated him with a careful mixture of gratitude and deference.

By February 1944, her hesitations overcome, Lydwine van Kersbergen had agreed to the purchase (with considerable financial help from the archbishop) of a 183-acre farm in Loveland, Ohio, twenty miles northeast of Cincinnati. With this land and its buildings the Grail acquired full title to "1 Bay Mare, 1 Sorrel Gelding, 1 Registered Guernsey bull, 1 farm wagon, and 200 rods of new wire fencing, an undivided one-half interest in and to certain livestock, consisting of 30 cows, 10 heifers, 28 hogs, and 15 pigs," and a one-half interest in the crops already planted on the farm. So far from abandoning its alliance with the rural life movement, the Grail had given it a new dimension, for this farm offered the prospect of self-sufficiency.[4]

Archbishop McNicholas himself dubbed the new headquarters "Grailville" and officially blessed it on July 17, 1944, using an English translation of blessings from the Roman Ritual prepared for him by a Grail member.[5]

While negotiations were in progress for the purchase of Grailville, a smaller property in the nearby town of Foster was used as yet another temporary residence. The Grail acquired this site too, and it soon became an integral part of the community's enterprise. Christened "Super Flumina" because it overlooked a stream, it was transformed into a place of retreat for leaders and for the more intensive spiritual formation of those who wished to commit themselves fully to the movement.[6]

Three training courses were offered amid the refurbishing of Grailville in the summer of 1944, but its still limited facilities prompted the Grail to organize courses in several other parts of the country as well. With the cooperation of local priests and religious these were given in Frontenac, Minnesota; Rugby, North Dakota; New Orleans, Louisiana; and Suffern, New York – all under the title "The Christian Conspiracy." Publicity for the courses indicated that Jacques van Ginneken's concept of the "elbow of time" was still very much on the Grail's mind. After pointing out that America was in a woeful spiritual condition (seventy percent of the population did not believe in God, it was alleged), brochures for "The Christian Conspiracy" went on to claim that nevertheless, "the old order of worldly values and spiritual apathy is dying out." There was still time, for women especially, to lay the foundation for a better future. "Young women of America," Joan Overboss wrote, "Awaken, Arise, and Act!"[7]

With a permanent home at last, the Grail now sought to make itself even better known to the American Catholic world. One perhaps myopic effort resulted in failure when Lydwine van Kersbergen appealed to the Benedictine community at St. Meinrad, Indiana, to change the name of its magazine, which to her dismay she had found to be *The Grail*. The abbot of St. Meinrad's reported to her, quite apologetically, that his chapter had considered her suggestion but rejected it. The vote was forty-one to none with one abstention.[8] Before the year was out, however, the Grail succeeded in achieving a measure of national prominence in another way, through its participation in the convention of the National Catholic Rural Life Conference held in Cincinnati.

Convention delegates were introduced to the Grail on "Rural Life Day" (November 12). A Mass was celebrated at St. Columban's Church in Loveland; a luncheon followed at Grailville; and then in Cincinnati in the afternoon and evening the Grail's young women gave a lively demonstration of folk dancing. The dancing, young Grail member Barbara Ellen Wald explained, was "a symbolic act expressive of the joy of accomplishing a common achievement." The *Catholic Action News* of Fargo, North Dakota, reported that "these young girls, the Ladies of the Grail, literally stole the show."[9] Edward Skillin, writing in *Commonweal*, agreed: "Striking as was the obvious zest, devotion to their leader [Lydwine van Kersbergen], and unfailing cheeriness of these young students, it was the poise of each and all which was most impressive." Skillen also took Wald's point approvingly: "In this atomistic, self-centered world, the Grail believes that we must rediscover how to accomplish things together."[10]

The NCRLC convention also got to hear the Grail's first really public statement in America on the nature and special role of woman. Janet Kalven began her address, "Woman and Post-War Reconstruction," with an echo of the British distributist, Vincent McNabb: "The problem of the hour is the problem of the land, and the problem of the land is the problem of the woman." Woman could be the key to a new pattern of life on the land which was the "indispensable foundation on which to build a new Christian social order." But to pursue her "real career" as wife and mother—Kalven strongly implied that business and other professional work should be temporary at best—woman required a new kind of education, an education on the land itself. The small, diversified family farm, Kalven argued, permitted woman to develop her intellectual gifts, which lay in the "practical realm"; it helped her to understand herself as "a universality and a personalist"; and it supplied her with the strong community she vitally needed—since women did not have "the temperament to sustain the life of a desert father" and could not bear the isolation the farm too often imposed.

Kalven's address achieved wide circulation when it was subsequently published by the NCRLC and reprinted in the *Catholic Worker* and the *Catholic Mind*. Later Grail statements on woman lacked its strong focus on the virtues of rural life, but its basic contention, that woman's nature was fundamentally distinct from man's and therefore required a unique form of education, continued to govern the movement's thinking.[11]

The 1944 NCRLC convention, then, was a major public event for the Grail. But there was also rejoicing behind the scenes. "The Grail girls" (as they were often called) were particularly elated just at that moment by news that a young couple (the wife a product of Grail training) was planning to set up a homestead adjacent to the Grailville property. The couple's decision marked the beginning of a significant development in the movement's vision of the lay apostolate.[12]

Back home, the Grail was soon ready to take a major step forward: establishing the full-scale training center which the trials experienced at Doddridge Farm had forestalled. The land was there, the Grail had no extraneous responsibilities, and its numbers were sufficient to form a viable community. Besides a few "free workers," among them Mary Louise Tully, about to go to Philadelphia to engage in Catholic interracial work, and Jane O'Donnell, who had been sent to assist the Catholic Workers at Easton, Pennsylvania,[13] thirteen young permanent Grail members were now on hand to assist Lydwine van Kersbergen and Joan Overboss. Thus on October 1, 1944, the movement opened its first Year's School of Formation (or, as it was also called, the Year's School of the Apostolate). Here was the new kind of education of which Janet Kalven had spoken, a system designed to free the American Catholic young woman from arid intellectualism, to strengthen her too frail body, and to prepare her for an active life in the lay apostolate.

The Year's School was a nearly year-round program (several weeks at the end of the summer being set aside as "closed season," during which staff members rested and planned for the future). Its "curriculum" incorporated the Christmas and Holy Week sessions and the summer courses (which remained as times of introduction to the Grail and the lay apostolate), but it consisted fundamentally of the everyday life of Grailville's farm laced with lectures, meditations, and other religious exercises. It was anything but a casual program. An average day at Grailville began at 5:30 A.M. After farm and household chores had been taken care of, the entire community walked in silent procession (about a mile each way) to Mass at the parish church in Loveland (immediately causing wonder—and later consternation—among some of the townspeople). Breakfast was at nine, also in silence except for a reading—in carefully measured tones—by one of the students. Then there was more work until eleven when a two-hour period of study and meditation began which proceeded partly in private, partly in the group, and often included a lengthy reflection by Lydwine van Kersbergen on such spiritual texts as the *Parochial and Plain Sermons* of John Henry Newman. After dinner came more work and study projects until five, and then another hour of prayer. After supper there was a recreation period (often given over to a lecture or discussion with a distinguished visitor); then night prayers, and finally, at 9:00 P.M., silence until the next morning.[14]

Time for the affairs of the world was obviously minimal at Grailville. But such concern was also firmly discouraged. Newspapers and radios were not available to students (although an oral summary of news was sometimes given at Sunday breakfast), and frequent correspondence was understood to be inappropriate. Even further removed from the world was Super Flumina, where those "making a beginning on the way to perfection" were introduced to the ascetical theology of the sixteenth-century Jesuit Alonso Rodriguez.[15]

Just three students were accepted for the 1944–45 Year's School. But the pattern of the school's daily life was firmly established at once and numbers soon increased. Twenty-five students were enrolled for 1945–46.[16]

The multi-faceted life of the Grail presented by Lydwine van Kersbergen and Joan Overboss made a powerful impression on these first few dozen American young women. One of them found that "the confined cramped little 'alley' " of her spiritual life had "suddenly and miraculously expanded."[17] Another was attracted to the Grail's integration of the practical and the theoretical.[18] A third discovered that she was being given the means to discern the causes of chaos and injustice in the modern world.[19] Several others delighted in the contrast between the Grail's clear philosophy of work on the land and the "non-philosophy" which governed the lives of city dwellers. "When I picked the typewriter in preference to the mixing bowl," one of these women wrote, "I had chosen the poorer part."[20] Manual work, said another, "brings freshness of insight and renewed energy to prayer, and prayer brings vision and motive to work."[21]

For all, the Grail was something new on the horizon of

Catholicism: an exciting alternative to the convent (which some of them had considered and a few later joined) and to ordinary parish life. Some came to Grailville after high school, some after college, others interrupted their college studies or abruptly left their jobs. They hailed almost exclusively from urban backgrounds.

A decision to join the Grail (or at least to attend the Year's School) was nevertheless frequently beset with difficulties. Some parents, who might have been happy to see their daughters join an order of nuns, raised questions about this new community which strove to live such a serious life but neglected the usual vows and distinctive religious habit. They were further distressed by the problems they experienced in learning exactly what the life of the Grail was like. They received relatively little mail, they were not encouraged to visit Grailville (though they were not prevented from doing so), and their children did not come home at holiday times.

Besides this parental anxiety, some of the young women had to deal with sharp criticism of the Grail which had begun to surface in other lay organizations to which many of them had previously belonged. While personally painful, this criticism reflected a growing rift in American Catholic Action circles between groups which included a rural life, or as one might say now, a countercultural element in their philosophies, such as the Grail and the Catholic Worker, and those which did not, especially the Jocist YCW and YCS.[22]

Jocist leaders found the Grail's worldview and training methods simply wrongheaded. As one of them put it, Grail members were no help to the apostolate when they

> go to work on the girls and try to take them out of the environment by advising them to go around *sans* lipstick, attractive clothes, and all the other marks of our devastated civilization (!), when they tell girls that the modern economic system is basically evil and that they shouldn't work in offices, but should go back to the land.[23]

A more prominent figure, John Fitzsimons, author of a volume on Catholic Action in Europe, told the Grail bluntly that the lengthy periods of training it was now offering at Grailville were premature. There were as yet no people in America, he thought, who had sufficient experience of "the environment" to benefit from training outside it. In his opinion the Grail would merely wind up transferring the "accidentals" of Grailville to the city where they would certainly be perceived as out of place and bothersome.[24]

Agreeing with Dorothy Day, who declared the Jocist goal of sanctifying the surroundings of the workingperson hopelessly unrealistic, the Grail was unmoved by Fitzsimons' argument.[25] It wondered if he and his colleagues appreciated the extent to which "our existing economic institutions like the soap operas, the making of vitamin pills, the manufacture of white flour, etc." needed radical transformation. The Jocists seemed to be thinking exclusively in terms of their highly urbanized backgrounds and appeared unduly attached to "various gadgets with which industry provides them." Fundamentally, the Jocists seemed not to realize that a *very* great degree of sanctity was required to remain a wholehearted Christian while working in the world. "Don't you [first] have to take people out of the environment," Grail leaders asked Fitzsimons, "to give them experience of Christianity as a complete life and a common life?"[26]

The Grail also asked pointedly if Jocism—in which, it should be noted, each cell had a priest chaplain—had given much thought to the place of woman in society. It seemed to see her as just another worker, neglecting her role as consumer and "home producer."[27]

Underlying all this was an instinctive Grail reaction against Jocism's "specialization." Workers, students, artists, and others, ought not to be separated, but united in the interest of a total renewal of society and culture. Fitzsimons did not appear to be thinking in terms of "the organic units of society: the family and the human community as ultimate goals."[28] For Lydwine van Kersbergen, the Jocist par excellence, Reynold Hillenbrand, personally exemplified his movement's limitations. The Grail leader admired the monsignor for his advocacy of liturgical reform and the doctrine of the Mystical Body of Christ but found he had no "cultural dimension." He was "a very masculine type," successful mainly with priests.[29]

Grail-YCW tensions remained unresolved and were to crop

up again. But at present there were many more important considerations. The Grail had much work to do in building up its own community life and the task of "postwar reconstruction" was nearly at hand. In the summer of 1945 the movement again launched a series of courses. At Devil's Lake, North Dakota; Bristow, Virginia; Brookfield, Connecticut; and Cary, Ohio, it presented "The Task of Young Women in the Era to Come." At Grailville, it was "Women and the New Era."[30]

America experienced an enormous social transformation in the postwar years, and American Catholics were caught up in it to an unexpected extent. Thanks to the GI Bill, they went to college in unprecedented numbers, and, sharing in the nation's general prosperity, they joined a great movement of people to the suburbs. They moved easily among their fellow citizens as never before. These new experiences signaled the completion of the "Americanization" of the Catholic community. American Catholics had never thought of themselves as less than fully American, but now, it seemed, the social barriers to realizing this in practice were being removed. They could, and would, turn back to the question of how to be *Catholic* with a new critical eye.[31] But this development still lay in the future. In the late 1940s, the controlling ideas in American Catholicism were still those of earlier decades and still largely dependent on European sources. With Europe in economic disarray and the Soviet Union looming larger than ever on the international scene, "the crisis of Western civilization" remained a dominant theme and the apocalyptic warnings of the 1930s reappeared with even greater insistence. According to a typical contributor to the 1949 symposium "The Catholic Renascence in a Disintegrating World," a gigantic, inevitably destructive effort was in progress all over the globe to build "a new earthly city" inhabited by man "sadly dethroned and bereft of his spiritual nature."[32]

This was an outlook with which the Grail, schooled by Jacques van Ginneken in the three-pronged rivalry between "America and her capitalism, Soviet Russia and her communism, and . . . Christ," readily identified. The Grail had given voice to it even as the war raged on. At Libertyville, Illinois, in 1942 Joan Overboss warned that the next few years would be decisive as to when the crisis would really reach America, and she asked how well Americans would be prepared to deal with it. Janet Kalven, in a talk delivered to many wartime audiences, argued that "the world will not sway perilously at the turning point for long. Within our life-times, it will move one way or the other, toward the Kingdom of Satan or the Kingdom of God." The real crisis, she said, lay in the fact that the majority of Americans drastically underestimated the depth of the spiritual problem facing the Western world. They refused to believe that the war would bring about any social revolution and were naively confident that prosperity would soon follow. At Bristow, West Virginia, another early Grail recruit, Mariette Wickes, declared that the whole world was suffering from "spiritual anemia."[33]

The Grail's analysis of the crisis found its fullest expression in the 1946 booklet *Program of Action: A Suggested Outline for the Lay Apostolate of Young Women*. All doubts about the reality of the crisis, this work said, had been removed by the events which brought the war to an end. With a directness not frequently encountered at the time, the booklet stated that "the atom bomb may be seen as a final symbol for a basic truth: man, whenever he loses his center in God, will ultimately destroy himself." The root of the crisis was now clearer than ever. It was not so much communism as a more general secularism, "the separation of religion from every aspect of public and social life." Spawned by the Renaissance and the Reformation and unleashed by the French Revolution, secularism had produced aggressive atheism, extreme materialism, and self-destructiveness in logical sequence. The evidence was visible everywhere: the low level of church affiliation; the domination of spiritual and intellectual activities by business and advertising; the compartmentalization of the intellectual life ("Having lost contact with the invisible world, the individual no longer has any vantage point from which to see the universe as a whole"); the almost complete breakdown of family life in America; and finally, the unrest and dissatisfaction of the individual, who was "threatened with the disintegration of his personality."

One's first obligation, the *Program of Action* said, was to verify personally the low state of religion in her own milieu, and then to become familiar with the literature of the Catholic Revival and allied material—such works as P. A. Sorokin's *The Crisis of*

Our Age, Nicholas Berdyaev's *The End of Our Time,* and Jacques Maritain's *The Twilight of Civilization*—upon which the Grail drew for its analysis. Having become acquainted with the disease, one could then proceed to the remedy, "the answer of the Church to the world crisis of secularism," the lay apostolate, which the Grail booklet described as the successor to the Desert Fathers, Benedictine monasticism, the Franciscans, the Dominicans, and the Jesuits in the long line of instruments of the Holy Spirit for the renewal of the Church.[34]

To reinforce its points the *Program of Action* also included essays by three laymen of the Grail's acquaintance, Emerson Hynes of St. John's College, Collegeville, Minnesota; Carl F. Bauer, founder of the Center for Men of Christ the King in Herman, Pennsylvania; and Frank O'Malley, professor of English at the University of Notre Dame. O'Malley, who also lectured at Grailville on the Catholic Revival, contributed a particularly stark sketch of the modern condition. León Bloy, "a primitive Christian in an alien world," had seen clearly, O'Malley said, that "the choice of this century and every century was chaos and death or the Church and life." The secular mind, lacking the resources to deal with "a large complex, technological civilization, constructed without consideration or design, and so creative of destruction," could end only in despair; it was epitomized by the suicide of novelist Virginia Woolf. One could find a way out, however. Converts Jacques and Raissa Maritain, who had made a pact to do away with themselves if their search for meaning proved fruitless, had found it in the personal and intellectual riches of Catholicism.[35]

The crisis of the West also involved the fate of "the womanly ideal," according to the Grail. Janet Kalven took up this question again and produced the movement's most comprehensive treatment of it thus far, in *The Task of Woman in the Modern World* (1946).

Recapitulating Jacques van Ginneken's portrayal of the Reformation and the Industrial Revolution as ultra-masculine, Kalven lamented the consequent relegation of woman to "kirche, küche and kinderstube." The worst aspect of this situation, however, was not, as the feminists would have it, that public opinion looked down upon women, but that women themselves had lost touch with their true nature. This was the heart of the matter, and it remained so in all the Grail's reflections on woman until a much later date.

Kalven argued that finding themselves in "a culture of the assertion of man; of man's reason and scientific method in the intellectual sphere; of man's will to power and conquest in business and world affairs; of man's independence of God in all aspects of life," women unfortunately had tried to beat men at their own game. Unfortunately, first, because they had failed; G. K. Chesterton's observation, "Twenty million women rose to their feet with the cry: 'We will not be dictated to' and proceeded to become stenographers," Kalven said, was "more than a witty pun." But second and more importantly, because feminists had unwittingly deprived women of their real powers of recovery; they had "simply helped to destroy the difference between the sexes." The way to the future was rather (as Chesterton had also said) that "the men should be manly, the women womanly."

The starting point for social and cultural recovery, according to Kalven, was recognition of the fact that the deepest difference among human beings was the difference of sex: "In the whole range of her being—her mind, her senses, her emotions, her will, her interests and reactions—woman differs profoundly from man." The problem was not that man was theoretical, ambitious, self-assertive and oriented to power; he was these things by nature. It was rather that woman, by living outside her true nature, failed to complement, modify, and restrain the nature of man.

What then was the proper role, or the "essential mission" of woman, as Kalven called it? It was, in essence, "to be for mankind a living example of the spirit of total dedication to God." It was true that every person was created for the love of God, but "man the lover" as distinguished from "man the maker" was most perfectly realized in woman; it had always been recognized that "love plays a far greater role in woman's life than in man's." From this vantage point, since her "masterpiece is life itself," woman's prime task was to be "the great inspirer" of man, intuitively perceiving what was best in his ideas and encouraging him in it. It was superficial, Kalven argued, "to think as women that we must be in the forefront of public affairs, politics, or business to influence the course of the world." Women were not interested in abstract or technical achievements, but in persons. As Gertrud von Le Fort (with Chesterton, a major source of the Grail's thinking) had put it, "Not in the branches of a tree but in its roots do force and power reside."

Of course woman had to give direct service to humanity as well as example. She might do this, Kalven said, in the religious life, in marriage, or as a single person, but only in occupations "in which she can use her womanly talents and develop her woman's nature," such as social work, agriculture, medicine, and education. Even to these, woman would not bring expertise so much as her maternal life, with its "warm personal devotion and generous self-sacrifice." It was, however, in marriage and the family that woman was most in her element. This was not to be understood as "küche and kinderstube" all over again, Kalven insisted. It was, in fact, a matter of high spiritual and cultural purpose. As an intellectual and organizer on her own ground, the wife and mother was a great educator, "transmitting the fundamental heritage of civilization, the traditions of culture and religion, to the new generation." Modern woman's abrogation of this traditional role, Kalven concluded, was a tragedy.[36]

Something of a crisis arose within the Grail itself at the end of World War II. In August 1945 Lydwine van Kersbergen journeyed to London to attend a reunion of Grail leaders held concurrently with a centenary celebration of John Henry Newman's conversion to Roman Catholicism. There she saw Jacques van Ginneken for the last time (he died just two months later) and found him singularly unimpressed with what she told him of the Grail in America—especially about its close involvement with the rural life movement.[37] European leaders were also perplexed, not least by van Kersbergen's further revelation that none of the young American women who had become permanent members of the Grail had been required to make formal promises of poverty, chastity, and obedience. Margaret van Gilse, still the Grail's international leader after more than two decades, decided immediately to travel to the United States and form her own judgment.

Arriving at Grailville with two Dutch women who were to join the staff there, van Gilse soon became aware of a still more curious fact: the presence at the Grail's headquarters of a number of men.

Besides farmers and guest lecturers, most of these men were part of what Lydwine van Kersbergen called "the Christian community apostolate." Noticing that many of the young women who came to the Grail in the early 1940s maintained a strong commitment to a full Catholic life and to the ideals of the movement in their married lives, van Kersbergen had seen no reason why they should be lost to the lay apostolate or to the Grail itself. She had also been struck by Luigi Ligutti's remark that "there are no old people at Grailville." When a number of Grail-trained wives and their husbands proposed to settle on lands adjacent to the movement's home, therefore, she encouraged them. These people were not old, but they could be expected to bear a convincing adult witness to Grailville's young women.[38]

The first of the married couples (the ones referred to in Edward Skillin's *Commonweal* article on the 1944 National Catholic Rural Life Conference convention), Daniel Kane and Mary Cecilia McGarry of Philadelphia, took up residence on a thirty-five acre parcel down the road from Grailville on February 1, 1945. Within the next two years they were joined (on separate properties) by a half dozen others. The couples formed a kind of federation of their own, aiming to share goods, labor, and farm tools—though, like the Grail, they came to the land not so much in search of self-sufficiency as an opportunity to cultivate "a whole and holy life."[39] This led naturally, as van Kersbergen had hoped, to a close association with Grailville—an association in which the men were most visible. Daniel Kane, who had toured the country for some years as an "apostolic lecturer," continued his efforts, now on behalf of the Grail (and the National Catholic Rural Life Conference); William Schickel, an artist, began to work with Grailville students and introduced a course on "The Visual Arts and the Christian Restoration"; and James Shea, a journalist, besides giving instruction in writing, contributed articles to a number of periodicals describing the Grail's life and program. It was Shea who gave the most enthusiastic estimate of the couples' experience in Loveland:

I have discovered it is possible to make a beginning of living a Christian life, because we are *making* that beginning. For me it is quite a change. And for anyone who plans to live the life of the Church more fully, I would suggest as one possible means: marry a girl from Grailville![40]

After observing the beginnings of "the Christian community apostolate" and the rest of life at Grailville for a full year, Margaret van Gilse remained uncertain about the viability of the American Grail. It seemed so blithe about its future: it lacked visible organization, and what if everyone married a girl from Grailville? But van Gilse decided to intervene only to a limited degree, requiring that Lydwine van Kersbergen and Joan Overboss spend time reviewing the course they had taken: van Kersbergen was to have a sabbatical year at Super Flumina beginning in October 1946 and Overboss was to take the following year at leisure in Europe. Van Gilse was moved, perhaps, by the lively spirit she encountered at Grailville, and by Lydwine van Kersbergen's argument that she wished to promote the lay apostolate as widely and variously as possible. Laying heavy emphasis on permanent membership, van Kersbergen thought, might diminish the Grail's attractiveness for women preparing for married life. (It might also have lent further credence to the erroneous image of the Grail as a community of "nuns in mufti.") Van Gilse was also aware that the Grail in Europe was beginning to feel the winds of change (the name the Society of the Women of Nazareth was shortly to disappear from view). At any rate, she demanded no major changes at Grailville and van Kersbergen resumed charge there in mid-1947.[41]

There was one area, however, in which Margaret van Gilse insisted that the American Grail not so much change as grow. Peacetime had opened new horizons for "the conversion of the world" and the international movement looked forward to reviving the missionary outreach which had been frustrated by the bishop of Haarlem in 1928; a mission school was soon to be opened in Ubbergen, Holland. To impress the Grail's global ideals on America, van Gilse assigned its most seasoned native, Mary Louise Tully, to work with Father Nicholas Maestrini, the general secretary of the Catholic Truth Society in Hong Kong. Arriving at her destination together with a large contingent of

Protestants on the Feast of the Epiphany, January 6, 1947, Tully became "possibly the first American [Catholic] lay missionary in China."[42]

Joined later by another American, Veronica Forbes, and the Australian Grail member and journalist Elizabeth Reid, Tully remained in the Orient until 1950. During her stay two young Chinese women were sent across the ocean to enter training at Grailville. It would not be long before the American Grail became a full partner in the lay mission apostolate.[43]

With the return of Lydwine van Kersbergen to Grailville its growth as a fully integrated Christian community and a training center for laywomen went forward with renewed intensity. Numbers were on the increase: the 1947–48 Year's School of Formation boasted a population of sixty (including old members and new recruits), divided into "families" of eight to ten living in buildings named "House of Joy" and "Metanoia." Van Kersbergen had also worked out a plan according to which the School of Formation was to develop in a multi-faceted way:

> Ultimately, we see a number of semi-independent schools for writing, arts, agriculture, recreation, etc., arising around the school of the apostolate, each with its own house and its own program. The School of the apostolate will give the basic vision: the principles of Christian life, the fundamental spiritual training, the understanding of the crisis, the task of woman, the role of the family and the community. The specialized schools will apply these intensively in a particular field. Each school will have a permanent staff to carry on the work and to train the apprentices.[44]

In the earliest days of Grailville its many activities had been arranged according to a system of guilds, "flexible groups . . . reminiscent of the organizations of medieval craftsmen." There were guilds for agriculture, weaving, sewing, cooking, baking, laundry, writing, and the "guild of Good Samaritans" whose members offered assistance to distressed families in the Loveland community.[45] Now the guilds were on the brink of achieving the greater organization and semi-independent status of which van Kersbergen spoke. The Agricultural School, the first to establish a more formal program of its own, was housed in a building called "Pneuma." The "Logos" guild, living in "Parousia," was about to become the School of Writing. A Center for the Womanly Arts and a School of Missiology were in the planning stages.[46]

The structure described by van Kersbergen in fact embodied the Grail's response to the crisis of the times. Secularism could not be thwarted by mere economic recovery (which was deemed unlikely in any case). The reconstruction of society had to be conceived in the broadest spiritual and cultural terms, with the "complete and common life" of Catholicism as its unique and indispensable wellspring. As one Grail brochure put it:

> On the one hand there is the richness and beauty and meaning of the Church. And on the other is the life of the Church leading to order and peace. Through the mediums of ART, MUSIC, DRAMA, WRITING, we must bridge the gap between the Church and the people, so that in the world we bring forth from the crucible of the times the life of the Church and the life of the people are one. Our task is one of integration.[47]

The Grail was here expressing its version of another ideal generated by the Catholic Revival and popular in the whole American Church in the postwar era: the renewal of Christian culture, the building of a "new Christendom." The very name of a new lay-edited periodical, *Integrity*, expressed this ideal (the magazine called for "a new synthesis of religion and life").[48] The recently established Catholic Commission on Intellectual and Cultural Affairs discussed it frequently, as did writers in the new journal of the Catholic Renascence Society.[49] And it was employed by the bishops of the United States. Secularism, the hierarchy declared in 1948, was destructive of "our heritage of Christian culture, which integrates the various aspects of human life and renders to God the things that are God's." The individual Christian, the bishops said, "must get the full vision of Christian truth."[50]

In the life of its headquarters the Grail sought to integrate what it considered the fundamental areas of human existence into the heart of Catholicism, the liturgy, and create new expressions of Christian culture. The new Christendom would be danced, sung, woven, and even cooked, as well as written and talked about. "The life of the Christian community," Lydwine van Kersbergen was soon to say, "is fertile soil in which traditions will sink fresh roots, and new customs and ceremonies will flower forth organically."[51]

And so it began to happen. Dramatizations of passages from the literature of the Catholic Revival became regular features of the Grailville curriculum, with Frank O'Malley supervising readings from such works as Paul Claudel's *The Tidings Brought to Mary*. Folk dancing, long a Grail specialty, now became "Christian recreation" with the help of a young (and headstrong) teacher and journalist, Leonard Austin, who directed a mid-summer festival at Grailville and accompanied Grail dancers to the 1947 convention of the National Catholic Rural Life Conference in New Orleans.[52] The movement's practice of Gregorian chant also took on a new dimension, in connection with dance. Under the Benedictine Dom Ermin Vitry, an annual visitor to Grailville, a 1947 summer course called "Full Christian Living" included a "rhythmic festival" focusing on the themes of marriage and virginity. On the premise that chant offered "unsuspected opportunities for a form of spiritual ballet," students were taught how to express both the "soft contours" of the virgin and the mother and the angular movements which symbolized their "surrender" and maternal fruitfulness — all this to the chant notation of psalms and hymns from the Latin liturgy.[53]

The Grail had its writers, too, to promote the many aspects of Christian life and culture. Transformed into a full-time operation by 1948, the School of Writing, "with its own mimeograph, addressograph, and small offset printing press," soon became Grailville Publications.[54] Among its earliest efforts were a collection of folk melodies, simplified versions of papal encyclicals, a tribute to work on the land, and a pamphlet on Christian family life.[55]

Most of the Grail's published material, however, was designed to draw its readers — in the lay apostolate and in Catholic families generally — into the liturgical life of the Church. Reporting in Lent of 1949 that "there have been so many requests coming in from all over the country for ideas and suggestions for celebrating the feasts of the Church year," the writing group

PERMANENT ROOTS 61

was delighted to respond.[56] It produced several pamphlets which gave not only ideas but descriptions of how they had been put into practice at Grailville. *The Christian Observance of Candlemas*, for example, was based on the celebration of Mass, a procession with candles in Loveland on the morning of the Feast of the Purification, and another ceremony which "recalled in a very real way the presentation of Christ in the Temple by his mother" conducted at Grailville in the afternoon. The latter ceremony, preceded by another procession across the Grail's property and followed by a festive supper, involved the already growing families of the married couples living nearby. Each mother made an offering of her child to God with a simple prayer of her own; a visiting priest gave a short homily and blessed the children; and the afternoon closed with Vespers.[57]

The most ambitious of the Grail's efforts to emphasize the central place of the liturgy was *Restore the Sunday* and its companion volume, *Toward a Christian Sunday*, published in 1949. Following several essays by scholars on the theological and liturgical aspects of the Christian Sabbath, Part II of *Restore the Sunday* presented three articles by members and friends of the Grail on practical ways in which Sunday could be celebrated in the parish and the home. As no part of life should remain unrelated to the liturgy, so every hour of the Sunday should be filled with some activity related to the day's sacred meaning. A full celebration should begin with "the sanctification of Saturday night": after "Mass preparation" (the reading and explanation of the Scripture passages for the following day's liturgy), meals could be prepared in advance and clothes selected and laid out; then a vigil service might be held, followed by silence until morning. The Sunday Mass, the central act of Christian worship, should ideally be sung by all and include the sprinkling of the congregation with holy water (the "Asperges") and a procession at Communion time. After Mass the family should assemble for a festive meal (hints for which might be gleaned from a volume called *Cooking for Christ* by Mrs. Alfred Berger of Cincinnati). The family should also take its recreation together (perhaps a hike or a picnic, with song, dance, and dramatizations) and should complete the day with the praying of Vespers.[58]

The Sunday was a major concern of America's lay apostolate

and liturgical movements in the late 1940s because it focused the then more frequently heard call for informed participation in the life of the Church and for the creation of a new Christendom. It was a "constantly recurring theme" at Grailville in the summer of 1949, where it was explored with the help of the itinerant pastor and writer H. A. Reinhold and the celebrated German historian of the liturgy Josef Jungmann.[59] And it was the subject of the 1949 National Liturgical Week held in St. Louis. Lydwine van Kersbergen took up both the theological and cultural aspects of the Sunday in a Grailville publication, *The Normal School of Sanctity for the Laity,* and in an address delivered at the Liturgical Week.

In her booklet van Kersbergen noted that in America there was still a scarcity of material which dealt with the meaning of the Christian Sabbath, and consequently, "for most of us lay people, the concept of Sunday is a sadly impoverished one." The Grail leader herself, however, had access to European sources and proceeded to draw upon them, especially the resolutions of the 1947 French Liturgical Conference. The Sunday, she wrote, possessed a wealth of theological dimensions: it was at once the weekly memorial of the Resurrection; the sacramental presence of the Risen Christ in Mystery; the anticipation of the final revelation of the glory of the Lord at the end of time; the "assertion of our unity as the family of God"; and finally, a participation in "the divine repose of God."[60]

In *The Normal School* van Kersbergen referred to the Sunday as "a second integrating principle in the Christian life" (after the Mass itself),[61] but it was in her Liturgical Week talk that she related it more fully to the need to "rebuild paganized institutions on Christian foundations." Catholic leaders in France and Germany had devoted much study to the intellectual background of the Sunday, she explained, because they were convinced from their daily experience that "the deepest need of our time is the spiritual integration of modern culture." Van Kersbergen herself referred to the Sunday as "at once a great source of spiritual renewal and the symbol and starting point of a new Christendom." The impact of Sunday was both religious and cultural, she argued, because it "not only sets the pattern for our holydays; it reaches out to the rest of the week, governing the rhythm of work and rest, regulating the pattern of business, recreation, family life." Secularism, by contrast, had made of the modern world "one wild divorce court . . . separating religion from every sphere of life." Van Kersbergen hoped that as Christians began to grasp the theological richness of the Sunday and put it into practice, they would construct a pattern of life which would counter secularism's influence and begin to eliminate the cultural contradiction in which modern Christians tended to live.[62]

Even as the Grail was laying the foundations of its program for Christian cultural renewal, the movement's missionary aspirations, spurred by Margaret van Gilse in 1946, were also beginning to take concrete shape.

With Dutch Grail teams about to embark from Ubbergen for Indonesia, Lydwine van Kersbergen reported in the spring of 1948 to van Gilse's successor, Rachel Donders, that America would soon be ready to follow suit. Nicholas Maestrini had returned to the United States on a lecture tour and was assisting in the development of a plan for a mission training school at Grailville. The Chinese students who had come from Hong Kong were also touring the country and, according to van Kersbergen, creating great interest in the apostolate in China.[63]

Things moved ahead slowly but surely. The Grail's first formal mission course was given in October 1948, at the beginning of the Year's School of Formation, by a faculty including Maestrini and Monsignor Edward Freking of Catholic Student Mission Crusade.[64] The first lecture officially sponsored by the School of Missiology was delivered by Father Xavier S. Thani of South India late in 1949. And the school itself was formally opened on January 18, 1950. On that occasion Monsignor Freking told the members of the Year's School and their guests that "we are making history tonight. This is the first course of training to be offered [in America] for laywomen who will work in overseas missions." The world, he added, was looking to the American Church for the very things it had to offer: "a spirit of enthusiasm, the ability to organize in a practical way the activities in the missions, and lastly, our Catholic way of life." Lydwine van

Kersbergen also spoke that evening. Declaring that the Grail had always had as its ideal "a two-fold training, that of preparing young women to be whole-hearted Christians and the formation of lay apostles for foreign mission service," she went on to describe the modest beginnings of the School of Missiology. A mission "guild" would be established at Grailville; one "mission day" a month would be held for all Grailville students; weekend courses would be started for students from foreign lands; and finally, a course of training for young women who wished to go to the foreign missions for two years or more would gradually be developed.[65]

Freking was quite correct about the pioneering nature of the Grail's mission program. The missionary outreach of American religious communities was just then in its organizational infancy (the United States bishops had approved the establishment of a Mission Secretariate in Washington in November 1949). And the concept of lay missionaries was virtually nonexistent (a 1950 inquiry showed that for most religious orders, lay workers were "not needed and not wanted").[66] The Grail seemed never to doubt, however, that it would meet the challenge.

By the end of the 1940s Grailville had attracted substantial notice in the American Catholic community. Writing in the Jesuit magazine *America*, Joseph T. Nolan confessed that "personally I like to go there for bread," but he also expressed admiration for Grailville as "a beginning, not a finishing school." Its young students were learning well "the value of their traditional womanly role in contrast to the movie and magazine version of the Junior Miss and the successful woman."[67]

H. A. Reinhold told the readers of *Orate Fratres* that the Grail was a forward-looking and realistic Christian movement. Its name, which suggested "just that kind of bourgeois escape religion which became crystallized in the 'music drama' of Wagner," was unfortunate, he thought, but the simplicity of the Grail's life belied it. Neither could the movement be viewed any longer as a foreign importation. It was in fact "an answer to American needs" with some of its young women dedicating themselves to "religious life" and others "willing to marry," the Grail exhibited an attractive and appropriate "pluralism." "This was the way," Reinhold said (a bit at odds, perhaps, with the Grail's own thinking) "before the confusion of Christianity with Christendom caused by the Byzantine Emperors."[68]

The Benedictine scholar Godfrey Diekmann took the time, also in *Orate Fratres*, to review his acquaintance with the Grail over the past decade and offer another distinctly favorable view:

> I used to suspect that the whole thing was pitched too high; that it was removed from the pressing problems of industrialized, urban life; that it was too "ivory tower." Well, maybe. But then, the Blessed Virgin herself is *turris eburnea*. And we badly need "places of escape" where the spirit can be refreshed and the vision enkindled. That has been a traditional apostolate of monasteries in regard to the laity. Perhaps in this more complicated age, the laity themselves must help, in a more definitely practical way.[69]

Diekmann also ventured to say that his initial reservations about the Grail might have betrayed his own shortsightedness. "Our . . . reactions," he supposed, "are not uninfluenced by the fact that we are living in what European writers call the post-Christian age." However that might be, Diekmann concluded that "[The Grail's] apostolic spirit seeks its equal anywhere. They constitute the sort of argument that is difficult to refute."[70]

The Grail was brought to the attention of a still larger readership by the British novelist Evelyn Waugh. Commissioned to write an article for *Life* on the Catholic Church in the United States, Waugh was persuaded to visit Grailville, where, astonishingly, he was reduced to tears on hearing a portion of his *Brideshead Revisited* read aloud.[71] In his article he pleaded that space was lacking to describe many of the movements he had observed in America, but "something more must be said of the Grail." In a homestead, "unhappily named Grailville, Loveland, Ohio," Waugh wrote,

> . . . 30-odd girls at a time, of widely different social origins, are being intensively trained in the 'lay apostolate.' Their life is in startling contrast to the ideals of the advertisement pages of the women's magazines. Strenuous rural pursuits, periods of silence, plain dressing, liturgical devotion prepare them for life in the world as wives or workers.[72]

Not everyone was quite so enthusiastic about the Grail. The strong objections of the Jocist YCW/YCS have already been noted. Some others were disturbed by what they considered the excessive secrecy surrounding the movement. Among these were the parents mentioned earlier and some priests who visited Grailville in hopes of learning more about what was happening there. Even invited clergy were seldom made privy to the inner workings of the Grail, especially the nature of Super Flumina, where the ascetical practices noticed by Dorothy Day in 1943 were inculcated. There was also the seemingly uniform demeanor of the "Grail girls." *Commonweal's* Edward Skillin admired their "poise," but for others (Godfrey Diekmann's comments reflected this) the carefully measured tones in which they read—and spoke—and an everpresent "Grail smile" appeared overly stylized and artificial.[73]

Nevertheless, the Grail's evident ardor for the apostolate and perhaps especially its creativity in regard to the liturgy carried the day. By 1950 the movement had attracted more than its share of recruits. It had gained the support of many priests and the blessing of some bishops (notably McNicholas of Cincinnati). And, in the face of some obstacles, it had forged and maintained its own distinct identity. Resisting the "in the environment" strictures of the Jocists it had established its own permanent training center with its "complete and common" Christian life. It had also come to the fore, virtually alone, with a forcefully articulated philosophy of woman's role in the lay apostolate.

The Grail seemed just about ready, then, after six years of building up the facilities and the ethos of Grailville, to step back out into the world, where the real challenge of the apostolate was to be met. Three small steps in this direction had in fact already been taken. Two Grail members had looked into the possibility of a base of operations in Detroit; another two had quietly taken jobs in a Cincinnati shirt factory with an eye to organizing groups of workingwomen;[74] and (as will be seen in chapter 4) a third pair had been sent off to take charge of a Catholic Action center known as Monica House in Brooklyn, New York. The Cincinnati enterprise was short-lived, but the Grail's efforts in Detroit and Brooklyn became part of a veritable flood tide of activity in the 1950s.

4
"Cannot America Give More?"

As the Cold War grew colder and the fear of communism at home gave rise to widespread support for the crusading Senator Joseph McCarthy, American Catholic intellectuals and spiritual leaders continued to speak of the crisis of the West and its possible resolution in a new Christendom generated by the Catholic faith. Frank O'Malley, in a representative article, wrote that "we look out . . . upon a more or less devastated civilization and brood about the possibilities of universal catastrophe." But the Notre Dame professor was not without hope. Theologian Romano Guardini was correct, he thought, in noting "the stupendous Fact that the Church is once more becoming a living reality, and we understand that she is truly the One and All."[1]

There was indeed some basis for a claim that Catholicism was making a new and deeper impression on American minds in the early 1950s. Vast television audiences listened attentively to the lectures of Monsignor Fulton Sheen. Novels like Franz Werfel's *The Song of Bernadette* and Bruce Marshall's *The Word, the Flesh, and Father Smith* were popular; and Thomas Merton's account of his conversion and entrance into monastic life, *The Seven Storey Mountain*, became a runaway best-seller. The very revival of anti-Catholic sentiment, epitomized by Paul Blanshard's *American Freedom and Catholic Power*, testified to the nation's new awareness of the Catholic community—which had doubled in size over the previous twenty years and now numbered more than forty million.[2]

There were, on the other hand, some indications of a new, countervailing spirit within American Catholicism. Most visible in the pages of *Commonweal*, it claimed that many Catholics were coming at the task of influencing society wrongheadedly. They realized correctly that the secular mind had its grave defects— its "doctrinaire democracy" lacked any real foundation for spiritual and moral values. But they failed to appreciate the legitimate autonomy and limitations of the secular order—especially as these were set forth in the American Constitution (the United States was not a "laicized" state on the European model; it did not "establish" secularism any more than a particular religion). These Catholics mistakenly imagined a direct translation of Catholic teaching into the fabric of American society. They preferred to operate, furthermore, out of strictly Catholic organizations. They thus constituted a "ghetto"—a less humdrum ghetto than previously, but a ghetto nevertheless. Catholics, *Commonweal* editor John Cogley said, ought to come forward as individuals and play their parts in the "pluralistic" structures of American life.[3]

The Grail, however, seems to have taken little note of this new spirit when it first appeared. The movement's own experiences led it eventually to a similar point of view, but as the Grail entered upon its second full decade in America it was filled with determination to apply the comprehensive Catholicism it had cultivated at Grailville since 1944.

Immediately added to the growing list of Grail admirers was Jean Daniélou, the distinguished French theologian. In his travels in America Daniélou found only a few places remarkable for the richness of their Catholic life, especially as far as liturgy was concerned. One of these, however, was Grailville, which he visited in the summer of 1950. Making the standard Catholic Revival link between worship and cultural renewal, Daniélou neatly described Grailville as

> a city which is being built where souls weary of jazz, television and restlessness come to seek an integral Christian atmosphere. This atmosphere is based on the liturgy, for in our completely secular world, in a civilization standardized by science, souls thirst ardently and above all for the sacred.

The most impressive aspect of the Grail's liturgical life, for Daniélou, was precisely its participation in Sunday Mass at St.

Columban's Church in Loveland: "It was a sung Mass, full of spirit, in which the Grailville students and the parishioners participated." The Grail had no private chapel, he noted, no other church but the parish church. "That," Daniélou concluded, "is what can readily be called putting into practice the principles of the liturgical movement."[4]

Yet this very relationship with the parish presented the Grail with its next serious problem. Grail leaders and their trainees had never been just so many Loveland parishioners, and in May 1951 the vicar general of the archdiocese of Cincinnati informed Lydwine van Kersbergen that numerous representations had been received about them from unhappy local people.[5] Shortly thereafter Archbishop Karl Alter (who had succeeded John McNicholas in June 1950) was obliged to meet with a delegation which complained bitterly about "the usurpation of their parish by the students of Grailville."[6] The Grail, it was said, made disproportionate demands on the services of their pastor. It had privileged access to the church buildings and their facilities (the organ and the mimeograph machine), and it did not contribute its fair share to the financial support of the parish.[7]

Although van Kersbergen considered the complainants an unrepresentative minority, she nevertheless saw to it that Archbishop Alter received an immediate and full rebuttal of their charges. In addition to its many details, the document which the Grail submitted contained another revealing apology for the movement's aims.

It was true, the Grail said, that it had consciously chosen to train its young women outside "the environment." But it harbored no intention whatever of alienating them from ordinary parish life. On the contrary, it sincerely wished to form lay apostles who "will see the parish as the center of our Catholic family life, who will be aware of the obedience and reverence they owe to their pastors, and who will be prepared to give active cooperation in parish life." The Grail hoped that the Lovelanders would understand this. It also hoped, the document went on to say rather pointedly, that the local people would realize what a benefit the Grail's presence was not only to Grailville's students but to themselves. So far from being intruded upon, the parish had been given an opportunity to share in an exciting and significant development in the lay apostolate. After all, "visitors [such as Daniélou, Reinhold, and Waugh] from many parts of the country and from other nations have come to St. Columban's to participate in the services and to observe an active parish at prayer."[8]

Apparently the aggrieved parishioners were unmoved by this argument, and their continued "determined hostility" forced Lydwine van Kersbergen to consider her situation carefully. If the Grail chose, or was forced, to sever its connection with St. Columban's, there could be painful consequences. Obviously, the movement would lose some of its attractiveness to priests and lay leaders. Less apparently to others but more importantly to van Kersbergen, the Grail stood to lose a measure of its autonomy. With a chapel of its own, it might well be obliged to accept the appointment of a priest chaplain who would become its official spiritual director. Archbishops McNicholas and Alter had refrained from making such an appointment, but this need not remain the case. Reluctantly, and after consulting with international leader Rachel Donders, van Kersbergen decided to request permission from Alter to withdraw from St. Columban's at least "until the violence of passion has the opportunity to grow calm."[9]

The situation was set in order, however, and in extraordinary fashion, by a visit of Archbishop Alter himself to Loveland on July 20. In a prepared statement the prelate declared that determining the exact cause of the disagreement was no easy task, but he had concluded that most of the parishioners' complaints were based upon "misunderstanding and a misrepresentation of facts." After citing the Grail's rebuttal verbatim, he told the parish that the Grail did not have the resources to build its own chapel and that he was unable, because of a shortage of priests, to assign a chaplain to the movement. (Such a step had clearly been considered.) Some adjustments were to be made: the times of the Grail's participation in the parish liturgy would be limited slightly and better defined, and the movement was to make a fixed financial contribution. But finally, the archbishop said, the parishioners should give way. The Grail had been "especially approved by the Church for the purpose of participating in the life of the local parish" and they should consider it "a privilege and an honor to give assistance to this program."[10] It was as nearly complete a vindication as the Grail could have hoped for. Tensions would arise again in Loveland but the archdiocese of Cincinnati proved to be the home Chicago never was.

Just a few months later the Grail received another and perhaps even more significant vote of confidence. Rachel Donders, speaking at Super Flumina in October 1951, called the American headquarters "really MAGNIFICENT! fifty times MAGNIFICENT!" The Dutch leader expressed her pleasure with the integrity, richness, and variety of life at Grailville—even its previously mystifying emphasis on agriculture. ("In America," she said, "the apostolate needs that emphasis more than in Europe.") Donders found that Grailville had been built up very much in the spirit of Jacques van Ginneken. ("He was irritated if you were too much in one line, and immediately he created ten [new ones].") It also seemed to her a real community, with even the youngest members assuming some responsibility for the whole group. Despite Lydwine van Kersbergen's strong leadership, Donders could not see "the slightest suggestion of a mother superior with her chickens around her."[11]

Donders, however, had not come merely to praise. Margaret van Gilse had refrained from placing restraints on the Grail in America, but since her visit the international movement had experienced increasing tension between those who laid stress on centralized authority and those who favored a looser structure emphasizing the baptismal dignity of all laypeople. The Grail had actually undergone its first "schism": its English branch, acceding to the wishes of its local hierarchy for a more traditional lifestyle and greater ecclesiastical control, became autonomous and accepted the status of secular institute in 1949. Rachel Donders told the Americans that the time had come "to realize more fully the inward bond, the unity among the inner circle of the Grail everywhere"—to forestall further division, of whatever kind.[12] For the American Grail this meant informing its permanent members, at last, about the promises prescribed by Jacques van Ginneken for the Society of the Women of Nazareth, and urging them to make formal dedications. The dedications would make them members not of the Women of Nazareth— with its obsolescent "religious" connotations, the name was to be discarded—but of "the nucleus" of the Grail. (A review of van Ginneken's conferences turned up this new name: "Indeed, that is what I have wanted to found, after all: a fiery nucleus of women who dedicate themselves totally to Jesus Christ and who create a movement for the conversion of the world.")[13]

Donders conceded that the new approach might have "disadvantages for America"—running contrary, apparently, to the American preference for freedom and flexibility. But, she insisted, the good of the Grail all over the world had to be given priority, and "the stronger the nucleus is in every country, the more we can achieve internationally." The Americans themselves would benefit: they had a great contribution to make on the international scene which would be channeled through the nucleus; and they needed the nucleus dedication to strengthen their commitment as they moved out from Grailville into the world. The Grail wanted women, Donders said, who

> really see the lay apostolate as their complete vocation for all their lives, a vocation to which they give themselves with the same depth and surrender as a Trappist, and with the same love with which a girl gives herself in marriage, with the same zeal— or rather more zeal—than that which a communist gives himself to the party.

The international president (as she was now known), whose influence in the United States remained strong for more than a decade, concluded her remarks with a question that rang in the ears of her audience. "Cannot America give more?" she asked.[14]

Whatever had been its own thinking to this point, the American Grail responded instantaneously to Donders' call. On October 9, 1951, twelve women who had been with the movement for some years made their dedications in the nucleus. They were followed by a group of seven on January 13, 1952, and another of eight on April 10 of the same year. With the nucleus formally established, its members could be assigned with confidence to the foreign missions and to leadership positions in the broad spectrum of apostolic works for which the American Grail had been preparing for more than ten years.[15]

The Grail's missionary efforts were guided by a principle set down in the earliest days of the Society of the Women of Nazareth by Jacques van Ginneken. Exemplified by the plan for a woman's university in Indonesia based on Eastern language and thought patterns, it enunciated the ideals of true respect for and careful adaptation to foreign cultures. These ideals would best be realized in receiving as well as in giving. Thus the American Grail proceeded to work simultaneously at two interrelated programs, the training of American women for work in mission fields and an apostolate among foreign students attending American colleges and universities. Women from other lands were to be offered training in the lay apostolate and helped to understand American society, but they would also, it was hoped, impress the reality of their countries on the minds of Americans, especially aspiring missionaries. This had already been the aim of bringing the Chinese young women to Grailville from Hong Kong in 1947; these two were now, in fact, to form the core of an Oriental Institute conceived as an integral part of the School of Missiology.

THE SCHOOL OF MISSIOLOGY AND ORIENTAL INSTITUTE (GRAILVILLE)

Following the opening of the School of Missiology in January 1950, the Grail's mission program developed rapidly. By the summer of 1951 the movement announced that it was "prepared to train and place women in apostolic positions in foreign lands" and soon afterward reported "a surge of interest among young women across the nation."[16] The Oriental Institute, beginning with just two staff members and five students, was publicized at the same time. It was intended, the Grail said, to "prepare young women from the Orient to help in the conversion of their own countries by assuming leadership in the lay apostolate."[17]

The mission training program was described as "a course of intensive spiritual and intellectual formation for young women who want to play a part in the conversion of the world" and offered two avenues to apostolic service: a lifetime commitment in the Grail, or a temporary commitment for a definite period— three to five years. Women between the ages of seventeen and thirty were to be accepted for a training period of one to three years, depending upon their previous experience and maturity. The School of Missiology also announced that preference would be given to college graduates and women with professional backgrounds, since mission authorities were looking for teachers, social workers, and other trained personnel. But if a young woman without a profession wished to devote her entire life to the mission apostolate, she could receive a thorough spiritual and apostolic formation at Grailville and then be sent to a university or specialized school to acquire other needed skills.[18]

Despite the previously mentioned reservations which many had about the value of lay missionaries, the Grail's school did not want for champions. Archbishop Alter lent his support at once. Monsignor Fulton Sheen, director of the Society for the Propagation of the Faith, contributed an introduction to *Through Eastern Eyes*, the published version of conferences given at Grailville by another of the Grail's mission contacts, Henry van Straelen of the Society of the Divine Word. Nicholas Maestrini, now superior of the Sts. Peter and Paul Mission Society headquartered in Detroit, also provided encouragement, as did Bishop Raymond Lane, superior general of Maryknoll. The standing of the School of Missiology was further enhanced when Grailville was granted affiliation as a junior college with the Catholic University of America in November 1951.[19]

Just two years after the establishment of its school the Grail was ready to send its first trainees overseas. In February 1952 Helen Veronica Kelly of Brooklyn and Lorraine Machan of Milwaukee, both nurses, sailed for Johannesburg, South Africa, where they joined Grail members from other parts of the world.[20]

Africa, it seemed, was an especially fertile field for lay missionaries, and the Grail wasted little time in further exploring its possibilities. Lydwine van Kersbergen herself soon set out for that continent, where she glimpsed "a providential moment, but perhaps no more than that"—a "fleeting instant which may determine the course of the African Church for centuries." Uganda, in particular, attracted van Kersbergen's attention.

There, despite British rule and the heavy involvement of Asians in business and trade, the native African was "at home, independent and free, unsuppressed." In Uganda, at least, Catholic laypeople might be able to offer a Christian alternative in the struggle between communism, the newly awakened African nationalism, and the secularism and individualism emanating from the West. Van Kersbergen returned home echoing the challenge laid down by Rachel Donders. "America must give more," she declared.[21]

And America did give more. In 1953 Lorraine Machan moved on to Uganda, where she was joined by Marie Therese McDermit; and Mary Imelda Buckley, an early recruit from Brooklyn, and Mary Emma Kuhn left for Basutoland. (Buckley assumed the post of dean of women at Pius XII University, established some eight years before as the first Catholic university in Africa.)[22]

American Grail members were soon to be found in Latin America as well. From Colombia, Josephine Drabek and Priscilla Rivera reported that the potential of women there was high. Possessed of a deep faith and "a natural endowment of womanly qualities," Latin American women, they said, were "coming to the fore, especially in the large cities."[23] Bishop Lane of Maryknoll acknowledged that his community was indebted to the Grail for a "successful experiment in the lay apostolate" being carried on in the town of Bacalar, Mexico, by two native women trained at Grailville.[24]

These were to be just the beginnings of the Grail's involvement in Latin America. To lay the groundwork for the future, two young Grail leaders, Barbara Ellen Wald and Kay Walsh, embarked on an exploratory tour of Central America in the spring of 1955, and shortly thereafter Lydwine van Kersbergen set off on another extended journey, this time to Brazil.

INSTITUTE FOR OVERSEAS SERVICE

In September 1956 the Grail opened another mission training center, in Brooklyn, New York. The Grailville School of Missiology continued its own full program (and students from

Brooklyn spent several months there), but the new Institute for Overseas Service was deemed necessary and desirable in view of the growing response to the idea of lay missions which marked the mid-1950s. In an urban center, especially the heavily Catholic Brooklyn area, the Grail felt it could attract greater numbers, " 'boatloads' of high caliber young women," as the institute's first director, Janet Kalven, put it.[25] The majority of these women would probably choose the Grail's alternative track, that is, a limited period of service without further commitment to the movement itself. But, initially at least, the Grail was no less anxious to offer its services to the American Church at large.

In fact, the Brooklyn institute accepted forty women without previous Grail experience between 1956 and 1960, of whom just a handful actually wound up in the missions.[26] Its program, however, was not at all unproductive. Training more nucleus members and others closely associated with the Grail, it succeeded in sending a number of mission teams abroad. The group for whom a departure ceremony was held on June 3, 1958 (at which Brooklyn's Archbishop Bryan J. McEntegart presided) was typical: a team of four (two nurses and two teachers) headed for Brazil: a team of two (a nurse and a laboratory technician) for Rubaga, Uganda; and one member of the institute's staff for Ethiopia, where she took up the position of dean of women at the University of Addis Ababa.[27]

By 1960 the School of Missiology and the Institute for Overseas Service had made a significant contribution to the lay mission effort. Thirty-five American nucleus members were working overseas and more than one hundred women, all told, had been prepared to serve on Grail teams abroad.[28]

The Grail was generally enthusiastic about the growth of the American mission apostolate, but in a sign of things to come, it was never quite satisfied with it. Grail leaders wondered, first of all, if many of the new volunteers fully appreciated their right and responsibility to participate in the apostolate precisely as laypersons. It was quite fascinating, one of them observed, to see that while the term "missions" always elicited a positive response, the notion of "the lay apostolate at home and abroad" usually drew "a polite and uncomprehending stare." The "non-Grail" trainees were also frequently found wanting in the deep spiritual life which the Grail considered indispensable to the lay apostolate. They were, for the most part, "devotional" (rather than theologically informed) in their religious outlook and possessed "a somewhat limited background culturally." Many of them demonstrated a sincere desire to grow, but "their attitudes toward work, discipline, self-giving generosity, teamwork, sacrifice, are those of the ordinary American girl who is challenged very little if at all on these points." Finally, the Grail began early on to ask if the very term "missions" had any value at all. Some Latin Americans, they discovered, considered it demeaning. "International cooperation," Grail leaders now said, "is the key to the right approach."[29]

The Grail's critical edge was sharpened further in the late 1950s and early 1960s as a result of increased competition with other new lay missionary organizations, among them the International Catholic Auxiliaries, the Association for International Development, and the Lay Mission Helpers of the archdiocese of Los Angeles. These groups, the Grail noted, offered relatively brief training courses and "immediate placement"—not the kind of thing which promised adequate spiritual formation or preparation for working in unfamiliar cultures.[30] The creation in 1960 of the Papal Volunteers for Latin America (PAVLA) by the Pontifical Commission for Latin America in Rome gave rise to still more concern. PAVLA also espoused short-term training, and it threatened, by means of a network of priest-directors in many dioceses of the United States, to dominate the lay mission market.[31]

Despite its worries the Grail made no immediate, drastic moves. It compromised, in fact, by abbreviating its own program somewhat and opting for cooperation with PAVLA (which for a time recruited through existing lay mission organizations). At its third training center in San Jose, California, for example (see below, chapter 5), the Grail organized a four-month residential training program for papal volunteers, beginning in September 1961. And, despite its own expressed dissatisfaction with the conventional "missions" approach, it resisted the view of Monsignor Ivan Illich (who established his Center for Intercultural Information in Cuernavaca, Mexico, in 1960) that volunteers from outside might no longer be desirable in Latin America.[32] Grail mission training programs continued in Brooklyn until 1963 and in

California until 1964. But the questions raised by the mission experience lingered and were reinforced by problems encountered in the movement's parallel apostolate among foreign students.

INTERNATIONAL STUDENT CENTER

Soon after the founding of the School of Missiology and the Oriental Institute (which was broadened to include students from other continents but failed to sustain itself for more than a few years), the Grail proceeded to expand its efforts in "the foreign missions at home," the increasing number of students seeking higher education in the United States. The movement again chose New York City as its locus of operations.

Working at first out of an apartment in midtown Manhattan, the Grail cooperated with other agencies in providing the usual services to foreign students: finding them accommodations and jobs, orienting them to the city, and helping them with English. Its primary goal, however, was apostolic in nature. Despite the fact that a substantial number of the newcomers were "the fruits of generations of missionary labor," they were seen by the Grail as potential victims of the "secularist and positivist atmosphere of much of American higher education." They were ever in danger of "overlooking the best and imitating the worst in our Western culture." They were also subject, the Grail said (with a sensitivity not yet widespread among their co-religionists), to experiences of racial discrimination which might leave them "bitter toward American democracy and American Catholicism." At the Grail's own center these students would be provided with the means to "fill the spiritual vacuum of their lives with a fully-lived Catholicism." They would be helped to learn how to "evaluate Western civilization from a Catholic point of view" and to "distinguish which cultural elements [of their own societies] will harmonize with Christian teaching and which will ultimately hinder the work of the Church." The presence of these young people would also serve, in accordance with the Grail's principle of international cooperation, "to acquaint Americans with the treasures of other cultures."[33]

The Grail in New York also looked forward to the establishment of a student hostel for young women. Here too the aim would be properly that of the lay apostolate: "not so much the offering of hospitality to a large number of foreign students . . . but to draw the best of them . . . into an intimate family pattern of life . . . where they could be deeply formed as apostolic Catholic lay leaders." By this means an elite of foreign students would be prepared for their return home and in the meanwhile would comprise "an apostolic nucleus to reach out to the students of their national groups in this country."[34]

With the support of Archbishop Alter of Cincinnati, who declared that the Grail was "giving young people a thorough grasp of the positive Christian and democratic values as an effective antidote for the menace of communism," a substantial grant was obtained from the Raskob Foundation for Catholic Activities, and the Grail moved its International Student Center into the area of Columbia University in August 1953.[35] Dolores Brien, a young woman from Brooklyn who had spent time at the Grail's mission school in Holland (where she made her nucleus dedication in October 1952), served as the center's first director, with four other Grail members and four Oriental students constituting the resident community. The hostel concept was also implemented by means of another nearby apartment.

The International Student Center offered a wide variety of programs: "Catholic Europe Lives," a "new kind of 'Grand Tour,' with an introduction to the sources, ancient and new, of today's Christian rebirth"; a dramatization by African students of Alan Paton's *Cry the Beloved Country*; a seminar for Far Eastern students in cooperation with the Catholic Students Mission Crusade; an "International Party" for six hundred people on the campus of Columbia University, with doctor-missionary Tom Dooley as guest of honor; an annual International Student Day (with Francis Cardinal Spellman presiding on one occasion); and "Welcome to a City Parish" (St. Michael's on Manhattan's West Side), during which one hundred students attended a Mass celebrated by Father George Barry Ford (pastor of Corpus Christi Parish near Columbia) and heard a lecture given by the Grail's own world traveler, Elizabeth Reid.[36]

Lively participation in the liturgy, so highly developed at Grailville, also stamped the life of the student center—especially the celebration of Sunday. After Mass at Corpus Christi, Grail members and their guests returned to the center for "a long meal together, with songs, readings of the Mass of the Sunday, and contributions by way of 'talk and talents' on the part of the students."[37]

Such activities were carried on throughout the 1950s, and in 1960, according to one report, the Grail student center was still very much alive: "phones are ringing, girls are rushing about preparing for banquets and receptions, rehearsing songs and hymns for evening programs, typing out invitations for coming events, answering the door bell rung by a platoon of unexpected guests." It was "not uncommon to see some seventy-five students milling their way about, while the piano strikes familiar melodies."[38]

A further expansion of the apostolate to foreign students was undertaken in March 1961 when another apartment on Manhattan's upper West Side was rented and the Grail Inter-American Center opened. With a staff of four and several students in residence, the new center aimed to serve the special needs of Latin American women studying and working in the New York area.

Despite their apparent success in working with foreign students, Grail leaders once more confessed a certain lack of satisfaction with the progress of their apostolate. American life, despite their best efforts to filter it through the prism of Catholicism, continued to work its materialistic way with many foreigners who "lacked sufficient maturity to discern true from false values." The Grail's vision of full Catholic living and the building of a Christian culture often failed to make an impression even on those, Latin Americans especially, to whom it should already have been familiar; these students seemed not to realize "the lack of vitality and genuine conviction behind their customs."[39]

In the foreign student apostolate the Grail also found itself again in bothersome competition with other Catholic groups. Even as the International Student Center was being established, the arrival from Belgium of the Lay Auxiliaries of the Missions gave rise to concern among Grail leaders and (they said) to confusion among their supporters and the students themselves, as to whom the apostolate really belonged. Even greater tensions flared between the Grail and the Catholic Center at New York University, where the priest chaplain set about organizing "a kind of YCS" for foreign students. Faced with this new appearance of historically unfriendly Jocism, the Grail complained that it seemed "a waste of effort to begin from scratch" when the NYU center could utilize the International Student Center's "experience and accomplishment." Fortunately, Columbia University and NYU were sufficiently distant from one another and the two efforts moved ahead independently. The Grail thought it necessary nevertheless to plan a systematic program of "contacting priests and of trying to win them" to its side.[40]

The problem of cross-cultural communication also plagued the Grail's foreign student apostolate, as it had its actual missionaries. In 1956 Dolores Brien observed that "it still remains to be seen whether we can achieve . . . a true meeting of minds and hearts between Catholics and foreign students."[41] Her successors discovered that there were greater differences among Latin Americans themselves than they had anticipated and, most significantly, that anti-American feeling was "more deeply rooted than supposed." North Americans, they concluded, would have to study Spanish more diligently and spend more time learning about Latin America from Latin Americans, rather than attempting prematurely to organize them into a movement. "Complementarity, the meeting of two persons as persons, products as they are of the culture and milieu which has deeply formed them," these Grail leaders reported, was "still far off."[42]

As in the case of the Grail's foreign missions, these questions remained for the most part the private concern of the movement's leaders, and the foreign student apostolate continued on into the 1960s. But the experience of the dual mission/foreign students apostolate was a critical one for the future of the Grail. Begun with great determination and enthusiasm, it was accompanied as time passed by a growing sensitivity to the depth and complexity of the tasks at hand. This sensitivity frequently expressed itself at first in criticism of others' lack of zeal and insight, but gradually it gave birth to something new: a measure of self-criticism. Some Grail members, at least, began to raise questions about their understanding of the human situation in general and their own identity as Americans in particular.

5

Radiating from the Center

Obviously, Lydwine van Kersbergen and Joan Overboss had not attempted to realize Jacques van Ginneken's vision of "a hundred houses at a time" in America. But at Doddridge Farm and then at Grailville, they worked steadily to build up a corps of trained leaders whose task it would be to establish a permanent Grail presence in at least a good many locations around the country. By the early 1950s this leadership, strengthened in most cases by commitment in the nucleus, was in place, and America was able to "give more" at home as well as abroad. Within a span of six years, with Grailville continuing to operate at full capacity, "city centers" were opened in New York (the International Student Center, described above), Brooklyn (where the Institute for Overseas Service was also housed), Detroit, Cincinnati, Philadelphia, and Lafayette, Louisiana.

These centers, established in cities which "represent a large percentage of the population and are almost solidly Catholic," had as their overriding goal the introduction of young women to the life of the Grail and the apostolate of the laity. Their success, it was said, depended on the dedication of their leadership and on the quality of community life lived within them. They would work best, one Grail leader declared after a year's experience, when "we draw . . . twelve or fifteen girls to live together in the center with an all-around Christian Life."[1] Each center also sought to focus, however, on the particular needs of its local area which could be met by lay apostolic action. True to the schema presented to Bishop Sheil in 1941, the Grail was eager to respond to a wide variety of challenges in pursuing "the conversion of the world." Plenty of challenges were forthcoming, some of them from the world and some from within the Catholic community.

BROOKLYN

The early development of the Grail's center in Brooklyn was unique insofar as it was guided, initially at least, by a priest, the movement's oldest American friend, James Coffey.

During the war years and afterward a tentative coalition of Catholic Action groups existed in Brooklyn within which some young people (and their priest and nun advisors) gravitated toward the Jocist YCS/YCW, and others, owing to Father Coffey's influence, toward the Grail. The ideological differences between the two movements soon became apparent, however, and the young women who opted for the Grail proceeded to set up their own, independent meeting place, which they called Monica House (it was located across the street from St. Augustine's Church).[2] Coffey succeeded in persuading a number of these women to attend Grailville's Year's School of Formation and they returned to take charge of the new house—but, to the Grail's worry, under the priest's supervision and that of several other diocesan clergymen. The situation was further complicated by the fact that Coffey, rather than Grail leaders themselves, functioned as liaison with the local bishop, Thomas E. Molloy.[3]

Although the Grail was unprepared at this point for permanent ventures outside Grailville, Lydwine van Kersbergen did not wish to pass up the opportunity Monica House presented to extend the movement's influence and attract recruits; and she trusted Coffey implicitly—he understood that a priest's role in the Grail was to advise rather than to rule. Still, van Kersbergen was not anxious to see Coffey's position, however valuable, established as a precedent. She therefore took the bold step in 1947 of assigning a team of Grail members, headed by Mary Imelda Buckley, a native of Brooklyn, to take charge of Monica House. The move brought a variety of tensions to the surface.

Father Coffey was concerned about maintaining his bishop's approval of the Grail (which seemed more likely if a priest were involved), but perhaps even more so with prodding the Grail to adapt itself to "the Brooklyn city mentality." "Grailville patterns," he thought, were not sufficiently oriented to existing family and parish groups in his diocese. In a similar vein, another Brooklyn priest, George Fogarty (who also became a lifelong friend of the Grail), asked whether the movement should concentrate on bringing people to Monica House or, "in addition, bring what we have to offer them in their own groups and places."[4]

These tensions, perhaps inevitable as the Grail re-entered "the environment," were for the most part resolved following a dialogue between Coffey and van Kersbergen, and the further activities of Monica House embodied a positive response to the priests' concerns. Seeing in 1949 that "most of the girls who come to Monica House with any frequency are leaving their parishes," Brooklyn Grail leaders agreed to conduct programs at local churches and give greater attention to the apostolate among Catholic families. They did this using *Love, the Chief Instrument*, created by the staff of Monica House, which contained "a series of practical programs [eight weeks] . . . meant especially for groups with little experience in the apostolate." This booklet attempted to lead young women (high school students for the most part) to a sense of personal charity, through "the apostolate of friendship," and on to a wider view of lay involvement in the Church and the world. Other programs held outside Monica House were Advent and Holy Week paraliturgies at Catholic high schools and "A Challenge to Adventure," a weekend for teen-age girls given at the Catholic Worker's Maryfarm in Newburgh, New York.[5]

Monica House itself continued to offer an introduction to the integrated Catholic life which was the hallmark of Grailville. The center's program, it was reported, was "dominated by the liturgical year, its themes, its moods, and the graces offered at special times." A series of Sunday evening lectures was devoted to such topics as "Wellsprings of Christian Literature" and "The Role of the Catholic Intellectual." The Grail's international dimension was also made plain by occasional lectures and, as the movement's mission training program developed, by farewell ceremonies for those going abroad.[6]

Rapidly the Monica House community (or rather "several

communities . . . joined together in ties which vary considerably") took shape. At its heart was the small group of staff members and other young women living together in a nearby apartment who formed "a kind of nucleus to feed the rest of the organism with ideas, example, encouragement, and prayer life." This was in some manner the Super Flumina of Brooklyn. A second group was comprised of "the militants," those who had spent time at Grailville and although now living at home, took responsibility for one or another of the programs of Monica House. A third was made up of "beginners" who attended a weekly meeting and special events and who might eventually be "won" to the militants. Around the edges were the Grail's supporters, some four hundred priests, nuns, and lay people who attended occasional meetings, contributed money, and steered young women toward the Grail.[7]

After several years of work at Monica House the Grail decided it was time to secure its foundation in Brooklyn. Informing Archbishop Molloy in 1953 that six thousand women had participated in the American Grail's programs so far, it requested permission from him to expand Monica House into "a Grail Residential Training Center" and to purchase property for this purpose. With the encouragement of James Coffey, the archbishop responded generously. His offer of two large brownstone houses in the neighborhood of his own residence was gratefully accepted, and in September 1955 Grail members moved into "our own house—22 rooms, a nice large lecture room and a big dining room." Molloy was also the heaviest contributor to the fundraising campaign which the Grail immediately undertook to cover the cost of renovations, and he extended a large loan at minimal interest. "It was good of the Lord to get us all set," a Grail leader remarked, before the archbishop died in November 1956.[8]

With the opening of the Institute for Overseas Service on the same premises in September 1956, life became quite hectic at the Brooklyn Grail Center, as it was now known. (As will be seen, the original names of the city centers were dropped in the mid-1950s in the interest of making it clear that the houses were part of the international Grail movement.) Nevertheless, the center's programs continued to proliferate. Lectures were opened to the general public; "expansion teams" organized study-action groups in parishes, schools, and homes; and "outposts" were established in the poorer, Puerto Rican (Williamsburgh) and black (Bedford-Stuyvesant) sections of Brooklyn. A beginning was also made in Queens, the adjoining, more affluent county.[9]

As the 1950s drew to a close the Grail had succeeded in wining a considerable following in Brooklyn, which provided a great part of the movement's next generation of leadership. There were a few dark clouds: the center's staff had to operate under "a terrific strain"; money was often in short supply, and "vast social problems" were beginning to appear in the center's neighborhood. But spirits remained high.[10]

DETROIT

The Grail center in Detroit was the special creation of Joan Overboss. Following the sabbatical ordered by Margaret van Gilse which began late in 1947, the cofounder of the Grail in America remained in Europe, mysteriously, for two more years. Hindsight, informed by the later comments of some of her colleagues, indicates that even at this point, before Rachel Donders' intervention concerning the Grail's nucleus, Overboss had her reservations about the direction in which the movement was headed—toward seeking large numbers, acquiring property, and creating a tighter organizational structure.[11] At any rate, when she returned to the United States in 1950 Overboss proceeded to Detroit and announced shortly afterward that she thought it necessary to "abandon to a large extent . . . any plans of organized activity, parish work, expansion teams, youth movement techniques, etc."—the kinds of things which had begun to happen in Brooklyn. Overboss' idea was to learn as much as she could about the city and its people, and only then begin to plant the seeds of an organized movement by gathering together "a small group of capable leaders in a program of serious spiritual formation, prayer and meditation, study and discussion." She began her stay in Detroit, therefore, by working first in a restaurant, then in a laundry, and finally on the assembly line of a (Dodge) automobile factory. Overboss' approach bore remarkable similarities, probably not coincidental, to that of France's worker-priests.[12]

Joined after a year by Grail member Petra Coyle, a native of Detroit, Overboss took up residence in the parish of St. Leo, "one of the grand old parishes—predominantly Irish in its hey-day" (so its pastor said), which had fallen on hard times. With whites fleeing to the suburbs and poor blacks moving in, the number of Catholic families in the area had shrunk from twenty-five hundred to a thousand. Here Overboss began to conduct her small group meetings and, after another year had passed, rented a store with an apartment above it which became the Grail's center in Detroit at Pentecost 1952. It was called (at Rachel Donders' suggestion) the Gateway, honoring the Virgin Mary, "the Gateway to Heaven."[13]

Under Overboss' vigorous leadership the Grail's first real venture into the "inner city" developed rapidly as an "experiment in Christian living."[14] Within a year a community of four-teen women, seven from Detroit and seven from Grailville, was hard at work in the neighborhood of St. Leo's, and Overboss could list "five particular activities in cooperation with others which have flown [sic] from our living up to now." They were a cooperative buying service, to which Detroit college students volunteered their time; a family service program, with two staff members assigned to provide emergency aid; a social service program with staff and volunteers visiting homes and working with public agencies ("but in a very personal way"); a program of Christian culture: play-readings, musical evenings, and experiments in dance; and a program of education in the liturgy. Among these, Overboss seemed to have a special predilection for the expressions of Christian culture. They were needed, she said, to balance and complement the Grail's other works, but they were also practical realizations of the "full, positive Christian vision" required by the times.[15]

Active participation in the liturgy was an especially powerful factor in Detroit, owing to the Gateway's discovery that local priests were keen to use it as a means of gaining acceptance of the increasing black population by remaining white families. Father Walter Schoenherr, later an auxiliary bishop of the arch-diocese of Detroit, remembered that

after a great deal of praying, reading, thinking and discussing . . . with others and especially the members of the Grail, who had moved into the parish, we decided that the best approach would be through a greater emphasis on the spiritual life of all. No better means could be applied than by making the parish liturgically minded. Everything would be centered around the Mass. The church year must be something alive and meaningful for all. They must learn to live it.[16]

Grail members and the women they attracted to the Gateway contributed heavily to the parish effort by organizing Saturday night Mass preparation groups, designing cards to facilitate lay participation, and by helping with Holy Week celebrations which culminated in the baptism of a growing number of black converts at the Easter Vigil. Notes and mimeographed copies of the liturgies at St. Leo's were retained at first for the benefit of the priests and Grail leaders, but they were soon put together in booklet form and, according to Father Schoenherr, "the Grail center . . . distributed them to the four corners of the world." This was *The Church Year in a City Parish*, of which, the Grail told Detroit's Edward Cardinal Mooney, six hundred copies were distributed in its first year of circulation.[17]

In 1954 the Gateway was expanded to include two adjacent store/apartments. The first became a full-time workshop and retail store in which bread, woven materials, ceramics, and woodcuts were made and sold. The second served as a community service center where lectures, plays, and large-scale breakfasts, such as that following the Easter Vigil, were held. Teams of young women were formed to work on the many aspects of the Gateway's program, giving them, it was said, "a sense of 'belonging' to the movement, and putting as much responsibility on their shoulders as they can carry." An international students program was also begun in cooperation with groups at Wayne State University, the University of Detroit, and the University of Michigan.[18]

In the midst of all this activity, after giving a course on "Leisure and Culture" at Grailville (where she had seldom been since 1950), Joan Overboss left for Holland in the summer of 1955 and never returned to the United States. By this time the Grail had cultivated an even stronger emphasis on organization (especially of the nucleus), publicity, and ownership of property (see chapter 7). Overboss' departure seems to have been directly related to her dissent on this emphasis. In later years she retired to the fringes of the movement.[19]

The Gateway lost no momentum, however, after the loss of Overboss. The center's new leader, Mariette Wickes, soon announced that further efforts to expand its program were underway. These included the formation of a council on career services for women, programs for girls attending public high schools, and "the development of Negro religious art as a means of fostering the contribution of Catholic Negro women to the Church and building interracial unity."[20] This last aim was realized most fully in "New Born Again," a stage work described as "the story of mankind's creation and redemption, told in Negro folk verse, Negro spirituals, and modern dance." "New Born Again," which was performed at the Gateway and several other places in Detroit (on one occasion for an audience of five hundred), was directed by Elaine Jones, one of the handful of black women who actually became members of the Grail, and was narrated by a young black priest from Cincinnati who was later to achieve a reputation in the field of liturgical music, Clarence Rivers.[21]

The Gateway's success prompted the Grail to tell Cardinal Mooney in April 1957 (despite the prelate's earlier recommendation to the contrary) that it wished to settle more permanently in St. Leo's parish by purchasing property of its own. What actually transpired, as "social problems" similar to those in Brooklyn escalated, was the removal of the Detroit Grail Center (the "Gateway," too, was dropped) to an entirely different area, the city's more stable East Side. The new center was opened in October 1958 and blessed in May of the following year by Mooney's successor, Archbishop John Dearden. Successful fund-raising efforts soon enabled the movement to acquire and refurbish still another facility, which became an art and book store in prosperous Grosse Pointe.[22]

What these moves might have meant to Joan Overboss is not known, but the next wave of Grail leadership in Detroit was undeterred. The new shop, it was sure, would become a center of cultural education and "an atmospheric meeting place for all the teams and programs" operating in the immediate area. Plans were laid to seek further funds "to expand our program and undertake new projects." As the 1950s came to a close, the Grail in Detroit, too, seemed to be on the upswing.[23]

CINCINNATI

The city center located nearest Grailville was established in September 1951 in a three-room Cincinnati apartment "with a telephone, a wobbly table and an ancient refrigerator as its main assets" by Mary Brigid Niland, an early Grail recruit with a background in social work. Its primary apostolic task was defined as family service, especially aid to mothers in need of help in caring for their young children. Niland therefore dubbed it Gabriel House. (This was another gesture of homage to Mary. Having been informed by the angel Gabriel that her cousin Elizabeth was with child, the Mother of God had "hastened over the hills and . . . brought Christ with her.")[24]

The Grail evidently hit upon a real need in the local community, for in their first year the three women who comprised the staff of Gabriel House assisted an estimated seventy-five families and were forced to turn down three times that number. A larger facility was obtained, therefore, and officially blessed on May 25, 1952. At this new and permanent Gabriel House another "experiment in Christian living" was launched: the earnings of staff members who held outside jobs were voluntarily pooled and all received "according to their needs" from the common fund.[25]

Naturally, Gabriel House was to serve also as a center for the advancement of the lay apostolate, and it did not hesitate to combine this function with its efforts in social service. As one acute observer noted, "The families visited became . . . a part of Grailville's wider circle." Clients were encouraged to carry the message of the apostolate to their local parishes and especially to "initiate discussions" with pastors about active participation of the laity in the liturgy. This approach was appreciated by some but regarded as "meddlesome" by others. Cincinnati, in fact, semed in general to have little feeling for the Grail's religious aims and its "elitist" training methods. Despite the support of a number of prominent Catholics who served on the board of Gabriel House, the city contributed few recruits to the movement.[26]

Gabriel House persevered nevertheless, and by 1957 its program had grown and diversified. A Grail course on family life entered the curriculum of the high schools of the archdiocese of Cincinnati; and a substantial program involving high school and college students who taught catechism to public school children, conducted Saturday morning play schools, and provided hospitality to foreign students, was set in place. The Gabriel House community, including staff, students, and "working residents," grew to number more than twenty-five. By 1960 its leaders reported some anxiety about their ability to hold all these activities together, but they too looked to the future with determination. In Cincinnati, they said, "the Grail as a movement has a foothold now and it is very important to build onward."[27]

PHILADELPHIA

The way was prepared for the Grail in Philadelphia by two important local residents, Mrs. Anna McGarry, a pioneer in Catholic interracial work whose daughter had attended Grailville's Year's School of Formation, and Archbishop (later Cardinal) John F. O'Hara, C.S.C., whose godchild was the movement's first American-born member, Mary Louise Tully. With the archbishop's approval, given in September 1952, two Grail women, Gabriel Miner and Ivy Alves, living at first with Mrs. McGarry and then in a house provided by a parish located in "a growing negro district," surveyed the scene for a full year. Their observations, undoubtedly influenced by McGarry, convinced them that the Grail should concentrate its apostolate in Philadelphia on the black community.[28] The movement's ensuing request for permission from Archbishop O'Hara to establish a "Grail Center for Negro Young Women" therefore included a carefully laid out plan to that end. The Grail hoped to purchase a house for as many as twenty full-time residents who would benefit from the "all-around Christian life" generated by a half dozen staff members. It hoped also to acquire another smaller residence which would enable the movement to "continue its foothold" in the black community. From this strategic point the Grail would be able to discover potential leaders among black women and help them to take "preliminary steps toward the lay apostolate"; subsequently these women would "naturally be drawn into the entire program of the Grail Residential Center."[29]

After an intensive search—led by Lydwine van Kersbergen herself, with Janet Kalven and Barbara Ellen Wald—the Grail settled on a three-story, twenty-room house, formerly (movement members were warned not to be shocked) a home for the elderly run by Carmelite nuns. It was located, however, in a neighborhood which, though it included a number of black families, was identified as "very Catholic." And when the house was formally opened in September 1954—it was called simply the Philadelphia Grail Center—its effort to attract young women from the community was less pointedly described as "residential adult education." Local Catholics, it appeared, were less than enthusiastic about the mixing of races.[30]

Soon after the center was in operation, its leader, Anne Mulkeen, declared that the Grail's work in Philadelphia lay in two major areas: social and interracial action and the renewal of family life. She also noted, with both enthusiasm and a measure of concern, that staff members had begun to show great interest in joining forces with non-Catholic and even secular university people and social activists.[31]

Galvanized by the success of its art and book store (which "kept contact" with an estimated 4,000 people) and a performance in December 1955 of the Advent drama "The Desired of the Nations," the Philadelphia Grail Center went on to develop its own multi-faceted program, which included music and dance groups, a service career group, community development teams working in two parishes, and an international student apostolate. By the early 1960s hundreds of young women had shared in the center's life. As elsewhere, the leadership in Philadelphia experienced some difficulty in coping with so much activity. But opportunities were not to be lost, and Cardinal O'Hara's successor, Archbishop John Krol, soon found himself presented with a request to help the Grail expand its efforts in his see.[32]

LAFAYETTE, LOUISIANA

The Grail's apostolate in the South focused on students attending Southwestern Louisiana Institute. It also involved the movement once again with a number of priests whose support was much appreciated but, in the Grail's view, slightly off the mark.

Grail courses were given in Louisiana in the 1940s and the movement found a warm welcome there, especially from Alexander Sigur, at the time a seminarian and later chaplain at Southwestern Louisiana Institute's Catholic Student Center. On the strength of these early contacts the Grail received an official invitation from the diocese of Lafayette in 1950 and immediately sent out two young women from Grailville, one to serve as secretary-coordinator at the Catholic Student Center and the other as student coordinator on the campus of the institute. Shortly thereafter, two more Grail members arrived to devote their energies to a "state-wide woman's apostolate."[33]

At Southwestern Louisiana Institute the Grail attempted to help students with their immediate concerns, centered in this case around the transition from rural Louisiana to the college campus. But, as always, its primary goal was the introduction of more young women to the lay apostolate, for which a center of the Grail's own seemed desirable. It was not until 1957, however, when relations with the local clergy had become strained, that the center was established. Over the next three years, Shadybrook, as the rented facility was called, offered forty residents "a preparation for the lay apostolate, as far as it has been possible to work within a full program of studies."

Besides providing a home for the Grail's student apostolate (which included a program for foreign students and a variety of discussion groups), Shadybrook also became the hub of the movement's outreach in the diocese of Lafayette. With local women, both black and white, involved as "team members," discussion groups and short courses were organized at parishes and schools in Lafayette itself and in neighboring towns. These soon led to more elaborate programs in "parish community development," notably in Kaplan, where the Grail worked with a black priest, Albert McKnight, C.S.Sp., who had made the movement's acquaintance some years earlier at Monica House in Brooklyn. The apostolate in Kaplan included marriage preparation courses for teen-age girls, an adult education program, and a parish credit union and cooperative grocery store. Team members were also placed as teachers in several schools of the diocese.[34]

The Grail's relationship with Alexander Sigur and three other Louisiana priests during this time was complex, and perhaps a bit mystifying to the clergymen. Sigur, the brothers Marvin and Roland Bordelon, and J. B. Gremillion were all keenly interested in the lay apostolate and they admired the Grail immensely. Its spirit, they were sure, was more than compatible with their own ideal of "the Christianizing of the social order," and it had great potential for broadening the horizons of Catholics in Louisiana. As Gremillion put it in his widely read *The Journal of a Southern Pastor,*

> If the South tends toward narrow provinciality, the Grail tends to embrace the whole world: extensively, the world of geographic continents; intensively, the world of women in all its diverse cultural creations and human concerns.[35]

Problems arose, however, on two fronts. First, the priests continued to lend their support to other lay groups. Sigur championed the cause of Caritas, for example, an organization (some of whose members were Grail-trained) which was in process of becoming a secular institute. He apparently thought that a young woman could belong to Caritas and the Grail. Grail leaders of course disagreed.[36] The priests' encouragement of other groups also seemed to deprive the Grail of some of the local women most suited to the lay apostolate. "Louisiana has not really produced as far as we are concerned," Marvin Bordelon was told.[37] Second, the priests' approach to "the Christianizing of the social order" appeared inadequate to the Grail. Evidently they rushed too quickly into discussions of concrete social and economic questions. "This satisfies their practical, masculine mind," a Dutch Grail leader remarked after a meeting with the Bordelons and Gremillion at de Tiltenberg in 1954, "but I cannot imagine that it could ever satisfy a woman's heart." The Grail was fully committed to the transformation of the world, this leader added, but it insisted on giving first place to "the spiritual mission of women." "Sacrifice, prayer, dedication, holiness, God-centered-ness, and bringing Christ to people" were the movement's main concerns.[38]

In 1954 the Grail felt that despite these differences in understanding, patience might still produce "a beautiful example of cooperation between the masculine and the feminine and work a mutual inspiration and help."[39] And in 1957 the local Grail leadership was advised to avoid confrontation. "We can *never* make issues with priests or men and prove them wrong," they were told. "That is gaining a battle and losing the war."[40] But the movement's patience was not rewarded and the Grail was forced back upon its customary approach to the clergy, a direct appeal to the diocesan bishop, in this instance Maurice Schexnayder of Lafayette. With Schexnayder's help, a new center, accommodating sixteen residents, was opened in the town of Lafayette in 1960. Management of the student residence at Southwestern Louisiana Institute was abandoned, relations with the Catholic Center improved, and the Grail concentrated on its parish programs and training women to serve the diocese of Lafayette as teachers and social workers. The center in Louisiana, like all the others, had up a full head of steam as a new decade began.[41]

Beyond the organized city centers, Grail teams, small groups living in common, were to be found in more than a half dozen other places. From these two more centers emerged in the 1960s. Under the leadership of Brooklyn-born Dorothy Rasenberger, an art and book shop was opened in Toronto, Canada, in October 1961, and a residential center was established in that city's downtown area in May 1964. In September 1961 the California Grail Center was opened in San Jose. As mentioned previously, it offered a training program for missionaries in Latin America; it also focused its attention on the local Spanish-speaking community.

Without doubt, the Grail's city centers exerted a powerful influence on a wide constituency—clergy, families, and especially the thousands of young women who took part in their programs. Much of what they offered was new to the majority of American

Catholics. Their vision of Catholic life centered in active and imaginative participation in the liturgy was still seldom to be found in a local parish in the 1950s. And the apostolic works in which they engaged, inner-city renewal, interracial cooperation, community development, and the secular university apostolate, had entered the consciousness of very few.

The city center experience generally proved exhilarating for Grail members as well. But certain tensions also began to appear along the way. Those involving priests and competing groups were resolved satisfactorily enough, or put aside. But others continued to give trouble. Foremost among them was the fatigue city center leaders suffered as they tried to cope with a myriad of tasks in settings which lacked the concentration of Grailville. These young women, many of them holding positions of responsibility for the first time, had to pursue a full spiritual life (Mass and daily spiritual exercises), coordinate an ever-increasing number of programs, and (as will be seen in chapter 7) recruit new members of the Grail. Some of them, encountering urban life for the first time as lay apostles, also began to wonder a little about their appreciation of the secular world. Was it in such decay as people like Frank O'Malley said? Did they not meet non-Catholic and even nonreligious people who were nevertheless concerned about the world? Such questions, like those occasioned by the Grail's mission experiences, were seldom entertained openly. But they were there.[42]

6

The Heart of the Movement

As the Grail built up its network of city centers its headquarters at Grailville literally overflowed with aspiring lay apostles, and with ideas and materials for the advancement of the movement across the country.

Throughout the 1950s Grailville's elegant old farmhouse, now christened "House of Joy," and its many other green- and white-trimmed buildings were fully occupied, and then some. Each Year's School of Formation accepted approximately forty new students; and in the summers, when sometimes more than three hundred women attended courses, all of Grailville's barns were transformed into dormitories and the House of Joy's dining room spilled out onto the porch and surrounding lawns.[1]

These nearly overwhelming numbers seemed ample justification for Lydwine van Kersbergen's claim made at the 1951 National Catholic Youth Conference in Cincinnati that American young people were waiting to be asked for great things. Serious young women, van Kersbergen said, would surely answer a call for "sanctity, a spirit of sacrifice, a live Catholicism which integrates daily life, and a goal of nothing less than the conversion of the world."[2] The reflections of many students on their Grailville experience seemed to support her contention.

One woman from Louisiana discovered on a visit to Grailville that she was no longer "just a young girl lost in the complexities of modern life" and decided to enroll in the Year's School. As she prepared to return to Ohio, equipping herself with books on the Catholic Revival, the liturgical movement, and the cultures of the Orient and Africa, she was convinced that her previous world had been very small and that she now wished to live on a "world scale." Back at Grailville, her days took on an even greater "new sparkle." "Just try being bored," she exclaimed, "when you are living the life of the Church." This young woman was preparing for marriage, but Grailville helped her to see that in her own home and neighborhood she could participate in a larger Catholic effort to "restore family life to its proper level of Christian sanctity."[3]

A second student, from New York, was equally impressed. At the International Student Center she encountered the Grail's "normal, attractive young girls living on principle and being utterly wholehearted about it," and made the difficult choice to drop most of her "exhausting social life" in favor of a more "balanced" Christian existence. At Grailville she found an even greater order—and its source. "In spite of the great variety of backgrounds, interests, and talents," she said, "there was here a great unity of spirit, a very special unity and love which came from sharing in Christ's sacrifice and in a common life of work, recreation, study, and prayer."[4]

A third young woman, from Chicago, who had "never particularly wanted to be a secretary" and was saving money for college, experienced "a taste, the promise of something rich and full" on her initial visit to Grailville. Later, at the Year's School, she too identified the source of her feeling. Life had taken on a new rhythm. Before it was erratic, dependent on "moods and circumstances, successes or failures, friends, and family." But now it had the "graceful, flowing rhythm . . . of the Church's liturgical year which springs from the life of Christ within his Mystical Body."[5]

Grailville was perhaps most appreciated as "the Mystical Body in miniature," the place where the Grail's integrated Catholic life was most fully realized. But it remained "the heart of the movement" in another important sense—as the spawning ground for the broad spectrum of apostolic projects the Grail had been preparing for years to implement. City center leaders visited Grailville frequently in the 1950s. The ideas and activities they brought back to their centers grouped themselves around four major themes: world vision, Christian culture, woman, and modern catechetics.

WORLD VISION

The Grail never ceased to insist that all its activities be seen in the perspective of world conversion through the lay apostolate. Specialization in any area, such as family service or assisting foreign students, was never to become an end in itself—for the movement as a whole or any of its members. As has been seen (and will be again later in this chapter), specialization was regarded warily as a masculine tendency which limited the range of the apostolate and obscured its spiritual foundations. Female lay apostles were to be personalists and universalists.

As the Grail extended its own reach in the 1950s it became increasingly preoccupied with the need for breadth of vision in the apostolate—and with the apparent failure of some other lay organizations to promote it. With an obvious glance in the direction of Jocism, the Grail declared outright in 1953 that "Americans are tired of over-activism and are dissatisfied with the narrow provincial 'in the environment' focus of the average Catholic Action group." That year's "closed season" at Grailville was devoted, therefore, to a discussion of ways to recover "a world vision, a universal mindedness, a truly missionary spirit." For an hour after breakfast every day (while they sat in a circle cutting up apples and tomatoes for canning) and at other meals and in the evening, Grail members asked themselves, "What is a world vision? Why do we need one? Do we personally have one? How can we get one? How can we help others to get one?"[6]

These sessions soon gave rise to a new Grailville publication, *Towards a World Vision—An Apostolic Program* (1954). The Grail's world vision, this booklet said, was simply that of the Church "seen in all her universality." Its authors conceded that recent events—World War II, the atomic bomb, and the expansion of communism—had lent themselves to a rediscovery of Catholicism in worldwide terms. But such events were incidental at best to the Church's self-understanding. The world vision of Catholicism was "not simply a beautiful idea manufactured in order to meet the challenge of the present day." It was, on the contrary, *"our birthright as Catholics"*; it was "implicit in our faith long before the world became chaotic and troubled, and its re-emergence is one of the signs of a new springtime in the Church."[7]

For these Grail writers, instructed by the literature of the Catholic Revival, the Catholic Church alone possessed the inner strength and global reach to answer the challenge of the whole modern world. Other religious traditions were limited. Islam had a deep sense of the greatness of God but was flawed by a certain "moral laxness." Protestantism had a great missionary sense but exhibited a dangerous "watering down of doctrine"; its "union with the forces of secular humanitarianism," furthermore, made it the adversary of the Roman Church "on many points . . . crucial to her existence and welfare." The real problem, however, lay with the lack of appreciation which Catholics themselves displayed for their "birthright." To make this point unmistakably clear, *Towards a World Vision* presented a "play in one scene" in which "Comrade Mike" of the United States tells his fellow members of the Kremlin's Center for the Liquidation of Catholic Power that American Catholics have been infected with "the typical bourgeois mentality"; "they no longer have the aim of world conquest." "Comrade Pedro" agrees: rank and file Catholics have no conception at all that "theirs is a universal ideology which they must bring to all men."[8]

"Has the Catholic Church renounced her goal of winning the world?" *Toward a World Vision* asked. And would the Church be able, in practice, to match the power and scope of communism, which was attributable to "what it retains of Catholic doctrine?" The booklet, which was widely used at the Grail's city centers, called urgently for a process of re-education of Catholic people which would center on the social character of the Church (as the Mystical Body of Christ) and on a Catholic view of history.[9]

CHRISTIAN CULTURE

Behind the Grail's ideological discussions and its antipathy to specialization lay the movement's desire to bring the Christian spirit to bear on a full round of human pursuits ("unwomanly" work excluded), and thus to assist in achieving the Catholic Revival's ideal of a new Christian society. "We must work for a new Christendom," Lydwine van Kersbergen said again in 1950, "for recreation, drama, art, literature, music, and objects of daily life which express Christian values." Building on foundations established in the late 1940s, the Grailville community greatly increased its productivity in just these areas over the next decade. Frequently its practical efforts were accompanied by further elaboration of the Grail's approach to spiritual and cultural renewal.[10]

Gregorian chant had always been a major component of the Grail's training program. Everyone at Grailville continued to sing, but some now received more intense instruction in theory, polyphonic singing, and choir direction at the Grailville School of Music, established in 1953 "in response to the urgings of leaders in the field of liturgical music." A choral group was formed which participated directly in the apostolate by means of several recordings which were produced and distributed commercially. The first of these, *Grailville Sings—Music of Advent and Christmas for Listening and Family Singing*, was made in 1955. It was praised by the *New York Times* and by *Caecilia*, a journal of Church music, though the latter's view was a bit more critical. "True [*Grailville Sings*] is the work of amateurs," *Caecilia* said, "but it is work of superior quality with a depth of feeling and evidence of real musicianship that would make the record good for a music appreciation class of secondary or collegiate level or for a parish choir." In 1959 engineer Peter Bartók (son of the renowned composer Béla Bartók) journeyed to Ohio to record the choral group, then called the Grailville Singers, in *Easter at Grailville*. The *New York Times* was again enthusiastic, calling this "one of the best Easter records that has been issued since the long-playing process brought the genre into being"; the recording's main impression was one of simplicity, "a simplicity that is animated by reverence and musical sensibility."[11]

These first two records included some folk songs in addition to sacred music and the Grail's next two albums, *The Grail Singers* (1959) and *One World in Song* (1961), were wholly devoted to folk material. *Saturday Review* noted the former's "verve, gusto, and warm spontaneity." The School of Music also cooperated with the World Library of Sacred Music in Cincinnati in producing the booklet *Feast Day Melodies, Scripture Themes in Song* (1957).[12]

Eleanor Walker, who had learned about the Grail through Jean Daniélou's Cercle de St. Jean Baptiste in Paris, became the movement's spokeswoman in the field of music. This facet of Grailville's life she wrote, was to be understood in light of the Grail's overarching goal: "the spiritual formation of mature, responsible Christian laywomen able to carry their share of the temporal and spiritual labor required for the extending of the Redemption to every sphere of human life." Music could contribute to this spiritual formation, even in modern times, Walker argued. In worship, it could "raise man here and now to the harmony and integration of being promised by the Redemption." But even in less exalted circumstances, in "the other normal and good human activities we are called upon to share while on earth," music performed a "similar unifying and integrating function."

Grailville, Walker explained, kept itself free of competition with secular institutions of learning. Its concern was not so much a question of "providing tools in the form of particular skills or knowledge, as of a lifting of these tools to a new level by consciously integrating the student's personality around its relation to Christ." A product of Grailville's School of Music, Walker thought, should arrive at both "a deeper awareness of the dignity of her craft and her responsibility for its Christian exercise."[13]

In 1950 St. Brigid's Guild, the weaving group, occupied the feed room in Grailville's chicken house. Two years later the chickens moved out and another art department moved in, involving Grailville students in ceramics, woodcarving, painting, and calligraphy. The weavers, headed by Dutch Grail member Lydia Mulders, created church vestments, wall hangings, and costumes for the Grail's dramatic presentations. The others, led by Fern Logan and instructed by neighbor William Schickel, worked at a variety of things, notably the clay statuary which became the mainstay of the Grail's artistic output. This second group included the most prolific and admired of the movement's artists, Trina Paulus. In 1956 the arts center undertook its first commercial venture, the design and sale of three Christmas cards. A year later the Grail's first art catalogue appeared, offering small statues of the Holy Family and the Virgin Mary ("Fiat") and more Christmas cards. For several years thereafter new items were introduced, among them plaques of the Sacred Heart, wall hangings for the Christian year, a Christmas crib set, and cards for various occasions.[14]

As explained by Jeanne Heiberg, an art student at the Cooper Union in New York before joining the Grail, the art program was also deeply rooted in Grailville's vision of the Church and Christian culture. Its students were fortunate, first of all, to find themselves in an "organic and living" atmosphere; they worked in close touch with nature and lived in small groups which both provided support and demanded personal responsibility. Students also benefitted from the fact that their work fulfilled a "genuine need"; the furnishing and decorating of Grailville brought the subjects of the community's reading and meditation to life for everyone, as well as giving "outlet and encouragement" to the artists themselves. An even greater impetus, however, according to Heiberg, was the liturgy, "the living education of the Church." Immersed in worship, one could grow not only spiritually and intellectually, but also develop "in the finest possible way the feeling and sentiment the artist should have." The liturgy, moreover, untrammeled by either sentimentality or puritanism, could become a home for *contemporary* artistic aspiration. "The restrained intensity, the deep disciplined feeling, and the austere, stylized expressions of the Mass and the Office," Heiberg asserted, "have a close kinship to what some of the best moderns are striving for in their art."

Heiberg also pointed out that the art center, like the music program, did not intend to provide "a complete training in itself." It offered rather "a very valuable and necessary complement to art education as it exists."[15]

The remarks of both Walker and Heiberg indicated that the Grail was interested in restoring "the balance of personal creativity" in an age of increasing mass production. But the renewal of Christian culture was a large task which demanded that Christian art find its way to the many, especially to Catholic families.

Grailville's production program was soon geared, therefore, "to meet . . . the need for good, integral contemporary work in sufficient quantities to keep costs low." Following this philosophy the Grail launched a sustained effort in the late 1950s (primarily at its own city center art and book stores) to market the work of Grailville's artists and of others who made "a serious attempt to give fresh expression to Christian concepts."[16]

Dance had also been an integral part of Grailville's life, nurtured in the early years by Dom Ermin Vitry and Leonard Austin. In the 1950s the Grailville community created a number of new dance-dramas on scriptural themes, reminiscent (though on a smaller scale) of those performed in Europe two decades before. Under Grailville's inspiration, city center leaders mounted similar efforts of their own.

The first of the new dramas was "The New Eve," with which Grailville marked the 1954 Marian Year (the one hundredth anniversary of the definition of the doctrine of the Immaculate Conception). In its rhythmic movement of silent dancers and the commentary of two grey-robed choruses of speakers and singers, "The New Eve" portrayed Mary in her "surrender and dedication to the will of God, as the exemplar of woman's vocation." It was followed by "The Desired of the Nations," a drama for Advent, prepared by city center staff members in Philadelphia, Brooklyn, and New York and performed in all those cities (in Manhattan in the Carnegie Recital Hall) in December 1955. "New Born Again," previously described, was given first at Grailville in 1957 and then in Detroit in 1958. In 1958 also, the Lafayette, Louisiana, Grail Center produced "The Cosmic Tree," a dramatic presentation on the mystery of the Cross.[17]

The Grail had a word, too, about the place of its dance programs in the Church and the lay apostolate. Calling itself "a pioneer among an increasing number of college and university groups discovering in rhythmic interpretation a strikingly effective medium for expressing great religious themes in vivid, dramatic terms," the movement cited biblical precedent (David's dancing before the Ark of the Covenant) for its new productions. It also noted that the early Church had made use of symbolic movement and gesture in the liturgy, and that dancing had been definitively banned from religious ceremonies only at the time of the Reformation. The liturgy still contained remnants, the Grail thought, of gestures which allowed "the whole man" to express "in a natural way the many aspects of his inner dialogue with his Creator," and the movement's dramas were designed to rehabilitate this aspect of Catholic tradition.[18]

The Grail also put its forces in the visual arts, music, and drama together for several gala presentations. Grailville, as usual, led the way with a Festival of Arts in August 1956. This weekend devoted to "a contemporary expression of the Christian ideal in various cultural fields" included a display of art pieces, a lecture by William Schickel on "The Role of the Artist in Life," a dramatic reading from Paul Claudel's *The Satin Slipper*, and a concert by the Grailville choral group. A similar festival was held the following year in Philadelphia, and in December 1958 and January 1959 a Holiday of the Arts, with concerts, poetry readings, and an exhibit called "The Incarnation and the Arts," was presented in New York, Philadelphia, and Boston.[19]

Although it was implicit in the discussions of Eleanor Walker and Jean Heiberg, the theory or theology of Christian culture received little elaboration within the Grail. (Woman's role, it will be remembered, was deemed more motivational and practical than synthetic.) But the concept remained prominent in Catholic circles in the late 1950s, and Grail members paid some attention to it. Eleanor Walker noticed that Jacques Maritain, in his "kind and hope-filled new book about the United States," *Reflections on America*, had suggested that a new and great development might be near at hand: "the flowering of a modern Christian civilization on a world scale, with America playing the lead role." Christopher Dawson, less sanguine about America than Maritain but writing more vigorously than ever on the West's need to recover its religious (Christian) worldview, also attracted the Grail's attention. Guided by Dawson's ideas, Janet Kalven offered a series of lectures on religion and culture at Grailville in 1958. And, during the 1960–61 Year's School (the theme of which was Christian Culture), Dawson himself, who had come to the United States to be the first occupant of the Stillman Chair of Catholic Studies at the Harvard Divinity School, appeared at Grailville to lecture.[20]

By the time of Dawson's visit, however, the Grail found that it was devoting much less effort to production and promotion in the arts. The 1961 recording was the last, and no more dance-dramas were forthcoming.

The musings of artist Trina Paulus in 1960 hinted that this falloff was related to a slowly shifting perspective on the relationship between the Grail, the Church, and the world. Walker and Heiberg had spoken confidently about the value for the artist of Grailville's liturgical atmosphere and about the subordinate place of knowledge and technique. Paulus said that imbibing the "beautiful and special life" of Grailville and putting one's talents at its service was wonderful and perhaps essential—"for a while." And, living in New York as she now did, Paulus wondered if serving the world community and the Grail might not demand something new, "a certain freedom of spirit." In New York, she also observed, "you have no chance to become a big fish in a small pond."[21]

Such thoughts were soon to issue in a clearer suspicion that the Grail's approach to Christian art and the very concept of Christian culture, comprehensive as it seemed, were less than adequate to the modern condition.

WOMAN

Building on the teaching of Jacques van Ginneken, the Grail labored long to impress "a positive and profound concept of woman's specific role in the work of redemption" on the American lay apostolate. Thus far it had embodied that concept in Grailville's program of womanly education and discussed it in such publications as Janet Kalven's *The Task of Woman in the Modern World*. Understanding and acceptance had come slowly, the Grail felt. But now, after a decade of effort, "the point of woman" was making some headway. "We are not as far as Europe," Barbara Wald told her colleagues in 1953, "but there is a turn here and at least American Catholic leaders are recognizing that women must be trained differently than men—and that there is such a thing as women's apostolate after all!" Grailville, she thought, had itself "shaken the ideas of modern educators on curriculum for women."[22]

Buoyed by these feelings, the Grail moved into the mid-1950s determined to strengthen its own sense of the uniqueness of woman's role and promulgate it ever more widely. The tenth anniversary of Grailville was celebrated with a summer program entitled "The American Woman," which included courses on "The American Woman in Teaching, Medical, and Social Work," "The Young American Woman and the Will to Community," and "Woman in an Apocalyptic Age."

An "ancient proverb" quoted in the publicity for this program indicated that the Grail's thinking on woman was still very much in tune with the Catholic Revival's "crisis of the West" mentality. "Woman is the last fortress of every people," the proverb said; "If the man falls, God punishes the man; but if the woman falls, God will punish the people." Modern woman had fallen, the Grail declared, and her spiritual confusion constituted an "ominous sign" for society as a whole. But the proverb's warning could also be reckoned "a tribute to woman's power." It even contained "the seeds of new hope"—if woman could recover her true self. As Barbara Wald's reference to "different" training for women showed, the Grail had not changed its mind either as to what constituted this true self. The movement's reflections on woman in the 1950s held fast to the conviction that the natures of man and woman were, though complementary, necessarily and fundamentally distinct. These reflections were put forward with great energy, however, and with the earlier rural life emphasis no longer in evidence, they were placed in a more elaborate theological context.[23]

The American Grail's principal spokesperson in this realm was its cofounder and president Lydwine van Kersbergen. Three of van Kersbergen's attempts to bring the question of woman to a wider reading audience were gathered with a previously unpublished essay into a small volume called *Woman, Some Aspects of Her Role in the Modern World*. John J. Wright, bishop of Worcester, Massachusetts, in his Foreword, called it "a theologically valid analysis of what God had in mind, so to say, when he created woman."[24]

Van Kersbergen began her analysis with yet another Grail repudiation of feminism, which had recently been cast in its "most extreme form" by Simone de Beauvoir in *The Second Sex*. Feminism, van Kersbergen wrote, was a fundamentally resentful phenomenon, exhibiting a "deep-seated, misogynous aversion for everything connected with the specific womanly role in love and motherhood." It also championed the erroneous and dangerous view that "the achievements which our society designates as masculine are the only valuable achievements." De Beauvoir herself had fallen into the now traditional feminist trap of identifying the human with the masculine; she offered no positive concept of woman, no recognition that women have gifts and qualities "different from men's but equally representative of humanity and equally valuable."[25]

Van Kersbergen was pleased, however, to see evidence of a growing reaction against feminism's errors. Helene Deutsch, Dorothy Thompson, and even Margaret Mead, she said, could be numbered among those beginning to realize that woman's inherent qualities had not been given their due. Working women, too, "restless and dissatisfied in routine jobs, or exhausted by the struggle for success in the highly competitive world of business," longed for more genuine fulfillment precisely as women. "We appear to be at the threshold of a new development," van Kersbergen concluded; "The way lies open for a genuine integration of woman's new found freedoms with a positive concept of her role."[26]

Valuable as psychological, biological, and sociological insights might be, however, only Christian theology could reveal the "ultimate metaphysical meaning of womanhood." An "unparalleled opportunity for Christian thinkers to take the initiative in the work of integration" presented itself. Van Kersbergen proceeded therefore to an examination of Scripture and Church tradition.[27]

In the Book of Genesis, according to the Grail's president, Adam and Eve stand "side by side as images of God, mirroring his likeness, endowed with the same gifts of mind and heart and will." But this equality does *not* constitute identity. Eve's peculiar qualities complement those of Adam precisely by standing over against them—they are "counterparts." Adam is the more active and independent of the two; he imposes his will on life, rules the family, defines principles, becomes an expert in "one specialty" or other. Eve, in contrast, is the more receptive and dependent; she is the "tactful and loving" companion of her spouse; she is the keeper of tradition and the home; she surrenders her will with "ready pliability" to a multiplicity of demands—she is in truth "the mother of all the living."[28]

Van Kersbergen insisted that the masculine and feminine are not mutually exclusive. Everyone possesses both, and the great person—the genius and the saint—usually develops both to a high degree. Nor should woman's qualities be considered weak in comparison to man's. Woman is not merely passive: she is "not echo but answer—the active, discriminating, sympathetic response, which inspires and encourages and fructifies." Neither does woman fail to play her part in intellectual and cultural life, though she does so as a "hidden collaborator." Her receptive nature actually enables her to take on the most important and demanding task of all, that of "safeguarding the Godward direction of mankind." It is woman's natural and supernatural destiny "to embody the free and loving submission of creature to creator and to inspire this surrender in others."[29]

Beyond all this explication, however, it remained true for van Kersbergen that "in man, the masculine should predominate; in the woman, the feminine."[30]

The divine idea of woman, van Kersbergen added, is to be found most perfectly realized in the "illuminating radiance" of the Virgin Mary. The "non serviam" of modern secularism might be overcome if contemporary woman rediscovered her "fundamental spiritual orientation" in the mother of Jesus, "the divine school in which humanity learns to say 'Yes' to God."[31]

Although the American Grail demanded no formal promise of celibacy in the 1940s, the movement was known to advocate the virginal life and received many invitations to speak and write about it. Great caution, however, seemed in order. The Grail had not wished to stress the value of virginity above that of marriage; and it had received little encouragement from priests and other Catholic leaders who had been "afraid . . . for years" of the idea of consecrated virginity for the laywoman. As late as 1953 the movement deemed it unwise to enter the public arena on the subject. But in the mid-1950s virginity, too, was gaining a hearing—Pope Pius XII issued an encyclical on it in March 1954.[32] Given this more favorable climate, and the Grail's recently announced need for a strong nucleus of totally dedicated members, it seemed time to change course. Lydwine van Kersbergen addressed the notion of virginity directly in the pages of *Woman*.

The Grail leader recognized that modern society ("today's de-Christianized culture") considered virginity "at best a deprivation of a natural function, a failure of life." But it was all the poorer for thinking so. Contemporary minds had much to learn from the Christian tradition, for which, van Kersbergen said, virginity symbolizes the absolute value of the person before God. The virgin's consecrated life indeed puts her outside the family— but only to demonstrate that "our human destiny is greater than the family circle, however valued that may be." It puts her outside the state as well—but only to "proclaim the dignity of the weak, of the aged, and of minority groups" over against "humanitarians and totalitarians." There could be little doubt, van Kersbergen said, that virginity had played a decisive role in establishing the spiritual equality of woman and man.[33]

Van Kersbergen also noted that the virgin plays a crucial part in the life of the Church, keeping in "delicate balance the scale of action and contemplation." The virgin withdraws behind the traditional symbol of the veil in order to "pierce through the shadows to the fulness of light"; she lives a life of atoning sacrifice, accepting the role of victim in reparation for the sins of the world. But she is not thereby confined or without impact on the world, van Kersbergen argued. Without contradiction, she can be an apostle, and a freer one than most. With "heart whole, all her energies concentrated immediately and directly on God's work," she is ready to go wherever she can be of service to others.[34]

Van Kersbergen again insisted, with respect to virginity, that she was following a "venerable Christian tradition" which calls attention to the differences between man and woman but does not dichotomize them. Fundamentally, the consecrated life is the same for both sexes. But different expressions of it for each are appropriate. The Church knows this, and in the liturgy therefore "sets before the man the pattern of the high priest and king, the ruler and the soldier of Christ, while for the woman she chooses the nuptial theme."[35]

Van Kersbergen concluded her study of woman by returning to the theme of motherhood, which Janet Kalven had stressed in the previous decade. The demand for "defense production" in the Cold War era had accelerated the trend toward "paid specialized employment of women," and this, coupled with the errors of feminism, had led to great confusion about the dignity and significance of woman's motherly nature. It was bad enough that this confusion adversely affected family life, van Kersbergen observed, but it also had negative implications for woman's larger contribution to the social order. Without an awareness and acceptance of the mother's qualities of fecundity, other-centeredness, compassion, universality, and stability, woman would fail to help the world see the weak, the helpless, and the poor "as children." She would not supply the necessary counterbalance of compassion and mercy to the sense of justice and the rule of law "which are man's contribution to society." The woman in politics, van Kersbergen said, suddenly making the Grail's first discernible allusion to the possibility of such a vocation, must exercise a form of motherhood and not be "a replica of the masculine legislator and politician."[36]

As a reader in the 1980s might surmise, van Kersbergen's theology of woman was eventually rejected, despite its emphasis on woman's strength, as an invitation to unwarranted self-deprecation and continued male dominance. But for the moment —and for nearly a decade—it elicited no visible criticism. In context this was unremarkable, for van Kersbergen's line of argument departed in no significant way from the few other Catholic treatments of woman's nature circulating at the time.[37] It also rode the crest of an ongoing and successful effort by the Grail (described in chapter 7) to increase the number of its lifetime celibate members.

Van Kersbergen's apology for virginity was, however, an element in a shift of policy within the Grail which eventually produced a reaction important to the movement's future. As already noted, the Grail in the 1940s sought to keep married women and even their whole families in close touch with its full-time, permanent members. In the early to mid-1950s, despite the formal establishment of the nucleus (or perhaps because of it), efforts were made to keep this spirit alive, primarily by Joan Overboss. Following the precedent set by the case of the families who came to live adjacent to Grailville, Overboss began a new attempt in 1953 to "integrate into the movement" the large number of families the Grail had encountered at its city centers. After a year of meeting with married couples from many parts of the country, she reported that although the "family apostolate" remained distinct from the centers' primary tasks, it was still developing in "close harmony" with them. It seemed to Overboss that the inclusion of Christian families was of the "utmost importance," both for the married couples themselves and for the Grail as a whole. She also led a weekend, therefore, at Super Flumina for twenty-five young married women (without their husbands) in February 1954, the success of which led to a similar meeting conducted for East Coast women by Lydwine van Kersbergen. Overboss noted that in these gatherings one point emerged most strongly: "the necessity of a close bond between those who are married and those who live in dedicated virginity." "Once we begin to see the unity among us all," she hoped, "we can see so much better that it is possible to create a current of womanly influence in our time."[38]

But it was not long after this that Joan Overboss left the United States, and with her the approach she wished to cultivate anew. In March 1957, in fact, International President Rachel Donders advised American Grail leaders to the contrary. They were to concentrate, she said, "more on the young girls and those who have no apostolic outlets yet and who can be used more." The married women actually were "a little bit of a problem," part of an "alumnae feeling" which the Grail should not encourage. They should be given consideration, Donders allowed, but "not the couples."[39]

At a reunion held in May 1958 for women who had attended

the Year's School, Janet Kalven told her audience that the Grail had evolved in such a way that all of them shared responsibility for it in some manner, but also to the point where the distinction between full-time celibate members and all others was firmly established.[40]

At the close of the 1950s the Grail's family apostolate had virtually disappeared from view and some of the married women were beginning to ask just what their standing in the Grail was.

MODERN CATECHETICS

The Catholic Revival, though it sought to skirt the problems which led to the condemnation of Modernism, succeeded in restoring a certain theological consciousness to the Church, especially to men and women involved in the lay apostolate. Even in the 1930s few Catholic Actionists were unaware of the Church as the Mystical Body of Christ and the possibilities of living out this doctrine through active participation in the liturgy and some kind of engagement with the world. In the 1940s Pope Pius XII attempted to nurture this consciousness in his encyclical letters *Mystici Corporis* and *Mediator Dei* (On the Sacred Liturgy). By the 1950s, moreover, a new wave of Catholic biblical studies had appeared, and some theologians had begun to glean insights from many other formerly neglected fields, especially psychology. With more and more lay apostles now in need of and seeking out a theological background, a reformulation of the ordinary means of teaching Catholic doctrine seemed much in order. "Modern catechetics," emphasizing the scriptural and experiential dimensions of faith, was the result.

Modern catechetics (or sometimes simply "religious education") was the last major theme to be sounded at Grailville in the 1950s, but it generated no less enthusiasm than the earlier ones. It was, in fact, "a case of love at first sight" since, as nucleus member Eva Fleischner explained, the Grail "had for more than fifteen years been trying to work out some of the most essential aspects of the catechetical renewal." Catching the new emphasis precisely, Fleischner cited the movement's long-standing concern for the liturgy as "the school of sanctity and doctrine," for Scripture as "the life-giving Word of God," and for Christian faith as "the response to God's love, flowing over into concrete commitment."[41]

Anxious to absorb the new catechetics, the Grail again followed the procedure adopted in its earliest days in America of inviting prominent scholars to bring their expertise to Grailville (and the city centers). Thus in the summer of 1955 the German Jesuit Johannes Hofinger arrived to give the Grailville community a survey of the contemporary theological situation and to lecture on "Theology and the Layman." In the following year French theologian Louis Bouyer came to speak on "The Bible and Liturgy in Our Christian Witness to the World," and two summers later he returned for more lectures and a retreat for thirty Grail members based on his study of Mary in the Scriptures, *Le Trône de la Sagesse.* In 1958 theologian and psychologist Josef Goldbrunner, with Hofinger a prime mover of the new *German Catechism,* came to lecture on "Depth Psychology and the Spiritual Life" and "Human Nature and the Mysteries of God"; he too returned to Grailville, in 1959, for a course on new teaching methods.[42]

Modern catechetics quickly took hold in the minds of Grail members, one of whom began to study with Johannes Hofinger at the University of Notre Dame in the summer of 1957 while several others entered training at various catechetical institutes, including Lumen Vitae in Belgium. Catechetics also soon found its place in the structure of the movement. In 1958 a catechetical department was formed at Grailville and rapidly grew into the Grail Council on Religious Education which coordinated new programs throughout the country. In November 1959 the first issue of this Council's *Bulletin* appeared, edited by Eva Fleischner. Consisting mostly of reprints of articles and reviews from European sources, the *Bulletin* was at first intended for circulation only within the Grail. But Father Gerard Sloyan of the Catholic University of America expressed interest in becoming a subscriber and the *Bulletin* was soon "happily surrendered to serve a more general purpose."[43]

In 1960 Fleischner reported that the Grail's city centers in Brooklyn (and Queens), Detroit, and Cincinnati were actively engaged in catechetical work. Seventeen parishes were being served in Brooklyn alone. Programs were being developed for primary school children (six Grail members were about to take over a school in Lawton, Oklahoma, as a laboratory for work at that level), and for teenagers (the Grail's Youth Leadership Program was aimed especially at Catholic young people attending non-Catholic schools).

As these efforts went forward, the Grail found "an immediate and wholly positive response" among its students and teachers. The reason, reiterated by Eva Fleischner, was that contemporary religious education at its best centered on the person. It was not, she said, concerned with "a series of abstract tenets that must be memorized and believed, but with *life*, the life of God communicated to man, and calling forth in man his wholehearted response in love."[44]

The Grail had always placed a premium on the development of each individual's gifts, but the personalism of the new catechetics, especially as it "linked psychological health or wholeness . . . to spiritual life and growth," seemed to bring a fresh dimension to the movement's thinking. Many Grail members later recalled that along with the writings of Teilhard de Chardin, modern catechetics started them along a path which led to a new view of themselves and of the Church's approach to the world.[45]

World vision, Christian culture, the nature and role of woman, and modern catechetics became elements of all the training programs at Grailville and the city centers, but the 1958 Year's School of Formation, called the Cooperative Community Year, brought them together in especially explicit, summary fashion. Staff members were in relatively short supply that year, since many had gone off to the missions or were in demand around the country, but the Cooperative Community Year nevertheless offered three "integrated programs" designed to "enable women to play their part in meeting some of the deepest needs of modern man: the need for an authentic Christian and apostolic formation [modern catechetics]; the need for true community on the family, neighborhood, national, and world levels [world vision]; and the need for cultural expression in accord with inner convictions [Christian culture]." The year's program showed, in other words, that Grailville in the 1950s had adhered tenaciously to its "task of integration," honing it to a fine point.[46]

Reports on the Cooperative Community Year also demonstrated that Grailville's commitment to maintaining "the Mystical Body in miniature" was still intact. There was, as usual, a Thanksgiving course ("Liturgy Builds Community"); a Christmas course (highlighted by a lecture by Clement McNaspy, S.J., on "Incarnation and the Arts"); Lenten lectures (given by Robert Lechner, C.Pp.S.); and weekends devoted to art, music, and dance (Dom Ermin Vitry was back for a workshop on "Music and Eurhythmics"). The daily schedule, too, remained virtually unchanged: the walk to Mass at St. Columban's in the morning, the farm work, the long periods of meditation, the festive meals, and the night silence. Radios and television sets, which now proliferated elsewhere, did not intrude.[47]

Consistent in all these ways, Grailville was counted a success. It had not been altogether untroubled. In 1955 and again in 1957 Archbishop Alter of Cincinnati was prompted to make new inquiries about some of the Grail's ascetical practices, its liturgical innovations, and its canonical status. Some of the observations he received from local priests were not especially flattering: one referred to "the untrained mind of the layman"; and another, alluding to the "unusual perfection" sought by the Grail, included a reminder that "they are a group of women being led by women, with a great deal of female emotions and instincts guiding them."[48] But none of these criticisms moved the archbishop to take action. Prospective lay apostles continued to pour into Grailville. As the Cooperative Community Year began, one hundred of the two hundred and fifty young women who had attended courses during the previous summer committed themselves to serving as team members with the Grail; twenty-six more entered training as members of city center staffs; and fifteen remained at Grailville for a year's stay.[49] On the assumption that these numbers would remain stable or even increase, and that "the heart of the movement" would continue to beat as it had since 1944, an Expansion and Building Program for Grailville was announced on December 6, 1959, just six weeks prior to Pope John XXIII's announcement that he planned to convene an ecumenical council in Rome.

7

"Which Only Women Can Achieve"

As the stories of Grailville and the city centers show, the American Grail took wing in the 1950s. Other lay apostolate groups did too, and the Grail's place in what one contemporary observer called "a vast surge of interest in the layman's role in the Church" will be examined later in this chapter.[1] But one more facet of the Grail's life remains to be uncovered: the deliberations of its leadership. Focused for the most part in what was called the Round Table, these deliberations reveal in their own way (as the Cooperative Community Year did in another) the Grail's most basic and fervently pursued aim: the integration of all its activities — and all its people — into an overarching framework of apostolic ideals. They also demonstrate how, following the establishment of the nucleus, the Grail in America came to see its future more and more precisely in terms of organizational strength.

The Grail's leadership was never quite satisfied that it was living up to Jacques van Ginneken's ideal of "a smoothly running organization and a flexibility which only women can achieve." In a period of rapid expansion its dissatisfaction was all the greater. As Barbara Wald said in a statement typical of the 1950s, "We feel that our pace is still too slow and that we must work with far greater energy and clarity of goal in the coming years, to take advantage of the golden opportunity that is ours in America right now." "A more structured approach in our work of building a movement," she added, was thought to be especially important. The Round Table was established, therefore, in November 1953, consisting of Lydwine van Kersbergen, her two assistants, Wald and Janet Kalven, and leaders of the then existing city centers. This assembly of nucleus members, which met in Burlington, New Jersey, was the Grail's initial answer to the need for greater organization. Its business was short- and long-range policy and planning.[2]

First on the Round Table's agenda were matters of real estate and finance. Lydwine van Kersbergen was especially concerned about them. It was a great lack, she said, that besides Grailville the movement as yet owned no property. Renting space, which offered little protection in time of economic depression, was "pouring money down the drain." The Grail should carefully but quickly acquire property of high resale value. Van Kersbergen also advised her cohorts to seek an adequate amount in donations. Leaders should make sure to gather "circles of friends on whom we can rely in every difficulty" and keep in touch with all the movement's benefactors, giving them "a good strong lecture from time to time." They should pay special attention to ecclesiastical authorities. "Learn how to visit them," van Kersbergen said; "Build up a psychological approach. . . . Do not go to them all the time with difficult matters. They are so weary of these problems. The next time you can go with a difficulty."[3] Van Kersbergen's desire to see the Grail purchase property of its own became the rule as the city centers were established in succeeding years.

At its initial meetings the Round Table also noted that the Grail lacked "mass techniques." Without better publicity it could not become a truly influential movement.[4] More pressing, however, was the question as to whether the Grail was making a sufficiently deep and permanent impact on the growing numbers of young women participating in its programs, especially at the city centers. The Round Table confessed that it did not think so:

> We do not have the sense that we must touch the heart of every single person who comes to us. We have a good sense about our own personal transformation; we have a certain sense about reaching leaders, but hardly any sense that every last person with whom we come in contact must be changed. . . . The spirit of the Grail is to ask sacrifice of everyone it touches, not just to lift or stir them with its message.

A list of "signs of transformation" was drawn up, therefore, to help leaders gauge the effectiveness of their efforts. A young woman experiencing a true "metanoia" (change of heart) should exhibit a spirit of sacrifice; a sense of wholeness; an awareness of secularism; an agreement on fundamental principles [of the apostolate]; a sense of apostolic responsibility; and a feeling for commitment to the Grail.[5]

Two years later, meeting with International President Rachel Donders, the Round Table was, if anything, more convinced that the Grail should "develop its scope as a movement." Donders herself was sure that the Americans were "at the verge of an important step ahead"; they had reached a point where they could expect a surge of growth, as when "the chestnut tree's slimy brown buds . . . burst with a 'ping.' " Lydwine van Kersbergen concurred. "A Benedictine monastery is an end in itself," she remarked, "a way of life, an oasis. But our vocation is to expand."[6]

The 1955 Round Table drew its conclusions in vivid arithmetic terms. "Multiply immediately" was to be the slogan of the movement, and "ideas and influence should spread out in geometrical progression." Specific numerical goals were attached to these generalities: a total of one thousand Grail team members by June 1956; one hundred participants in the next Year's School of Formation at Grailville; and fifty new members of the nucleus by October 1956.[7] Nevertheless (it was said), numbers were not to be overemphasized; they were not paramount, nor were the personal problems of young women attracted to the Grail ("although we must help to solve them!").[8] What really mattered was that each person be challenged about the seriousness of her participation in the movement. To this end the Round Table recommended a previously neglected instrument, a pledge of commitment for those who did not (or did not yet) intend to join the nucleus. "I believe that by my Baptism and Confirmation," one version of the pledge read in part, "I have been entrusted with a particular task in God's plan for the conversion of the world. In striving to fulfill this task, I freely pledge myself to work in unity of goal and action with young women of every race and nation as a member of the International Grail Movement."[9]

In 1956 the Round Table again focused on challenging all those associated with the Grail, this time on the need for a deeper spiritual life. It was decided that each Friday at the city centers was to be set aside for prayer; that those in the nucleus or preparing for it were to spend one month of the year in recollection; and that Grailville's training program was to be extended, ideally at least, to three years.[10]

Round Table discussions also reflected the concern (seen above in several connections) that the American Grail understand its position and its ultimate goals clearly: that it was part of an international movement, and that each of its apostolic works was but one facet of an attempt to renew all of society. Rachel Donders put these points forcefully in 1955. Undue attention to local problems, she said, could obscure "the uniqueness of the Grail . . . that we are aiming at the conversion of the world." The city centers (which had been founded in part to serve their surrounding communities or to house a special program) had "no meaning unless they are related to the total movement."[11] The Round Table responded to this admonition by agreeing to drop the distinctive names of the centers in Detroit, Cincinnati, and Brooklyn. The Gateway, Gabriel House, and Monica House became simply the Grail centers in those cities. But the underlying issue was not resolved, at least not to Rachel Donders' satisfaction. Two years later the international president returned with a similar warning. Five years into the future, she said, "maybe all there will be will be the centers." Citing the situation of the Institute for Overseas Service in Brooklyn as an example, Donders insisted that it was not enough "if people who come to work in the missions get their education in your institute"; they had to realize that they were coming into "a mansion and not into a little chicken coop."[12] The members of the Round Table once again took her words to heart. "In general," one of them confessed, "I think the girls feel that we are trying to draw them into a particular field." The assembled leaders agreed to place greater emphasis on the Grail's inclusive aims at all their centers.[13]

In accordance with this same emphasis, major steps were taken in 1955 to coordinate and consolidate the actual operations of the Grail on a nationwide basis. With Lydwine van

Kersbergen retaining final decision-making power as president, and Janet Kalven, Dolores Brien, and Jeanne Plante comprising its executive committee, the Round Table was assigned overall charge of the movement in the United States. And to coordinate and develop particular aspects of the apostolate, a series of councils was established, each body headquartered in one of the city centers. The Council on World Community worked out of New York; the Council on the Integration of Life out of Cincinnati; the Council on Christian Culture out of Philadelphia; and the Council on Work for Women out of Brooklyn.[14]

In succeeding years more measures were adopted in the interest of "a gradual growth of centralization" of the Grail's administration and finances, especially those of its publications and art production programs. In March 1957, at the suggestion of Rachel Donders, a Committee of Three, consisting of Lydwine van Kersbergen, Barbara Wald, and Eileen Schaeffler, was formed to coordinate these functions from Grailville.[15]

The leadership's desire to unify all the movement's activities eventually led to a more thoroughgoing structural reform. In 1959 the Round Table was succeeded, in effect, by two new groups. Its decision-making function was assumed by a National Committee through which the American Grail's president (van Kersbergen), two vice-presidents (Wald and Schaeffler), and three others (Jeanne Plante, Dorothy Rasenberger, and Audrey Sorrento) were to exercise "shared responsibility." And its original consultative role was taken over by a National Advisory Committee which included not only Grailville and city center leaders but heads of various committees and others, nucleus members only it should be noted, in the forefront of the movement.[16]

A separate committee was also established in 1959 to care for the "special interests" of those who belonged to the nucleus. The need for such a committee seemed clear, for with the strong emphasis placed on virginity and depth of commitment to the Grail in the mid-1950s, the nucleus had grown appreciably. The goal of fifty new members set for 1955–56 had not been reached, but eleven American women had made their dedications on February 14, 1955; another nine joined on March 2, 1957, followed by five more on March 25 of the same year; and a group of sixteen, making their promises of lifetime celibacy and obedience to the Grail's international president on October 2, 1959, brought the number of American nucleus members to more than seventy.[17]

The organizational structures at which the Grail arrived in the late 1950s, especially the National Committee and the National Advisory Committee, were apparently intended to *decentralize* authority in the movement and to provide opportunities for a new generation of leadership to emerge. But there were also the last steps taken in the spirit of "integration" which had guided the Grail so far and which had been invoked with such insistence throughout the previous decade. The movement's passion for personal commitment and for "unity of vision and action" (Rachel Donders' phrase) had reached its zenith.[18]

In the early 1950s advocates and practitioners of the lay apostolate in America were few. But by the end of the decade the idea, at least, of active lay participation in the Church's mission had begun to take hold. Several new lay-edited periodicals had appeared, among them *Cross Currents* (1950), *Jubilee* (1953), and *Apostolic Perspectives* (1956); and books like Louis Putz's *The Modern Apostle* and Michael de la Bedoyere's *The Layman in the Church* filled the shelves of Catholic bookstores. The idea had also received a tremendous boost from the papacy. Pope Pius XII, addressing the Second World Congress of the Laity in Rome on October 5, 1957, enunciated what was by far the most theologically positive description of lay action to date. "The 'consecratio mundi' [consecration of the world]," he said, "is essentially the work of laymen themselves, of men who are intimately part of economic and social life. . . . ." Ecclesiastical authorities, the pope continued, should "entrust the layman with tasks that he can perform as well or even better than the priest, and allow him to act freely and exercise personal responsibility within the limits set for his work or demanded by the common welfare of the Church." Pius XII even wanted to de-emphasize direct hierarchical mandates and to encourage "the free lay apostolate." The training of lay apostles, the pope also said, should be attended to by lay organizations themselves.[19]

Inspired by the new literature and this papal sanction, a

number of lay groups began to prosper from the mid-1950s onward. The Grail's old debating partner the YCS/YCW reported in 1959 that it had 3,000 members in thirty-five cities; its alumni and alumnae had also flocked into the Christian Family Movement (CFM), which in the same year claimed 50,000 member couples. The number of lay missionaries trained by the Grail and other organizations like the Association for International Development increased—not monumentally, but at a rate sufficient to constitute a "new boom" in the field and occasion a National Conference on Lay Mission Work in November 1959. More traditional, parish-based organizations also showed new vigor. The NCWC's National Council of Catholic Women and National Council of Catholic Men helped to stir interest in the lay apostolate with progressive programs in liturgy, social action, and family life. And the Legion of Mary and the Sodalities of Our Lady burgeoned. (The latter claimed 18,000 units and formed a national federation in 1957.)[20]

Not everyone was sure about the depth of this American Catholic phenomenon. One observer remarked that many people contracted an "apostolic itch" which quickly faded. Another felt that Americans were insufficiently aware that much of the literature concerning the laity's role emanated from Europe (especially France) and was therefore valuable only for inspiration—not for insight into America's problems. Others were vaguely disturbed about the "suburbanization" of some lay groups, particularly the CFM. Leo R. Ward, for example, in his impressionistic survey of contemporary lay movements published in 1959, allowed that the recently increased activity and confidence of American Catholics might be based in part on "a sort of general prosperity." But such qualifications did not coalesce into a major critique. The lay apostolate was still new to the general run of churchgoers and needed as much encouragement as possible.[21]

As noted above, the Grail entertained reservations of its own regarding their fellow Americans' ability to understand and commit themselves wholeheartedly to the apostolate. But in general its judgments about the recent rise of lay activity, and about its growth, were positive and hopeful. "The laity's coming of age," Dolores Brien wrote in 1957, "their ripening into mature, responsible members," was becoming an important factor in the modern mission of the Church.[22] This was also the view expressed by Lydwine van Kersbergen on her return from the Second World Congress of the Laity in the same year. Twenty or thirty years before, she said, the lay apostolate was in "the full flush of adolescence—full of enthusiasm and untried optimism"; now it could boast men and women "of wisdom and experience who are fully aware of their task and accepting the responsibility for Christianizing the modern world."[23] Rachel Donders, furthermore, was filled with joy that the Grail was part of a vanguard sure to shape the Church's future. "We are really in the Church, fully in it," she told the Round Table. Priests might continue to insist that they alone were theologically informed, but lay people actually engaged in the apostolate, especially the women, knew what they were doing. "In ten years," Donders asserted, "you will have another language again." Lydwine van Kersbergen picked up her superior's point one more time. "We are the doers," she said, "theology and canon law follow."[24]

The Grail did show some awareness in the later 1950s of new questions raised within the American Church regarding the proper relationship of Catholics and society. The call for Catholic self-examination issued earlier by John Cogley and others was now widely heard and debated, thanks primarily to historian John Tracy Ellis' 1955 essay, "American Catholics and the Intellectual Life." Ellis did not dwell on the value of an autonomous secular order but he claimed that a "self-imposed ghetto mentality" had severely limited the Catholic contribution to American culture.[25]

Perhaps conscious of its previous indisposition toward American higher education, the Grail took no apparent notice of Ellis' contribution. But when the Jesuit theologian John Courtney Murray, in a special issue of *Life* in 1956, acknowledged that a "certain 'group consciousness' " had inhibited a true sense of the Church, Dolores Brien hastened to agree. The time for Catholic "self-defense and self-protection" was past, she declared. The ghetto mentality of American Catholics, who though more than thirty-million strong sent only five thousand missionaries to foreign lands, was obsolete. A "more Catholic approach to life in America" was required. Brien's remarks here were perhaps "too Catholic" for John Cogley; and they pertained more to the Grail's global aspirations than to a new approach to American society. But they also included one Cogleylike perspective: Capable people, Brien said, especially in the lay apostolate, had "come out of the period when 'secularism' was the burning question."[26]

Brien went on to indicate how the Catholic freed from preoccupation with secularism might see the world anew in a 1957 Grail booklet, *The Laity and the International Scene.* There were factors at work in the world, she wrote, which were actually favorable to the Church's mission: "From a natural point of view, we can observe the evolution of certain attitudes in modern society which are fundamentally Christian. Although far from perfect they form the basis upon which the total Christian vision can be built." Among these attitudes were the unity of the human family, the dignity of the person (as affirmed in the charter of the United Nations), the political and social interdependence of the nations of the world, and the acknowledged right of all peoples to self-determination. A radical change—from "what is merely human to what is compatible with man's divine end"—had still to take place within this framework, and Catholics ought still to look for its source in the Church. They should attend especially to the lay apostolate among "the dynamic elements which are in motion in the Church enabling her to capture this moment of time." But the eyes of believers ought not to be averted from the world and its possibilities. It might even be, Brien mused, that "the deeper reality of the doctrine of the Mystical Body of Christ can never be attractive unless a need is first realized in the natural order."[27]

In their references to the "merely human" and a "total Christian vision," Brien's observations continued to reflect the Catholic Revival philosophy which had motivated the Grail through the years. Lacking an emphasis on the chaos of the modern world, however, they sounded a new note in the Grail's thinking on the relationship of Church and world.

It was not apparent in the late 1950s, however, that the new, more positive emphasis on the secular world would do any particular violence to the then reigning concepts of the Church or Catholic identity. The terms of the Catholic intellectualism debate were broadened significantly by Thomas O'Dea's *American Catholic Dilemma* (1958), which said that the American Church labored under the burdens not only of defensiveness but of formalism, authoritarianism, clericalism, and moralism.[28] But it took subsequent events to bring O'Dea's thinking to the fore. The American Church, and with it the Grail, approached the year 1960 with a mixture of impatience and confidence but no real prescription for change.

As will be seen in the next chapter, the Grail soon began to take a harder look at itself. But at this point there was little question that its future lay in a more intense commitment to the ideals it had adhered to and the forms it had developed during its first two decades in America.

The concepts of "the conversion of the world" and "Christian culture," after all, had served the Grail well. The movement had shown the way, almost alone at first, in the lay mission field; it had established a network of centers which introduced thousands of young women to a brighter vision of the Church and to a wide variety of apostolic projects; it had created and marketed a popular line of contemporary Christian art objects; it had articulated and put into practice—here again it was virtually alone—a theology of women's role in the apostolate; and, with the growth of its inner elite (the nucleus) and the development of coordinating councils and committees, it had achieved considerable strength as an organization. The Grail's leadership in the lay apostolate had also won further recognition. Not just a few would agree with Leo R. Ward that the Grail had become "a chief source of new life" in the American Church; Ward found himself hard pressed to name a half dozen groups who were doing more for "the restoration of a full blooded Christian community and a Christian culture in America."[29]

With the Grail's mission program in full swing and its city centers and Grailville looking to expand, and with the prospect of further encouragement for the laity from Pope John XXIII's ecumenical council, the future seemed full of promise. As things turned out, it was full of agony as well.

8
From Organization to Meeting Place

The new spirit generated but not fully comprehended by the elites of the 1950s, including the lay apostolate, burst upon the American Church in the new decade. It was abetted by the figure of John F. Kennedy, newly elected the first Catholic president of the United States, by a new wave of European theological literature prompted by Pope John's call for Vatican II, and by the surprisingly irenic social teaching and personal bearing of the pope himself.

The young president symbolized the realization of two major aspirations of 1950s progressive Catholicism: full involvement in American society and a clear focus on the Catholic layman. Kennedy was, to boot, a loyal (if not particularly zealous) Catholic whose public course of action was not (as he explained during his campaign) going to be determined for him by the Church's hierarchy.[1]

The new European literature, exemplified by Karl Rahner's *Freedom in the Church* (1960) and Hans Küng's *The Council, Reform and Reunion* (1961), focused attention more sharply than the Catholic intellectualism debate had on problems within the Church.

And Pope John's encyclical *Mater et Magistra* (1961), urged Catholics to take part in a wide variety of economic, social, and cultural organizations—to contribute to the great process of "socialization" in the modern world. The encyclical embodied the pope's soon-to-be-announced rejection of "those prophets of gloom" who saw "nothing but prevarication and ruin" in modern times.[2]

127

Conversation among American Catholics in the early 1960s about the Church's future course was greatly intensified and was generally optimistic about the possibilities of "aggiornamento" (updating), as John XXIII referred to his goal of bringing the Church into closer touch with twentieth-century society. This was certainly true with regard to hopes for recognition of the role of the laity. Reassured by the pope's statement in February 1961 that the lay apostolate would be the object of vital concern at Vatican II, Robert Graham, S.J., drew a conclusion with which few, and certainly not the Grail, would have disagreed: the age of the laity was arriving, or, "to speak more accurately, that day has already arrived. It remains only for the Fathers of the Council to give it formal recognition."[3]

Champions of the laity could envision some difficulties, to be sure. Graham noted that "the delicate balance between lay responsibility and episcopal control" had yet to be worked out fully. And Donald Thorman, author of the influential *The Emerging Layman*, wondered how the laity would be permitted to exercise free speech, since there were as yet "no clear-cut channels through which their voice may be heard." But neither man anticipated any serious problems. The laity, Thorman said, wanted "prudently and humbly [to] exert a beneficial pressure on the Church."[4]

Events at the council's first session, when it opened in October 1962, indicated however that the Church was in for far more serious trouble. With the approval of Pope John XXIII, documents prepared by the Roman Curia were remanded to committee and battle lines were drawn between "liberals" like Cardinal Leo Suenens of Belgium, who wanted the council to endorse a more sympathetic dialogue between the Church and the modern world, and "conservatives" like Cardinal Alfredo Ottaviani, who thought that the existing authority and teaching of the Church ought to be invoked more strongly.

The incipient conflict, which came into the open at the council's second session, was also reported in detail by the pseudonymous Xavier Rynne in the *New Yorker* and Robert Kaiser in *Time*. These popular accounts, widely read, gave many American Catholics the sense of a deeper problem in the Church, and in themselves.[5]

The Grail, meanwhile, was both consolidating its gains and quietly beginning to take a fresh look within. According to Lydwine van Kersbergen, the Grail was in 1961 "the fastest growing lay apostolate movement in the United States and Canada; 14,000 women, she claimed, had taken part in its programs so far and one hundred and twenty of its mission trainees were currently serving overseas.[6] The Grail's progress was clearly visible at its Ohio headquarters. Thanks to the success of the fundraising campaign begun in 1959, Grailville's great barn had been transformed into a modern place of worship called the Oratory and a gleaming new dining hall now adjoined the House of Joy.[7]

Behind the scenes, however, within the National Committee and the National Advisory Board created in 1959, conversations were taking place which were to set the Grail on a new course. Significantly, they were conversations of an emerging generation of American-born Grail members—women who had joined the movement early in their lives and now, mostly in their mid-thirties, were assuming leadership positions. Among them were Dolores Brien, elected an international vice-president of the Grail in 1961; Audrey Sorrento, placed in charge of Grailville in the same year; and Eileen Schaeffler. Schaeffler, having served at Monica House in Brooklyn and the Gateway in Detroit, was to be named president of the Grail in America in January 1962, succeeding the Dutch-born Lydwine van Kersbergen.

Schaeffler and her colleagues had undergone the trials of the mission and city center apostolates; they had been shaped by the personalism of the new catechetics; and they had shared in the Grail's high fervor of the late 1950s. In their discussions the lingering questions generated by these experiences mingled with those recently raised within the Church at large.

Some of the advisory board's deliberations reflected the Grail's approach of former years: the need for more strength in the movement's organizational structure; its responsibility to expand; the problem of eliciting a firm commitment from everyone it reached. But the meetings also broke new ground. The Grail had understood itself for decades to be in the vanguard of the Church and the lay apostolate. But now board members found themselves asking something new and unexpected: Was the Grail really in touch with the modern world? Was it "really 'in the current' of the time"? In particular, was the Grail sensitive to present social and political trends in America, the dangerous drift, for example, toward defending the country's "positive role" in the world with "self-righteous, conservative rhetoric"?[8]

Clearly, the advisory board suspected the existence of a serious problem: if the Grail's view of society were incomplete or anachronistic, the movement could not expect to be effective in transforming the world for Christ. The board decided, therefore, to gather more information, by means of a poll of its own members. The inquiry did not concern itself directly, however, with developments in the world but with the board members' personal histories in the Grail, especially perceptions of the training they experienced at Grailville. What had these women found most helpful in their formation? And what was lacking or "should have been better in your particular case"?[9]

From this point on the Grail pursued two constantly intersecting lines of self-questioning. On one it re-evaluated its image of the modern world. On the other it scrutinized the concepts of personal growth and community life which had governed its own program of spiritual formation.

The advisory board's poll evoked a clear consensus on the strengths and weaknesses of the Grail's training program. Grailville's precisely religious dimension was judged to be its greatest asset. Students were fortunate, one board member said, to have been immersed in "the *fact* of God, and Christ as a person." But beyond, or beneath, this dimension, life at Grailville was seriously flawed—it seemed, finally, to have sacrificed the individual in many ways. Undue emphasis had been placed on external conformity, too little distinction had been made between essentials and nonessentials, and not enough time allowed for "physical and spiritual relaxation." Personal relationships had not developed satisfactorily in this atmosphere, since "love was more centered on our work and our service," and Grail members tended too often to judge themselves and others in terms of visible accomplishment. Grailville had also been marked by "a certain lack of stimulus to think out personally."

Sounding a note which was heard throughout the Grail and indeed the Church generally over the next decade, advisory board members concluded that the movement's present need was a concentration on "human formation"; a "greater internalization of values"; "more freedom for personal choice." "I feel we are crying out," one respondent said, "for an understanding of our human nature—of our *human* potential."[10]

As a result of the advisory board's findings a Research Team for the Future Development of Grailville was formed which began to meet in January 1961. One year later an in-depth report, written by Mary Imelda Buckley, was ready for the board's consideration. Buckley's work called several of the Grail's controlling ideas into further question and offered a number of practical suggestions for reform.

The total transformation of culture as it had been envisioned in the 1940s was still a viable concept, Buckley said. But it had been too strongly conditioned by the rural life ideology which Grailville had espoused in that period. "It is no longer thought," Buckley declared, "that the answer to the problem [of cultural renewal] lies in the return to a less technological system or way of life." "Christian culture," too, was an ideal still to be reckoned with, but the Grail needed to pay greater attention to the complexity of the modern world, to its "variety in tradition." Consequently, Buckley recommended, there ought to be less manual work at Grailville and at least "a course or two" on contemporary thought, especially in the area of American culture.[11]

The Grail's educational method, geared to "practical" intelligence (the movement's "womanly education," though Buckley did not refer to it that way), also still had value. The Grail had seen correctly that academic institutions often fostered a sterile intellectualism. But it had erred, perhaps, in the opposite direction. "When the education of the whole person is emphasized," Buckley wrote, "the education of the mind is minimized." In the future Grailville's training should be "buttressed by greater knowledge and understanding," and more Grail members should be sent to pursue studies, especially in theology. The "integration of life" which the Grail sought would be all the more worthwhile.[12]

Buckley also issued a further call for the cultivation of personal responsibility in the training of Grail students. In the past, she said, "we have tended to rely more on . . . making an environment and atmosphere conducive to goodness, rather than on the formation of the creative and inquiring person." Grailville should therefore be redesigned to meet the needs of the mature woman more than those of the recent high school graduate.

The Grail ought not to forsake its most basic goal, the fostering of apostolic holiness, Buckley concluded. There was still no other organization in existence which aimed "to train all lay women (or nearly all) who wish to help the Church today." And Grailville should not become a conventional college—so two of Buckley's consultants, the Jesuits Walter Ong and John Courtney Murray, warned. Nevertheless, the need for deeper knowledge of the world and of the self within the Grail was clear. Grailville had been "an island of beauty" which must now modify its "monastic" tendencies.[13]

As the National Advisory Board deliberated, one of its new prime concerns, the relationship of person and community in the Grail, was raised in another, equally powerful way. A number of married women came forward to say that they were uncertain about their standing in the movement. Having been trained at Grailville, they had carried out their apostolic role at home and in their local communities, but it seemed to them that they had been relegated to the Grail's fringes. These women perhaps did not know of Rachel Donders' admonition to the Round Table about dealing with "alumnae," but they were aware that as the Grail consolidated itself organizationally in the late 1950s they had remained unfranchised. Unable of course to join the nucleus, they were neither considered for leadership positions nor did they have any say in who was.

The married women presented a statement of concern to the Grail's leadership at a meeting held in Burlington, New Jersey, in April 1961. Their primary objective, they said, was full participation in the spiritual benefits of the Grail: "a constant deepening in a life of prayer and worship; of continued spiritual growth through an ever greater love of the Cross and contemplation of the mystery of the Redemption." But they also sought an explicit affirmation of their membership in the movement, which they wished to see defined as "a worldwide community of women dedicated in virginity and Holy Matrimony." Such an affirmation, furthermore, ought to allow the married women themselves to determine the actual forms their membership would take; these would vary according to "the personal interests and inclinations" of their families. The married women also requested an official liaison with the Grail's National Committee and asserted that their future in the movement depended very much on their own initiative and on "a continued exchange of thought and study" among all Grail members.[14]

The married women's statement gave rise to some initial tension. But the movement's nucleus leadership soon reacted with overwhelming sympathy, recognizing the statement as an appeal for the personal freedom and diversity they themselves had been thinking about. Dolores Brien, for example, who represented the National Committee at the Burlington meeting, reported that she believed the Grail "must retain . . . the real freedom to carry out our apostolate in a way which would be compatible with the circumstances, interests, and the needs of the individual woman and her family." There was no need for concern about internal conflict, Brien added. The married women seemed to have a healthy bond with the members of the nucleus, even a "complementariness" with them.[15]

Four months later the married women had their liaison with the National Committee—in the person of Jeanne Plante—and they had their own newsletter which publicly proclaimed their desire for "a more intimate association with the Grail and a clearer formulation of their membership in the movement." Their initiative continued to elicit a positive response and kept the nucleus leadership moving in the direction suggested by the National Advisory Board's poll.[16]

The impact of the married women's challenge was most evident in Jeanne Plante's reflections published in the *Married Women's Newsletter* of February 1962. In their "wantingness" for a full share in the Grail which at the same time allowed them freedom to follow their own paths in the world, the married women evoked a similar desire previously buried in Plante's own consciousness. Her description of it, "that little feeling within you and me, that tiny flame of desire that spurts up because we sense that there is more meaning in our life and world that we have not responded to," was unspecific, certainly. But in this feeling Plante believed she could discern "the real starting point of the Grail."

The movement, Plante said, would continue to have an organizational dimension (at which it had worked so hard in recent time), and it would still undertake various apostolic projects under common policies. But the Grail was "primarily the discovery and cultivation of the spiritual bond among women." It should become, above all else, a "meeting place" for women of all circumstances and vocations. This new perspective, Plante conceded, would need time to develop; and it might not yield an immediate answer to the question, "What does it mean to be a member of the Grail?" But the married women, at least, must now be permitted to combine "outside" activities with formal participation, and all who belonged to the movement should "go forward discovering each other in friendship, supporting one another in difficulty, and encouraging each other to new possibilities."[17]

With the questions raised by the married women in mind, with Mary Imelda Buckley's report in hand, and Eileen Schaeffler installed as president, the Grail's leadership took some first steps toward reform early in 1962. Some of Grailville's formalities and ascetical restrictions were set aside, and means were sought to permit more members of the nucleus to pursue advanced studies. But, in accordance with the sentiments expressed by the married women and agreed to by Plante and other leaders, the Grail's future should involve everyone in the movement. Another unprecedented step was therefore in order: a national conference, set for October 11, 1962, just one day after the opening of the first session of Vatican II.

Invitations to the national conference went out to seven hundred women, married and single: all the alumnae of Grailville since 1944 and all city center team members. Including the nucleus, more than two hundred attended, causing an overflow into nine neighboring houses. In the course of the three-day meeting the sea changes implicit in the past three years' discussions came into clearer focus. For many, the conference marked a turning point in their perception of what the Grail had been and might now become.

Even before the meeting began it was evident that new perspectives were not the private preserve of the Grail's leadership. A "pre-conference dialogue" (conducted by mail) identified two especially strong desires which closely resembled those expressed by the members of the National Advisory Board. Prospective conference goers wanted to acquire "more formation in personal life for oneself and for other women . . . and to live more maturely, freely, even originally, when originality is necessary" and "to be fully in the 'inter' spheres—interfaith, intercultural, international, interracial relations; to be fully responsible citizens of 'the whole city' of this world and this time."[18]

Also employing a vocabulary which echoed the past but little and which became standard in 1960s America, the panel of leaders which opened the conference took up these points enthusiastically. "As lay persons immersed in the world," the panelists said, "we are seeking for a deeper theology of human effort. . . . We desire to be of relevance for the world in which we live. We seek to effect change in our environment. We hope that our own lives will take shape in being directed toward a meaningful goal." These women also declared, as had the National Advisory Board, that the Grail ought to take its American surroundings much more seriously. They were anxious that "our Catholicism not cut us off from our fellows as it has often tended to do." They wanted to "develop our 'personality' as a nation and come to the maturity necessary to carry the responsibility which is ours in this time of world crisis."[19]

Dolores Brien, in her keynote address, "The Grail: An Open Community," also stressed the need for relevance in delivering the Christian message to the modern world.[20] But the bulk of her remarks dealt with the increasingly dominant theme of personal development and interaction within the Grail itself. "We are on the threshold," she said, "of realizing ourselves in the fullest sense as a spiritual movement of women in the Catholic Church." But change, or at least an enlargement of vision, was required if the Grail were to go forward. The movement could meet the challenge of "a whole world in the making" if it could achieve a unity of commitment and collaboration which proceeded *not from a few but from all of us. . . .*" This unity, according to Brien, ought to arise from the Grail's "inner space" or "room to be" (Dutch, *ruimte*), which recognized the potential of every woman, "young and old, those in school, in business, in marriage, in the professions, those who have made their decisions about the future, and those still in the process of doing so." It should be the product, especially, of a closer and more conscious interaction between the movement's married and celibate members (urged years before by Joan Overboss). No blueprint for this interaction yet existed, Brien said, but one of the Grail's chief concerns at the moment was to create ways to make "shared responsibility" a reality.[21]

Rachel Donders had used the term "shared responsibility" some years earlier. But Brien's frame of reference was obviously wider, stretching beyond the nucleus to the Grail's total membership. Her address also signaled the Grail's most profound shift of emphasis in the early 1960s: from an urgent quest for commitment to the movement itself to a determined affirmation of personal freedom.

Following Brien's talk the conference participants broke up into working groups and in short order produced an answer to her call for a new order in the Grail. The movement, they agreed, should move formally toward decentralization—it should adopt a regional structure. Better plans of action could be worked out in this way (at least in terms of adapting national policy to local circumstances), and more adequate representation of the total membership at the highest levels could eventually be achieved. Twelve regions were tentatively identified, with each to have a local coordinator and a nucleus member assigned as resource person and link to the National Committee. Another national meeting was set for the following June (it was subsequently postponed for a year) to evaluate and incorporate the experience of the intervening months into a more definite scheme.[22]

With the "Program Material" from the conference in hand, those who had assembled at Grailville returned home to reflect on the Grail's new agenda. Most seemed pleased with it in principle but they found it did not translate easily into practice. The question of how membership was to be defined and shared responsibility exercised proved especially troublesome. Various ideas were advanced: drop the term "member" altogether; create a "core" of the Grail which would include married women as well as members of the nucleus; identify "responsibles" (anyone willing to participate directly in decision making) who would constitute "the nucleus of the movement functionally." But none of these proposals generated a consensus. Inhibiting this discussion, no doubt, was a lack of clarity about how far the Grail—in America and internationally—wished to go in the direction of democratization. The movement, it appeared to some as if for the first time, had been organized on strict hierarchical lines. In the United States the National Committee and the National Advisory Board remained restricted to the nucleus, and their members were appointed by the president. In March 1963 the possibility of non-nucleus participation on the National Advisory Board was raised and further discussion of it, involving women outside the nucleus, was held in the following June. But no action was taken.[23]

As the Grail struggled with its new self-image, the battle at Vatican II continued between the forces of "aggiornamento" and "non-historical orthodoxy" (as American writer Michael Novak labeled the conservative side). It seemed that the former was gaining strength. Pope John XXIII died in June 1963, but his successor, Paul VI, though a cautious man, made way for the discussion of a new set of documents containing a wealth of contemporary theological ideas. "The People of God" (supplying a communitarian emphasis) and "collegiality" (which put papal authority back into the context of the authority of bishops), dominated the new text on the nature of the Church; and support grew for an original statement on the Church's relationship with the modern world—with the Church seen as friendly critic rather than determined adversary. The laity, too, received a measure of attention. A chapter entitled "The People of God and the Laity" was inserted into the draft document on the Church, and Paul VI appointed a group of lay observers at the council's second session.

These developments could be seen, however, as painfully slow and perhaps not durable. The chapter on the laity, just mentioned, was there, but (according to Michael Novak) it was "negative, clerical, and groping."[24] Lay involvement at the council was a historic breakthrough, but it was minimal and, at first, all male. (Paul VI increased the number of lay observers at the third session of the council and included several women.)[25] The overarching question, it seemed, was the same as that facing the Grail: how far could (or would) the Church go toward modifying its centralized hierarchical structure? This was the question impressed on the minds of American Catholics when Hans Küng, strongly critical of the Roman Curia, came to lecture in their country early in 1963; Küng's own message was strong enough, but it gained added weight when his scheduled appearance at the Catholic University of America was canceled by the administration there.[26] The question may also have been reinforced in the Grail's mind by a bizarre but telling incident which took place in Rome during the second session of Vatican II:

> Journalists . . . had been invited to attend the Council Mass that morning. As about twenty of them rose to join the lay auditors at communion, a young American woman, Miss Eva Fleischner, a member of the Grail . . . , was the last in line on her way toward the communion rail. A male functionary motioned emphatically that she should stop. He motioned again, violently. Since the other members of the press, all men, were approaching the rail, she tried to hurry forward. The man physically restrained her; he would not allow her to receive communion. Elmer van Feldt of NCW News saw the incident from the tribune and later protested to the Council authorities. As the man had acted without authority, only on his own impulse, apologies were tended to Miss Fleischner. But the impulse was apparently widespread, for the next time the journalists were allowed to enter St. Peter's, women were expressly excluded.[27]

Amid growing unrest in the Church the Grail increased its efforts to absorb the new theological currents unleashed by Vatican II. It was already heavily involved in the renewal of the liturgy and recently ecumenism had appeared on its agenda; a Grail National Ecumenical Committee was formed which published the first issue of its *Ecumenical Notes* in October 1961.[28] The 1962–63 Year's School of Formation was conceived as "an adult-level course in Scripture and kerygmatic theology" and featured the Jesuits Bernard Cooke (who celebrated the liturgies of Holy Week when they were held for the first time in the new Oratory) and Walter Ong, Godfrey Diekmann, Monsignor John Oster-reicher of Seton Hall University, and the Passionist biblical scholar Carroll Stuhlmuller. In August 1963 a two-week institute called "Catechetical Crossroads included Joseph Goldbrunner, the Belgian catechetical theorist Marcel van Caster, and Gerard Sloyan of the Catholic University.[29]

The Grailville community's theme for the 1963–64 year was "The Christian in the World" and began with the study of Pope John XXIII's encyclical *Pacem in Terris* and Albert Dondeyne's *Faith and the World.* Also recommended to students were Karl Rahner's *The Christian Commitment* and the just published works of the new wave of American Catholic lay writers, including Daniel Callahan's *The Mind of the Catholic Layman* and Michael Novak's *A New Generation—American and Catholic.*[30]

The Grail's immersion in contemporary theology reached its climax in a four-day seminar in the spring of 1964 led by the liberal British theologian Charles Davis. Elaborately planned, this seminar attempted to attract a cross section of the American Catholic community and thus foster a dialogue on renewal in the Church. With respect to this goal the program was a failure, since none of the many bishops invited appeared and the assemblage included "no disciples of Ottaviani." Davis' lectures, however, elicited a strong favorable reaction from those who did attend. The battle within the Church was now firmly fixed in the consciousness of the American Grail.[31]

The new theology, focused on the Church as a community of persons reaching out to the world, seemed a fitting catalyst for the desired transformation of the Grail from movement to "meeting place," and the Grail pressed on with its task despite its initial difficulties. What ensued, however, was unexpected and disturbing in the extreme.

The Grail, first of all, began to lose members, and prominent ones. In March and April 1964, Jeanne Plante and Dolores Brien announced their decisions to withdraw from the nucleus, and both soon removed themselves altogether from active participation.

Some half dozen other women had quietly sought and been

granted release from their lifetime promises in the early 1960s, but their actions had been regarded as strictly personal; any disciplined community, lay or religious, could expect some losses.[32] But the two new cases seemed different. Could Plante and Brien, as leaders, have been concerned with a loss of power? Clearly, the Grail was moving toward some new form of government in which the members of the nucleus would be less dominant. Brien, however, had counseled the nucleus that they would have "a humble but indispensable place" in the Grail of the future; they would not be the center "around which all else orbits," but "a spiritual source which goes out from itself to strengthen, to give support, to work *with*, to pour itself out for the sake of all."[33] Perhaps the withdrawals of Plante and Brien were more directly related to "a general weakening in the health of nucleus members" and "a general feeling of lack of impact in the fields of the apostolate" which was reported to the Grail's international secretariate a year before.[34] No one, including Plante and Brien themselves, could or would say just what the problem was. Later it would appear that the steps they encouraged the Grail to take, and the questions raised in the Church at large about faith in the modern world, had led Plante and Brien to seek a radically new perspective on themselves. Dolores Brien said in 1979 that at the time of her decision to leave the Grail she felt the need to establish "an original relationship with the universe."[35]

As seen earlier, the Grail's city centers were operating at peak at the close of the 1950s. In the early 1960s they began to experience more acutely the tensions which accompanied their meteoric growth: competition with other groups, shortages of staff, and nagging doubts about the effectiveness of their programs. Into this situation the Grail, following its "meeting place" concept, injected a new definition of what a city center ought to be: "no longer a group living together, but a spark for local communities of faith at the service of the movement." This somewhat oblique description implied that the centers had become symbols of self-centeredness and institutionalism in the Grail. They should therefore be transformed into gathering places—as opposed to sites of an "all around Christian life"—to help women discover "what the role is of the Christian in the world." They should also enjoy greater autonomy, creating their own apostolic agendas rather than implementing ideas and programs emanating from Grailville and the Grail's national leadership. Staff (nucleus) members were to help, but mainly as advisors who conveyed the fruits of the local apostolate to the larger Grail community.[36]

Besides embodying the Grail's recent emphasis on relevance to the world, this concept also represented something of a return to the city centers' original inspiration: attention to local needs, which had been overtaken in the 1950s by a desire to create a sense of "the total movement" (Rachel Donders' "mansion" as opposed to a number of "chicken coops").

Relevance and local autonomy ought to have brought new prosperity to the city centers, but they did not.

In New York hopes were still high in 1963 that a full-fledged Grail center could be maintained there. But a lack of staff and a mysterious "lack of atmosphere" militated against them. Attempts to obtain property through the archdiocese of New York failed, and the Grail's apostolate to foreign students came to a halt.[37]

At the Brooklyn center, the Institute for Overseas Service, yielding to doubts about the value of American missionaries in Africa and Latin America, and to declining enrollment, terminated its training program in 1963. Leaders there still hoped for a renaissance in Brooklyn, where the Grail had made its "first effort to make a bridge into secular culture—into the world of the 'big city.' " But they also sensed "a general dissatisfaction with the way the Movement is going." Despite a substantial donation from Archbishop Bryan J. McEntegart, their program continued to diminish.[38]

There were also hopes in Philadelphia at the beginning of the decade as Grail leaders there approached Archbishop John Krol for assistance. Krol responded with a personal gift of five thousand dollars but said he could commit no more Church funds and added the suggestion that the Grail abandon its facility since it was in a changing neighborhood. After some hesitation, the Philadelphia Grail Center was sold to the Society of Jesus in 1966.[39]

In Detroit the Grail persevered a bit longer, partly on the

strength of an annual contribution (from 1961 through 1966) of five thousand dollars from John Cardinal Dearden. By April 1968, however, "there was a pretty clear feeling that the Grail was no more in Detroit." Longtime friend Walter Schoenherr was told by the Grail that "changes in us, in social patterns, in the Church, are affecting us all deeply . . . ; we can only be true to the present, hope in and prepare for the future."[40]

The Grail center in Lafayette, Louisiana, was disposed of in mid-1964. Only in San Jose, California, where "the House that Love Built" was opened in September 1961, did a Grail center flourish in the 1960s—though it too declined late in the decade.

In sum, the Grail's network of city centers disappeared about as quickly as it had sprouted up ten years before. As these "institutions" declined, the Grail strove to maintain less formally organized local communities of its members. But these communities were beset by a number of new problems. Local women, unprepared for or uncertain about what was really happening in the Grail, were in many cases reluctant to accept leadership positions. And many of the young people who would have been potential Grail trainees in the past seemed more anxious than ever to plunge directly into the secular world—in the Peace Corps perhaps. The basic difficulty, however, was the Grail's own prescription that its people turn outward into deeper involvement in the world's own helping agencies, such as community development and civil rights groups. Seasoned Grail members, especially, tended to spend more time in this way, "getting into our professions" it was called, or in pursuing the education which many had previously chosen or been persuaded to forego. They had less time—and less inclination—to promote specific allegiance to the Grail itself. The Grail's local communities became, in a real sense, "support groups," their members' attention focused on them only at times.

Grailville also continued to feel the impact of changing attitudes within the Grail and the American Catholic community. The 1962–63 Year's School still closely resembled those of the past: eighteen students remained from previous years for extended training, and forty-four new ones were accepted; Grailville's program continued to center on Catholic faith and fields of apostolic service—family life, religious education, art and culture, and missions. But some changes had been made. The formation program was now more precisely organized as "a course in theology applied to daily life," including weekend lectures which were opened to the public. In addition, the program was offered (in response to Mary Imelda Buckley's recommendation) on two levels, one for younger women and one for the more mature.[41]

In 1964 the continuing debate about the reform of Grailville was accompanied for the first time by a sharp reduction in the number of new applicants; the city centers were no longer producing recruits even if they were still trying to. Grailville's leadership reacted cautiously to this development, evidently hoping that quality, at least, could be maintained. They asked the women who did come to be prepared for the Grail's new concentration on shared responsibility; students were to understand that they were not mere subjects of training but contributing members of the whole enterprise, including its financial stability. Grailville's deficiencies in the "education of the mind," which Mary Imelda Buckley had underlined, were looked at again, but as Buckley also had recommended, Grailville was still not to become a conventional school. Its long-standing affiliation with the Catholic University of America was even to be reconsidered—in the interest of eliminating the "student-staff distinction" which had endured despite the Grail's best efforts and now seemed peculiarly foreign to the concept of shared responsibility.[42]

In January 1965 a "working team" reported that it had been grappling further with the questions of how Grailville could "belong more fully to all the members of the movement" and how its formation program might be improved. Answers to these questions, the working team said, was a matter of incarnating the trends of the past several years: greater diversification; greater freedom and flexibility; and preparing students to participate in— rather than "duplicating"—secular efforts to improve social conditions. Beyond these general principles the team noted that there were very practical problems to be solved at Grailville. The movement's headquarters, like the city centers, was understaffed; no one, it seemed, was interested any longer in working with girls of high school age; and if Grailville were to deepen its intellectual commitment, it would need a library and other study facilities.

With a shortage of working hands, and a waning emphasis on agriculture—this was no longer what the world needed—the question of maintaining Grailville as a farm also loomed large.

The working team went on to outline two possible approaches to reorganization. Grailville's training program could focus "not on learning how to live the Christian life, but . . . on growing as Christians through the discipline and contribution of their more individually determined work, . . . living together . . . sharing ideas, experiences, encouragement." Or, as some of the newer, younger people thought, it could be geared primarily to studying "the vital questions affecting the Church today." Either or both of these approaches, which were (however unspecifically) departures from the liturgy-centered, integrated life of the past, might give rise to a model for the future. Grailville might become a place for small groups of women fashioning their own programs and supporting themselves financially; it could become a new experiment in interdisciplinary study; it could adopt a seminar approach and become a meeting place for people to "come together with experts in the really live fields."[43]

Out of this welter of reflections, some decisions finally emerged. Enrollment in the Year's School of Formation would be deliberately kept small, and arrangements would be set in motion to keep Grailville economically productive but capable of being operated by "two steady farm workers" rather than the whole community. Grailville began to *purchase* its milk supply on May 15, 1965.[44]

It appeared, however, that the Grail was as yet unable to create a definitive new plan for its headquarters. While discussions continued, an interim arrangement was announced in June:

> In the coming year Grailville will be a center where Catholics and other Christians can meet as a community, exchanging [views] on questions of common concern.[45]

This statement effectively terminated the Grail's Year's School of Formation which had been in operation at Grailville since 1944.

In May 1965, with city center closings in progress and the status of Grailville in question, Dorothy Rasenberger attempted a summary/analysis of what was taking place in the Grail. Her letter to "Dear Everyone," the first of several perceptive essays she contributed in the 1960s, showed the community still hard at its new perspectives on personal growth and relevance to the modern world.

The Grail, Rasenberger said, had retained the lay apostolate's conviction that every baptized person is called to share fully in the life of the Church; it had also gathered strength from the notion of the Church as the People of God, and from a new awareness of the behavioral sciences. With these resources the Grail had deepened its understanding of how essential individual awareness and personal growth were to both human development and the action of the Holy Spirit. The "real continuum" of the Grail, Rasenberger declared, echoing the earlier sentiments of Jeanne Plante, was "the Holy Spirit acting through persons; persons relating to each other in friendship, in trust in the Spirit, in searching for the truth, in a variety of actions related to their common desire for the world." The Grail's "desire for the world," Rasenberger continued, had always been strong. But its understanding of the world was now "developing." It was already "a growing aspect" of the Grail's international concern, she said, to learn the political and economic realities of world trade and development more fully. Whatever the Grail's future apostolic work might be, it would be undertaken with "greater competency and realism."[46]

Conceding implicitly that the Grail had previously given the world less than its due, and that its institutional framework had obscured its "real continuum," Rasenberger remained hopeful. The movement as a whole did too, and it had already responded eagerly to the call of international president Magdalene Oberhoffer (who had succeeded Rachel Donders in 1961) for an "aggiornamento year" of the Grail's own, to culminate in the adoption of new guidelines at an international meeting in Holland in July 1965.

The process of preparation for the international meeting was welcomed by the Americans for a number of reasons, including the opportunity to move toward a more satisfactory expression of "shared responsibility." A decision was taken in September 1964 to circulate a digest of the international Grail's preliminary document known as "Basis for Consultation" to all the women then involved with the movement in some way. Those who responded were to be considered "responsible participants" and made eligible to submit nominations and be elected as delegates to the upcoming international meeting. One hundred and sixty-five (out of six hundred) replied, most of them offering nominations, and a special selection committee made the final choice of eight voting delegates. Two of these were married women. While permanent leadership positions still remained beyond the reach of most "responsible participants," this was a significant breakthrough. For the duration of the international meeting at least, married members of the American Grail would stand on an equal footing with the members of the nucleus.[47]

Eighty-five Grail members from many parts of the world met in Holland in the summer of 1965 "to consider the whole context of the Church and world in which we must place the life of the Grail today." The fourteen Americans in attendance—the eight elected delegates, five others not voting, and president Eileen Schaeffler ex-officio—found to their pleasure that the spirit of the meeting was closely akin to their own. The assembly was convinced that the Grail's original vision, that of Jacques van Ginneken, contained "the dynamic elements necessary for . . . continuing renewal," but that it must carefully review "those aspects of its life" which had been most affected by the Second Vatican Council (which still had one session to go). The result was new Guidelines for the Grail, under three major headings: The Conversion of the World; Communion with the People of God; and Christian Maturity.[48]

"The conversion of the world" was evidently a term too dear to many Grail members, especially the Europeans, to be dropped. But the statements made under this rubric clearly reflected the outlook of Schema 13, soon to become the Second Vatican Council's Pastoral Constitution on the Church in the Modern World. The Grail affirmed, for example, its awareness of "the oneness of God's action in the world and in the Church, calling for our openness to this action wherever we find it, and a recognition of the need for the continuing conversion of both Church and world." In this perspective, the Grail itself was to be understood (in terms bearing a remarkable resemblance to those of Dorothy Rasenberger) as

> . . . a woman's movement with a spiritual dynamism character-ized by an attitude of continual search and of openness to the Spirit, attentive to the signs which the situation of the world gives and to the action of the Spirit among the People of God.[49]

The new Grail guidelines chose the term "communion" rather than "some older and more familiar one, such as 'com-munity' or 'Mystical Body' " for a twofold purpose. It placed the movement's thinking "clearly in the context of the theology of the Council," and it conveyed a concept of unity which was interpersonal rather than "ideological" or organizational. The guidelines declared that unity in the Grail must be based upon "an acceptance of each other which respects both the uniqueness of each one's personal vocation and the common vision and task we share as our heritage." It should express itself in prayer, in the quality of personal relationships, and in "the tangible forms of various kinds of groupings through which members can be related to each other and the whole." This last expression was actually quite important to the American Grail since it was in-tended, however obliquely, to open the way for new definitions of membership and more inclusive forms of governance. The guidelines went on to state a bit more clearly that membership might be "elaborated at the national level" with the Grail's in-ternational president still to be recognized as "a final guarantee of our international unity." The Americans understood this as an avenue for greater, perhaps equal participation of non-nucleus members in the conduct of their affairs.[50]

"Christian maturity" was also described in the guidelines in a manner familiar to the Americans. It was meant to refer to "the whole process of personal development"; it involved "a ten-sion arising from the Christian's being present in the world and to the world, trusting its values and at the same time aware of sin at work in the world." Maturity should be fostered by sys-tematic formation programs and periods of reflection and prayer, but also, "as experience shows increasingly," by interaction within small groups. The experience alluded to here may in fact have been that of the Americans. Certainly their new regional structure represented such a turn.[51]

The guidelines, so congenial to the American Grail that Eileen Schaeffler was later asked if she and her fellow Americans had written them, were adopted on a two-year trial basis and were to be reviewed and confirmed at another international general assembly.

Schaeffler returned to the United States in a hopeful mood. Addressing the American Grail's second national conference in September, she said that the Grail had passed through a period of confusion and purification and was now ready to go forward again. It was true that many of its members were still having difficulty, "facing for the first time thoughts, ideologies, and practical consequences that they never dreamed of before." But in general, "I think we can say with relief that it now seems to be the time for affirmation . . . that we can . . . affirm with greater certainty the bases, the convictions, the elements of the vision which have attracted us to this particular way of realizing our Christian commitment."[52]

But the time of confusion and conflict was not over. Vatican II adopted its Constitution on the Church in the Modern World, and a perhaps even more critical statement on religious liberty, but not without intense debate. Several crucial topics had been held out of the council's reach by Pope Paul VI. And it remained to be seen whether and how the council's teaching would be translated in practice. Agreement on the Church's vision, and the Grail's, were not to come easily at all.

9

The Agonies of Openness

As the Second Vatican Council concluded, the "crisis of the West," to which the lay apostolate was to have been the antidote, gave way to an apparent crisis within the Catholic Church.

Donald Thorman, relatively optimistic in 1962, now observed that Vatican II had been "a traumatic experience for many." By "pull[ing] back the curtains on how the institutional Church works," the council had made it seem "something much more human and capable of human mistakes and manipulation." Many laypeople, Thorman said, were undergoing a crisis of faith, or at least a crisis of identity. Sociologist Andrew Greeley thought this was a "crisis of growth," but others were not so sure.[1]

At the highest levels the laity had not been ignored. Vatican II adopted a Decree on the Apostolate of the Laity, the first conciliar document ever to treat the subject directly; Pope Paul VI created a Council on the Laity in January 1967, and a third World Congress of the Laity met in Rome later that year. There were problems nonetheless. The Decree on the Apostolate of the Laity, with more than half its original text transferred to other council documents, was undistinguished, even a bit clerical, in its final form. And at the world congress, delegates (though generally moderates) insisted on raising the laity's most sensitive concern, birth control, which Paul VI had kept off the agenda of Vatican II. A "credibility gap," implicit in Thomas O'Dea's warnings in the late 1950s, was in the making: as the laity was encouraged to express itself and began to do so, even the most progressive of bishops became cautious.[2]

Frustration with the gap between what many took to be the spirit of the Second Vatican Council and its implementation was

149

also felt at the diocesan and parish levels. In the United States it surfaced most visibly in the National Association of Laymen (NAL), an organization formed in St. Paul, Minnesota, in 1967 without official connection with the hierarchy. At the NAL's 1968 meeting in Chicago it was evident that the attention of a good many laypeople, at least, was gradually shifting away from arguments with Church authorities and toward independent lay initiative and action. Even before the meeting Donald Thorman noted that concerned laypeople were finding it easier to set questions of Church reform aside and concentrate on being "practicing Christians in the secular city." They found it easier still, or more necessary, after Pope Paul VI issued his encyclical *Humanae Vitae* on June 25, 1968, affirming the Church's traditional teaching on artificial birth control. Rejecting the majority opinion of the pope's own special commission on the subject, the letter was arguably the major cause of alienation—or at least its increase—among American Catholics.[3]

"Practicing Christians in the secular city" was an apt description of the Grail in the postconciliar years. Its members became more and more preoccupied with involvement in the world, especially in the tumult of late 1960s America. They also spent great stores of energy trying to eliminate the vestiges of "institutionalism" within their own movement.

These preoccupations were already evident at the September 1965 national conference, and they came to dominate the programs and decisions about internal matters which followed in its wake. "Interest groups" at the conference explored civil rights, which had come to the fore with the arrest of Martin Luther King, Jr., in Birmingham, Alabama, two years before and the Selma to Montgomery protest march then in progress; peace, which had been championed by Pope John XXIII and taken up afresh in the Pastoral Constitution on the Church in the Modern World; and poverty, on which President Lyndon Johnson had "declared war" in 1964. Holy Week at Grailville in 1966 included a peace conference with speakers Gordon Zahn, James Finn, and others addressing issues of war, peace, and nonviolence. The following August Grailville hosted "Building the City of Man," described as "a Symposium, a Seminar, and a Gathering," at which sixty men and women examined the problems of urbanization.[4]

In the fall of 1965 a new form of Grail government was introduced, designed to facilitate greater participation of the total membership. Overall responsibility for the movement was now vested in a nine-member National Board (replacing the National Committee), for which all those designated "responsible participants" during the aggiornamento process were eligible to vote and—for the first time—to be elected. The initial board was constituted by means of the first direct election conducted by the American Grail, and one married woman, Mrs. Mary Cecilia (McGarry) Kane, was chosen to serve.

The National Board was to operate "in dialogue" with a Council (replacing the National Advisory Board), a consultative body made up of eighteen women representing various facets of life in the Grail, and with a general assembly (a formalization of the two previous national conferences) to be held periodically and open to all. Meeting for the first time in late November, the National Board saw itself as "a kind of continuum and underpinning for all the variety and free coming and going that makes up the Grail's complex reality." The whole Grail was now, the board said, "a free association of women of immense diversity of opinions, politics, professions and competencies, vocations, locations, religious perceptions, and futures." It even had two members on their way to doctoral degrees in theology.[5]

The American Grail's first general assembly, "The Grail for the World," was held at Grailville, August 20–31, 1966. Its advance announcements punctuated by such typical 1960s exclamations as "Stop the world, I want to get on" and "The world is not enough with us," the assembly provided another opportunity for reflection on the Grail's recent transformation.[6]

This time Alice McCarthy, a nucleus member since 1962, attempted to put things in perspective. Her address, "The History of the Grail as an Existential Movement," contained a nice mix of apology and self-criticism.

In the 1940s, McCarthy said, Grailville had indeed been a utopia, and some things about it "bothered us then and bother us now." The print dresses, the wholesome diet, the Grail smile, the slow and measured speech—all these could easily be caricatured. Nevertheless, the old Grailville had not been "a running away, or an escape"; it was rather "an attempt to put an evaluation on life." It had established the possibility of creating a "new polis" (a term McCarthy borrowed from Hannah Arendt), "a new group within the Church which made it possible for traditional religious ceremonies to be personal and relevant." From the social point of view Grailville had even been "a conscious expression of non-conformity." This was something to be cherished, for as Martin Luther King had said, the hope of the modern world lay with "disciplined non-conformists."

In the 1950s, McCarthy continued, the Grail had persisted in its utopianism but "they transferred the location—there was still a little utopia at Grailville, but it was moved to the city centers." Introduced to the complexities of urban life, the Grail began to adapt to them, developing new cooperative structures and probing more deeply into the realities of the world. This had been a wise and appropriate course; McCarthy thought that another contemporary voice she admired, Dag Hammarskjold, might have had the Grail in mind when he said, "In our era the road to holiness necessarily passes through the world of action."

In the previous two decades, then, the Grail "did meet both the identity and identification needs of people." But now, in the era of the New Frontier, the Great Society, the civil rights and peace movements, and Vatican II, the Grail had to move on. It was in fact already building another new polis or framework, "or rather the non-framework of the Grail at the moment—or rather the bursted framework, or whatever you want to say." In the 1960s, McCarthy asserted, it was necessary to find a way of "living spontaneously in action and reaction to life." Grail members ought to see their personal growth as central to the task of building a genuine community which was truly relevant to the world. Implicitly rejecting the Grail's prior view of what constituted spiritual growth and apostolic service, McCarthy ventured the opinion that

> . . . human fulfillment comes not in sacrificing for one another, but of realizing one's self for the other—and I think the emphasis on the study, and getting our roots in our professions comes from all this—that our greatest service for one another is finding ourselves.[7]

As far as relevance to the world was concerned, the Grail as a whole and its individual members pursued it unrelentingly over the next several years. In the summer of 1967 Grailville opened its doors to the Peace Corps' Advance Training Program.[8] Eva Fleischner marched with civil rights activist Father James Groppi in Milwaukee in September 1967.[9] And "there was Grail help all over the country" during Minnesota Senator Eugene McCarthy's campaign for the Democratic presidential nomination in 1968.[10] On the eve of that campaign American Grail leaders reported to their sisters in Europe that

> We feel it is a crucial year for us—with an election coming up that will affect our future approach to Vietnam and other areas of the world; with racial tension again threatening to break out in violence this summer; and with solutions to poverty (in the midst of affluence) not coming fast enough. These problems and the challenge they present to the whole value system of the country affect us very much and will affect the values we try to express as a Movement and the immediate goals we set for ourselves.[11]

One Grail leader had said without regret in 1957 that "We have not had much practice in being Americans." The movement was quickly making up for lost time.[12]

Just what further impact the encounter with the world might have on the Grail's internal organization was not yet clear at the 1966 general assembly. Speaking after Alice McCarthy, Wynni Kelly, a leader in Detroit, attempted to sum up the attendant problems in what she called "The Three Paradoxes." The Grail, Kelly said, had to deal with the desire for a defined membership and, at the same time, the desire for a "free flowing fluid and flexible participation"; a kind of utopian vision which "partakes of unlimited possibilities," on the one hand, and the desire for "immediate task-oriented action groups" on the other; and the uncertain relationship between diverse personal commitments and the need to sustain a corporate reality.[13]

In her summary of the assembly Mary Brigid Niland said that within the struggle with Kelly's paradoxes she detected "a new Grail emerging," even "a new optimism" about the movement's future. She added, however, that some participants were "not sure how they would fit into the changing Grail"; they exhibited a distinct "impatience for new structures to meet the new reality."[14]

Niland's latter observation was verified in the discussion which continued without letup after the assembly. For some Grail women the "three paradoxes" seemed more nearly contradictions, and a sharp division of viewpoints emerged. Anne Mulkeen, a member of the National Board, tried to describe this situation for her colleagues in terms of the differences between a moderate "Group A" and a more radical "Group B."

Group A, Mulkeen said, was pleased that the Grail had made "a fantastic change already from a rather authoritarian church structure to a more democratic, more 'secularly' oriented group." These women, who Mulkeen thought constituted a majority, were also open to further change. But they were deeply concerned that the Grail maintain "a central faithfulness" to Jacques van Ginneken's original vision. They were also worried about the transmission of that vision to succeeding generations and therefore saw a need for at least some full-time Grail staff, some kind of central administration, and a new formation program.

Group B, on the other hand, felt that the Grail would prosper "exactly by not having as a central concern . . . its own existence or continuity." Emphasis on government or formation was anachronistic. The Grail should become a kind of federation of "self-actuating individuals and small groups."

Mulkeen conceded that Group B's position, to which she subscribed, was "a very risky one." It raised the specter of anarchy and, given the current crisis of faith atmosphere in the Church, it might even result in "the Grail's ceasing to be Christian." Nevertheless, if the movement continued to demand "obligations, time expenditures, [and] endless discussions about 'Grail things' per se," it would suffer; professional women would not be attracted to it and many veteran members, who had abandoned the "mother of all the living" concept of woman in favor of educating themselves professionally, would withdraw.[15]

Mulkeen's assertions were not made altogether out of context. In the mid-1960s a shrinking of the movement had already begun, and by the end of the decade the Grail's overall numbers had declined by about half, with new recruits a precious few.

The nucleus suffered a "large exodus," counting fifty-nine members in 1970, down from a peak of about eighty. Anne Mulkeen was among those who withdrew, announcing that her original choice had been made "within a context I no longer see in the same way" and that she could no longer consider herself irrevocably committed to celibacy. Many former members of the nucleus subsequently married, one of them to some publicity: Florence Henderson, who participated in the Grail's short-lived attempt to organize women in a Cincinnati shirt factory in 1948, became the wife of theologian Charles Davis, who opted out of both the priesthood and the Church, levying charges against their impersonalism and lack of honesty.[16]

The crisis within the Church and the Grail naturally affected the members of the nucleus most profoundly. While many of them were most enthusiastic about the Grail's new emphasis on personal maturity and realism about the modern world, they had been most deeply formed in the movement's traditional mold— which, as it now seemed, entailed the overlooking of certain human factors in the interest of "carrying the [Grail's] structure." Among these neglected factors in the Grail's prevailing theology of woman was sexuality. In May 1967 remaining nucleus members finally discussed explicitly what they perceived as "the split in our lives between spirit and matter." They asked, "Does virginity really open the way to interior freedom?" and wondered if "sexual fulfillment was necessary to human fulfillment."[17]

In the later 1960s, with numbers decreasing, city centers in process of being dismantled, and its future so much a matter of debate, the Grail all but disappeared from public view. Articles in Catholic periodicals about the movement had abounded in the 1950s. Now there were next to none.

Following the 1966 general assembly the Grail pressed on with its search for a formula which would satisfactorily incorporate "the three paradoxes." A first step was the choosing, by election this time, of a new president of the movement in America. Eileen Schaeffler, whose term was to expire in February 1967, looked forward to such an election, and the Grail's new international guidelines now permitted it—though, to the displeasure of many, candidacy was still restricted to the nucleus.

The Grail seldom refrained from attaching a serious rationale to the reforms it adopted in the 1960s. Accordingly, Eileen Schaeffler said, the upcoming election involved more than the employment of a "mere parliamentary form." Rather, it constituted a symbol of the new Grail: it was "an expression of our striving for maturity and responsibility, for a personal share in leadership and authority, for a deeper perception of the action of the Spirit within us and among us." To reinforce this point, the election was preceded by still another evaluation process in which the Grail's women were asked to decide *for themselves* in what measure they wished to be active in the movement and, in particular, whether they wished to vote for the new president.[18]

In response, some two hundred and fifty women identified themselves as "responsible participants" and one hundred and seventy-nine chose to vote. A list of nucleus members was then circulated, and from the subsequent nominees Dorothy Rasenberger was elected to a three-year term.[19]

Following this exercise in democratization, however, the American Grail's leadership remained profoundly dissatisfied. The National Board reported its feeling that "the responsibility and authority that resides *in all who want it (i.e., the belief that each of us is responsible and has the right to breathe her own spirit into the Movement, to give it shape and form)* has not been expressed fully enough in our national structure in the last two years." All the consultations and elections of that time had not been enough to "bring forward the diversity of thought and involvement that is among us."[20]

The international general assembly held in Holland in July 1967, which confirmed the 1965 guidelines (and at which Eileen Schaeffler was elected international president) placed no barriers in the Americans' way as far as governance was concerned—it in fact clarified each country's responsibility to decide upon its own norms. The quest for a way to incarnate the authority of "all who want it" therefore could and did continue—but with difficulty. The National Board was by now asking itself some decidedly radical questions: was it even "a valid desire" for the Grail to try to say what it stood for as a movement? And could this be done "without limiting the meaning of value, without cutting off openness to others?" It was hard to see how a new organizational structure could be arrived at while the Grail's passion for freedom and diversity held such sway.[21]

The board adopted the tentative view that as a body the Grail needed "occasionally to test its values in relation to the efforts and struggles going on around us." But this testing should involve only limited goals which were understood by all movement members but to which they need not be committed "in practical ways." Some kind of national structure would be necessary to carry out the testing, but the structure itself must be limited, interim, and experimental. Guided by these criteria the National Board decided in 1968 to yield its place to a thirty-one member Task Force. President Dorothy Rasenberger and most of the women elected to the National Board in 1965 were to comprise its executive committee and see to administrative matters and relations with the Grail internationally. The Task Force as a whole would be "an instrument in finding new direction, developing existing possibilities for the 'forward thrust.' " As such it would not really be a governing body at all, but "a meeting place of different involvements or interests, to discern other or little known aspects of the Movement that need to be brought forward, to stimulate collaboration between persons and groups, works and interests."[22]

Those elected or appointed to the Task Force were to travel about "to meet and talk with persons in more isolated areas, consult with persons outside the Grail on social, cultural, and religious trends, and invite persons from the movement to consult on specific issues." Their findings would be addressed at a national assembly to be held one year hence.

"Identity crisis" is a much overused term, but something akin to it is necessary to describe the Grail as it searched for direction in "little known aspects of the Movement," in "more isolated areas," and in people outside its borders.

Meeting five times between December 1967 and the spring of 1968 the Task Force struggled mightily with the problems of the Church, the world, the Grail—and of itself ("No sooner were we born," one member observed, "than we began redefining ourselves"). Underlying the discussions of the Task Force were further manifestations of the Grail's current lack of clarity. "A certain unrest and a sense that we hadn't yet got to the heart of things" was present. This "Mystery item" was spoken of in a variety of ways, including "the basis of our unity," and " 'a quality of life' which we aspire to and sometimes share." There was also a feeling in the air, a fear, that if the Task Force really uncovered what movement members "want to give and get from the Grail," there would be (as Anne Mulkeen had already warned) severe differences to deal with. Nevertheless, it was the Task Force's job to "pull out all the stops on ways and means of communication." In the process the Task Force succeeded at least in identifying a number of "interest/problem/concern areas" in which greater communication ought to take place: peace; racism; the crisis in the cities; contemporary religious experience; full participation of "all Christian women" in the Grail; and the changing identity of woman in contemporary culture.[23]

After the Task Force had been in existence for a full year, Dorothy Rasenberger announced, as had come to be expected, that more time was needed before another general assembly could profitably be held. In the meanwhile, Rasenberger said in another of her summary essays, Grail members were continuing to develop a wide variety of vocations in the world — in politics, in education, and in other professions. This was entirely proper because since the early 1960s the Grail had, for the most part, "encouraged each person to do and be what she felt she had to and gave as much personal support as we could." As a result, however, the Grail seemed unable to achieve consensus on any particular issue. Rasenberger added her concern to that of the (now superseded) National Board about this fact: Weren't there some matters which the Grail as a whole could neglect only with "a violation of our integrity"? Rasenberger was referring to the social ills of American society, which had been brought into sharp focus by the assassinations of Martin Luther King and Robert Kennedy. But the way she phrased her next question showed that she — like the National Board in 1961 — had the Grail's own experience uppermost in mind. "Can we respect and live with differences," she asked, "avoiding new pitfalls of *group conformity*?"[24]

In her "Reflections on the Year '67–'68," Dorothy Rasenberger also noted that despite the stress created by the Grail's
dedication to diversity, the movement was still marked by a
strong "urge for openness to others." This urge now came to
focus on a critical question, full membership in the movement
for women who were not Roman Catholics.

The Grail had participated enthusiastically in the ecumenical
awakening fostered by the Second Vatican Council. Contacts
with Protestant women's groups increased, ecumenical conferences were held at Grailville, and a number of non-Catholics became closely associated with the Grail as the 1960s progressed.[25]
Possible broadening of membership was first discussed in 1964
and an Ad Hoc Committee on the Full Participation of All Christians was formed in 1966. Now, in 1969, two Protestant women
who had been living and working with Grail members in California and who had—with tacit approval—designated themselves "responsible participants," pressed their case for official
recognition.

The matter was taken up at the Grail's general assembly
of June 1969, which celebrated Grailville's twenty-fifth anniversary. (Balloons decorating the scene announced in 1960s fashion
that "We're still under thirty.") In the first written ballot employed at a Grail conference, the one hundred and fifty women
on hand adopted a resolution which affirmed "our desire to be
enriched in our search and work by full participation of women
from all Christian backgrounds."[26]

The vote was nearly unanimous, but the debate preceding
it gave vivid notice that the Grail's spirit of openness had un-
earthed still another problem—perhaps the deepest of all. The
discussion, it was reported, "blew the lid off" the assumption
of unanimity about the way the *faith* foundation of the Grail was
evolving. For some it was a shock to witness the formal transition from the exclusively Roman Catholic to the ecumenical—
the Grail could no longer be considered precisely an expression
of the lay apostolate. For others the vote seemed a mere form
which might obscure the need to re-examine questions of belief
and tradition in an even more thorough-going manner.[27]

Above all it appeared that despite Anne Mulkeen's earlier

remarks about the conservatism of the majority of the Grail's members, the movement was now possessed of a strong and widespread uneasiness with the Catholic tradition which had shaped it for so long. The sense of the 1969 general assembly was "to pursue religious questions in a more conscious way . . . including experimentation with new forms." A new term, which was to win a permanent place in the Grail's vocabulary, was introduced: "religious search" was intended to

> affirm those who were questioning the Catholic tradition out of which they had come—to the point of being unable to identify with basic beliefs, worship or teaching—and who yet felt that they continued to pursue the search for a spiritual dimension which they share with other Grail members, had a valid contribution to make to the communal understanding of religious faith, and to the purification and development of the Catholic tradition itself.[28]

Despite the fact that "religious search" was employed in various ways at the assembly ("in terms of Christian revelation, . . . personal insight, . . . and social responsibility"), discussion about it ended on an optimistic note. Those present recognized "how close to the heart and bone" of the Grail "religious search" was; and when asked how they wished to be related to the movement in the future, they made this search their first choice.[29] The underlying problem was not nearly resolved, however, and the first really public debate about the nature of the Grail's religious identity erupted some months later in the pages of the movement's newsletter, *Reaction*.

Barbara Ellen Wald, a member for more than twenty-five years and a protégé of Lydwine van Kersbergen, was particularly distressed by the talk about "religious search," writing that she had sensed "a weakening of faith and Christian basis in the Grail for a long time." Wald understood that some people in the Grail were going through crises of doubt and unbelief and that they deserved understanding, patience, and concern. But why, she asked, should they be allowed to "dominate the movement"? "Why do not those of us who believe in prayer—who have joined the Grail as a fundamentally Christian movement based on commitment to Jesus Christ—why don't we come out and say so?"

Wald could foresee only "what is already evident—a slow, weakening, disintegration, disunity—and what begins with a beautiful humanistic ideal of service turning into, in actuality, a service of *what pleases us*."[30]

Other long-time members responded sympathetically to Wald but exhorted the Grail to meet its future with hope, if not with the clarity of the past.

Eva Fleischner confessed that her experience in the Grail in the 1950s was precious to her, and that she still believed in Jesus Christ. But she was wary of nostalgia: "I do not dare impose this past upon the present." Fleischner disagreed with Wald's contention that the Grail was being dominated by "the doubters," but still less did she "dare . . . say that the Grail should be composed of or led (to use a concept of the past) by those who are sure of their belief in Christ and are able to speak of their religious experience only in Christ-centered terms." She too was worried about the possible loss of essentials but thought that doubt and unrest might also be interpreted positively: "Perhaps it is a response to the Spirit's challenge to let go, over and over again, to give up even our minimum securities of relying on old ways and forms, and to allow the new thing that is struggling for birth to come forth." Such an abandonment of power might be, Fleischner concluded, "a sign of faith and honesty, even of trust in the Lord."[31]

The American Grail's senior member, Mary Louise Tully, replied to Wald in a similar vein. She agreed that on its present course the Grail could disintegrate as an entity. But this was perhaps the way it ought to go: "Whether we should try to continue with a 'Grail Movement'—I don't know." The important thing for the immediate future was to avoid condescension toward "the doubters" and not to demand of anyone that she "see and state the meaning of life in the same terminology that is helpful to me." Tully added that she still liked "the pleasure from time to time, of Celebrating His Presence with Others who are Able to Recognize it now," but she was also inclined to the view that "the Reality of all that is, including the reality of Jesus Christ, is far beyond anything I can get into my concepts at this stage."[32]

The misgivings of Wald and others (including one who

recalled the days in which the Grail had "a special radiance and a special kind of boldness in speaking of Christ") did not effect a change in the Grail's course. If anything, the movement continued to broaden its theory and practice of "religious search." In 1975 the full participation of Jewish women in the Grail was officially affirmed. The vast majority of Grail members "are of" the Roman Catholic tradition, Eleanor Walker said subsequently; and it was recognized that Catholicism had provided "the basic concepts, symbols, and cultural forms for the corporate understanding and expression of the unity of the Grail." Nevertheless, Walker added, the movement was committed to trying to do justice to spiritual insights wherever they were to be found in the lives of women. "It would be an unimaginable impoverishment and a delusion," she concluded, "to think that we could abandon either the [many] traditions or the questions we and our world have to bring to them."[33] Pluralism, of a distinctly American sort, had found its place in the Grail.

An important factor in accelerating the adoption of "religious search" was the program the Grail finally created to replace its Year's School of Formation: Semester at Grailville (SAG).

Since it appeared that young women were more and more reluctant to remove themselves from the world in the mid-1960s, the Grail decided that it would do well to reach out to them. Beginning in April 1966 a number of consultations were held with college and university officials to explore the possibility of students' spending part of their undergraduate time with the Grail. The idea was to link "experiential inputs," the Grail's community life and volunteer work in both inner city and rural environments, with "systematic study," a series of seminars on contemporary social and religious questions.

The administrators responded favorably and SAG was officially launched on February 1, 1968. Constantly revised over the next seven years, its curriculum was a barometer of the times: seminars dealt with social change, "the God question," black history, the American Indian, death and dying, American cultural diversity, pottery making, socialism, and even Virginia Woolf rediviva.[34]

SAG's student body, two dozen or so women drawn from Ohio University, Ohio Wesleyan, and Antioch College among other institutions, brought a wide variety of attitudes toward religion and its relation to social problems to Grailville. Some were not pleased at all with the Grail's attempt to establish the relevance of "the God question," and others were uncomfortable with the liturgical celebrations which the Grail continued to offer as an integral part of its program. Disputes broke out, for example, as to how, or whether, to observe Easter. "Religious search" became a way of trying to hold all this diversity together and render it fruitful.[35]

SAG had several other significant effects on the evolution of the Grail. It quickened the "deinstitutionalization" process already under way in the movement, as Grail staff members gradually retired to advisory positions and SAG alumnae took charge of the program (this in accordance with the Grail's long-standing uneasiness with traditional educational forms, and with contemporary talk of "student power"). SAG also helped to sharpen the dual questions of what exactly the Grail was and how (with the Year's School of Formation a thing of the past) one became a member. A number of SAG students found their experience at Grailville challenging and they wished to remain associated with the movement. But the diversity they encountered was a two-edged sword, as a statement by one of them to the Council in 1971 revealed: "I don't know how to belong. . . . Where's the diversity that allows me—a college kid—to get into this thing? I don't even know what I'm asking to get into." This young woman had come face to face with the Grail's 1960s reticence—one far different from that of thirty years before, but reticence nonetheless.[36]

The quest for the relevance of religion to social issues continued unabated in the late 1960s and the 1969 Grail general assembly adopted resolutions on American defense spending, black economic development (in response to the recently issued Black Manifesto), community health, and communication among young people. Setting "religious search" and the internal reform of the Grail aside for a moment worked a welcome change in the assembly's atmosphere, it was said: "We were [then] a group, facing the vast problems of the world and wondering what we could do to help." The "structures" question remained, nevertheless. The Task Force structure had proved little more satisfactory than its predecessors—it still seemed too distant from the general membership. The assembly went on, therefore, to generate yet another organizational framework for the Grail. A committee was formed to put together a body to be known simply as the Council.[37]

As "an intersecting group representative of the live . . . interests in the movement," the Council differed little from the Task Force; it too had a Coordinating Committee (replacing the Executive Committee) to look after matters of finance, property, and communication with the Grail internationally. The one novel feature of the latest scheme was the provision that the Coordinating Committee implement policies determined not by the Council but by the general assembly. By implication, the general assembly—in which all could take an active role—was thus to become the actual governing body of the American Grail. (The Council was in fact described as "a kind of representative assembly between assemblies.")[38]

The Council began to meet in November 1969, but it too was found wanting; it failed to elicit any "dramatic actions or stands" on current social issues. A contrast was then noted, for the first time, between the sluggish deliberations of the Council and the efficiency of the Coordinating Committee. The Council was more representative but it was hampered by the Grail's self-imposed premium on freedom and diversity; as a report to the movement's international leadership put it, paradoxically: the American Grail's mentality *still* seemed to be "developmental, waiting for initiative from within, rather than [being] pushed from without." The Coordinating Committee, on the other hand, was less representative and less "spontaneous," but it was valuable as "a place of consultation for the stable, long-term commitments of the movement" and it produced concrete decisions.[39]

In 1970, therefore, another sustained effort was made to evaluate the Grail's structures—and to clarify its basic goals as a movement. At Grailville in June and October and in San Jose, California, and Cornwall-on-Hudson, New York, in November, nearly two-thirds of the Grail's "responsible participants" went through a series of "labs" or "process days," aided by "techniques of organizational development."[40] The program resulted in an affirmation, by 139 women, that the Grail was now to be understood in its essence as a "searching community":

> Responsible participation in the Grail implies a sensitivity to the Grail as a movement born of faith and of a desire to respond to the Spirit in different historical moments. This implies a continual search for the deepest meaning of life and work shared among women of different religious backgrounds, races, and cultures. Our commitment to each other and to our world and time asks an unprecedented religious questing and the facing of difficulties openly and as a conscious and common task.[41]

Another general statement of the quest for unity in diversity solved no particular problems, however, and in preparing for an open meeting of the Council early in the following year a committee wondered if it were time, at last, to re-examine the terms in which that quest had been defined over the past several years. Some Grail members, at least, had begun to feel "directionless and without purpose"; they seemed to be asking for something which emphasized "the integration of a religious and social vision which can be *identified and recognized by ourselves and others*." In the committee's mind the Grail's turn to "personal growth and the relational dimensions of participation" was "precious," and the value of personal freedom was not to be called in question. "But," these women said, "we have begun to question what this freedom is for."[42]

Still, the March 1971 Council meeting planned a further evaluation of Grail structures "in light of emerging issues and needs of the movement nationally." Worked on through the year, another new arrangement was in place in January 1972. The Council itself was retained, but two new bodies were created, a Movement Development Team and a Continuity Team. The former was to maintain personal contact with each Grail member, foster communication among all members and begin developing a new orientation program for prospective participants; the latter was to see to administrative matters. Three of the six members of the Movement Development Team and both members of the Continuity Team were to serve on a reconstituted Coordinating Committee which would "share . . . concern for the overall health and growth of the movement."[43]

Grail members themselves could not help but recognize that their search for openness, flexibility, and broad participation had brought the structure of their movement to a dizzying height of complexity. They smiled at the formula which expressed the relationship between its latest component parts: $C = \frac{1}{2}DT + CT$ or $3 + 2 = 5$.[44]

This, however, was not the last step. In 1975 "a completely decentralized structure for the U.S. Grail" was introduced, abolishing the Council and leaving the general assembly, to be held every three years, as the movement's sole policy-making body. In the meanwhile, in 1973, the Council established three task forces (the resurrection of previously used designations seemed not to bother anyone) to explore the three overarching concerns of the Grail in the 1970s: Woman, Search for God, and Liberation ("the transformation of the world into a universal society of justice, love, and peace"). The general assembly and what is basically a committee structure have endured.[45]

In the course of this process of revision upon revision the Grail also succeeded in eliminating its prime symbol of hierarchical authority, the office of president. The committee which organized the Council in 1969 was also assigned to supervise the next presidential election, and it carried out its task despite continuing strong sentiment that the office should be opened to women outside the nucleus; Dorothy Rasenberger was chosen to serve for an additional two years. But in 1972, though the Grail's international presidency was retained with "final responsibility for sustaining unity in vision," the American presidency was simply dropped.[46]

Reaction to a proposal circulated by one of the younger members of the Grail in March 1970 typified the state of the movement at the time. Mary Kay Louchart, soon to make her dedication in the nucleus (she was just the second American woman to do so since 1966), looked forward to establishing a new center of Grail activities in Saginaw, Michigan, amidst a heavy concentration of migrant workers, many Mexicans and blacks among them. Two or three Grail teams would live and take jobs in the area in order to "get to know and feel the culture and environment of the people"; after a while they would come together as a community and, while continuing to relate to the migrant workers, introduce programs purposefully designed to make the Grail known as an organization one might join.[47]

Despite their resemblance to those of Joan Overboss' (whose death in 1969 occasioned a round of tributes), Louchart's ideas were sharply criticized: "We don't think Grail centers can be set up the way they were years ago"; "It's the same old 'we've come to show you' approach"; if the Grail had something to offer, people would find out about it themselves – it shouldn't be hidden, but "we don't think we have to sell it either." Louchart's proposal was particularly self-serving, its critics said, because the Grail was presently "hung up about the lack of black and brown participation" in the movement. Gertrude Morris, a black member of the nucleus, agreed with this view: the Grail was, after all, a basically white middle-class movement which should look first to the quality of its own attitudes, and those of other whites, toward race.[48]

These responses made it clear that along with the conviction that the Grail had not really made way in the past for individual freedom and initiative, the feeling that the movement had imposed itself on the world, rather than serving it, remained powerful indeed. Together, these two reactions – revulsions, they may properly be called – overtook virtually all attempts not only to resurrect past approaches but current efforts to say what the Grail was and what it wanted to do. The problem of the Grail's identity remained largely unresolved as the movement observed the fiftieth anniversary of the founding of the Society of the Women of Nazareth on All Saints Day 1921.

Having brought itself to a near standstill, however, the Grail did not give up. There was still "religious search" to carry the Grail through the 1970s. As Dorothy Rasenberger put it, "the one truth that persists for me is that it was a religious experience that called us together, an insight perceived in common yet so uniquely that each one must speak of it herself. From what we have seen and heard we set out on pilgrimage. The task is still to reflect and act, act and reflect, giving shape and form to what we believe. In the action, belief itself—open-ended, often in turmoil, also 'on the way'—is refined and transformed."[49]

There was also, in spite of an ever-present fear of repeating the alleged mistakes of the past, a growing sense that the Grail needed to find out "what this freedom was for" and how the movement could be "identified by ourselves and others." In the fall of 1971 this feeling produced a "New People Weekend" and a "Grail History Teach-In" at Grailville. In succeeding years the Grail increasingly adopted the method of "telling its story," notably at its 1978 general assembly, where members joined in a session called "Cultural Roots," "a serio-comic episodic drama with musical interludes which provided glimpses of our corporate history, laid out in decades. . . ."[50] This approach, it was hoped, would at least make the Grail's history an explicit working element in creating the movement's future. But it was colored, inevitably, by contemporary perspectives. When Grailville's fortieth anniversary was observed at Christmas 1985 with a reunion of participants in the long defunct Year's School of Formation, a Eucharistic celebration was led by Nancy Richardson, an ordained minister in the United Church of Christ. Passing the soil of Grailville through her fingers, Richardson said "Earth, the roots of our faith and commitment," and lighting a candle sunk into the ground, she proclaimed "Fire, the passion for justice which sustains us." The minister herself and her words presented themselves as symbols of the Grail in its new life beyond the old lay apostolate.[51]

As the Grail struggled through the 1960s, immersing itself in American life, creating a long series of new organizational shapes, and altering its religious identity, it paid relatively little attention to one matter with which it had been vitally concerned in the previous two decades—the nature and role of woman. This was in fact a case of not-so-benign neglect, as a letter from a member of the Grail's National Board to the publisher of Janet Kalven's *The Task of Woman in the Modern World* made evident in 1966: the publisher would please discontinue the pamphlet because "it is no longer adequate to the complexities of the question in this day and age, and no longer reflects the author's thinking on the subject."[52]

With the rise of the women's liberation movement late in the decade, however, the Grail made a 180-degree turn in its attitude toward feminism. It embraced the spirit of Betty Friedan and the National Organization of Women, which aimed "to bring women into full participation in the mainstream of American society *now*, expressing all the privileges and responsibilities thereof in truly equal partnership with men,"[53] with something like the intensity with which it had previously dismissed Simone de Beauvoir's *The Second Sex*.

Janet Kalven, in explanation, said that in the past the Grail had been feminist, if one meant by that term "the affirmation of women as fully adult human beings." The movement's practice in many cases had also outweighed its theory, which held that male and female were equal but different and complementary. However, under the pressure of an ideology which taught women that their fundamental vocation was self-sacrifice and availability for any and every task (except those reserved to men), "we tended to be unaware of the misogyny in the Church and in our own teaching."[54] Another Grail writer made her point more bluntly: "As blacks have experienced, 'equal but different' has in reality always resulted in 'different but unequal.' "[55]

In the early 1970s the Grail set about the task of overcoming the theoretical and practical limitations of its former notions of woman. In the summer of 1972 at Grailville it hosted a conference, "Women Exploring Theology," sponsored by Church Women United. The context of this gathering and a similar one held in the following year was the participants' "increasing awareness of their identity as women in American culture," that is, "their consciousness of powerlessness and invisibility that characterizes a woman's existence" in society. This general consciousness was immediately seen to carry over into Christian theology, which, it was said, "has reflected male experience of the world—and of God."[56]

The Grail also provided facilities for and joined in the planning of an important outgrowth of the conferences just mentioned—the Seminary Quarter at Grailville (SQAG). This program, which began in June 1974 and continued through 1977,

drew women from some twenty-eight seminaries and universities and was described as "a substantial unit of theological education . . . in which women's concerns are central rather than
peripheral." SQAG offered "a focus on feminist perspectives,
both in traditional studies and in breaking new ground by
theological reflection on women's experience."[57]

Consciousness-raising for women has become the Grail's
principal activity in recent years. Grailville, which now functions
as a conference center and a place of "creative rest and relaxation" as well as a hub for the movement, has offered programs
on personal growth, including an introduction to Jungian psychology and an approach to "inner dialogue" called Psycho-
synthesis; on economics, liberation theology (reflecting a certain
desire within the Grail for a new critique of capitalism), and
sexuality; and on widely diverse feminist views of religion,
ranging from Elisabeth Schüssler Fiorenza's Catholic vision to
the neo-paganism of Starhawk.[58]

From the 1960s until quite recently, the Grail pursued this
new agenda at a distance from the public eye. In the mid-1980s,
however, it achieved new visibility when more than two dozen
of its members signed, and two veteran members helped to
organize, an ad in the New York Times which in effect supported
the legitimacy of dissent from the Catholic Church's position on
abortion.[59] The movement has also begun to attract new attention from opposing camps in the continuing post-Vatican II controversy about faithfulness to the Catholic tradition. In her New
Catholic Women, feminist Mary Jo Weaver admires the Grail of
the 1980s and calls it "true to its original vision."[60] In the conservative Catholic journal Fidelity Donna Steichen sees it rather
as "a point of intersection for every strand of lunacy afflicting
society and the Church in America."[61] One might expect such
disparate judgments on a movement which celebrates Holy
Week, as the Grail did in 1987, with a "non-traditional" Easter
Vigil and two Eucharists celebrated by a Jesuit priest.[62]

Afterword

The 1960s have been portrayed often, and correctly, as a watershed in American religious history. American Catholics certainly experienced an unprecedented upheaval in that decade—a "spiritual earthquake," as Philip Gleason has put it.[1] The shock and confusion of the average parishioner, largely unaware of currents of theological and liturgical renewal, is readily understandable. But if the Grail's story is a good guide, the undoubtedly more alert lay apostolate was also deeply affected, perhaps more so. At what seemed the moment of its triumph, the lay apostolate, which understood itself as an agent of renewal in the Church, was overcome by a blast of doubt and disillusion. The Grail, for its part, receded to the fringe of the Church and beyond.

What exactly happened? What generated the crisis of the 1960s? Full answers must await many more studies in the Catholicism of the 1940s and 1950s, but the Grail's history makes it clear that close attention should be paid to the worldview of the Catholic Revival, the ideological underpinning of the lay apostolate.

The Revival, it will be recalled, began as a vigorous attempt to overcome the "siege mentality" of nineteenth-century European Catholicism. At its core was the image of the Church as the Mystical Body of Christ, a figure which carried religious and social implications: sanctity and a sense of mission for all who belonged to the Church; and unity, in the Church and in society, with the Church functioning as a model for a new and just social order. By integrating all things in Christ, Catholics were to spearhead a new Christendom, replacing the old one which had been ravaged by the unbelief and materialism of the modern world.[2]

171

The ideals of the Catholic Revival began to attract American Catholics in the period between the two great wars. They were welcomed in the 1920s as a source of pride in the face of anti-Catholic prejudice. As appropriated by Peter Maurin, Dorothy Day, and others during the Depression, these ideals began to provide a basis for a Catholic prescription for America's social ills: an organic unity of owners and workers which would replace runaway capitalism. And finally, in the 1930s and early 1940s, the Revival's ideals were employed as a stimulus for Catholics to overcome the seeming complacency of their local parishes. A certain "mobilization" of American Catholics marked this whole era, the "active Catholic" becoming something like the norm. Much of the resultant effort was devoted to strengthening Catholic institutions and emphasizing Catholic achievement, but a growing part of it reflected the Revival's apostolic orientation. Some Catholics began to think that becoming more deeply Catholic should involve an attempt to close the gap between the Church and the secular world.[3]

The Grail brought powerful reinforcement to this budding apostolic consciousness. Geared to "the conversion of the world" by Jacques van Ginneken, the Grail presented itself as an embodiment, not merely a library, of the Catholic Revival spirit. It immersed its young recruits in the "complete and common life" of the Church at Doddridge Farm and at Grailville and, at war's end, began to send them out as missionaries both at home and abroad.

The postwar years witnessed the flood tide of the "mobilization" begun earlier. But the 1950s also saw the rise of new and disturbing questions about the "ghetto" quality of American Catholicism. It was now alleged that even avowedly apostolic groups were tainted by the "ghetto" spirit; they addressed the world, but from inside their exclusively Catholic framework. They thus "theologized" the world, making it an extension of the Church, albeit a recalcitrant one. The "new Christendom" concept was too closely tied to that of an enclosed "Catholic culture," resulting in a more benign but still distant view of society at large. The worldview of the Catholic Revival was, in other words, a well-intentioned abstraction which failed to appreciate or take seriously the particulars of the modern world, especially its in-

trinsic pluralism. The clear object of this critique was to propel
Catholics into closer association with other Americans, indeed
to encourage Catholics to participate — as individuals — in American institutions for the benefit of all citizens. Emanating from
young Catholics like John Cogley of *Commonweal* for whom the
postwar years had provided improved access to the mainstream
of American life — especially to higher education — this perspective was, it can now be said, at the cutting edge of developments
in the 1960s.[4]

There is no direct evidence that the Grail responded consciously to this point of view in the mid- to late-1950s, when the
movement was much taken up with expansion and tightening
its organizational structure. But indications are that the American
women who rose to leadership in the early 1960s had been sen-
sitized to it. They had been forced to think of themselves more
deeply as Americans (not only as Catholics) in their encounters
with African and Latin American peoples, they had had to face
many of the complexities of American urban life, and they had
been moved by an incipient democratic (read American) challenge within their own ranks — the desire of married women for
full membership in the Grail. In their first sustained discussions
about the future they arrived at the strong conclusion that the
membership's "human potential" had remained underdeveloped.
In terms of its mission, this meant that the Grail now felt that
it had, after all, taken too broad, too generalized a view of culture and thus of a "new Christendom." It had become the prac-
titioner of many trades but master of none, and it had neglected
the education of its members, especially in the "worldly" spheres
of politics and economics. It was attempting to speak to a world —
especially its own American world — which it did not sufficiently
know or respect.

Having formed these impressions, the Grail immediately
began to move toward professionalism and more explicitly intellectual training. But, more significantly, it also began a re-
examination of the brand of Catholicism which had brought it
to this juncture. What was it, its leaders asked, in the Grail's
own culture and its vision of Catholicism that had worked to
its detriment? The Catholic life of Grailville, it was decided, had
been cultivated in the isolation of rural Ohio with too great a

sense of self-sufficiency—mirroring perhaps the Catholic Revival's idea of the Church. The liturgical culture of the Church, *into* which the things of the world were to be integrated, had really been the focus of the Grail's attention all along. Moreover, the daily life of the training center was now deemed essentially monastic: The Grail, it appeared, was organized much like a religious order and had failed to achieve a distinctly lay spirituality; it had also, in its emphasis on the corporate (the Mystical Body, and the nucleus), inhibited the "human potential" of individual members.

How far these new views might themselves have taken the Grail on the path to radical change is difficult to tell. Grail members' feelings of surprise and perhaps embarrassment were strong, but the worldview of the Catholic Revival, which they were not yet ready to abandon, offered them no real principle of reform. ("Restoration" was more precisely its goal.) At this point, however, Vatican II, with its attendant controversies about authority and change, burst upon the scene. The Grail was favorably disposed to the council's attention to the laity and ecumenism, and was enthusiastic in its reception of the Pastoral Constitution on the Church in the Modern World. But the overall impact of the council and the controversies it generated was a fanning of the flames of discontent already burning within the Grail. While the Catholic Revival lacked full appreciation of the human, the council debates and resistance to implementation of the council's decrees at home revealed the all-too-human dimension of the Church, particularly its reliance on hierarchical power. This revelation seems to have opened another window into the Grail's past: the movement was as hierarchically organized as the Church itself; distance from authority had not prevented the Grail from reproducing its own inhibiting authoritarianism. With an enthusiasm equal to that which propelled its previous apostolic efforts, the Grail soon set out to eliminate all elements of hierarchy from its ranks. The movement's passionate, spiritually motivated search for a participatory (read democratic) structure, along with authentic, informed participation in "worldly" institutions, finally became the Grail's principle focus and led it beyond the bounds of explicit Catholic affiliation. A final discovery, that the freedom of women in the Church was radically circumscribed by (male) Church authority, accelerated this process.

One may say that there was and is a good deal of romanticism in the Grail. Its search for a re-Christianized world followed by disinvestment, followed by a new search for an ideal community of women, certainly exhibits a pattern of defiant, not to say naive, optimism. The problem with this pattern, of course, is that it demands leaving behind a place once visited. In the Grail's case this is now the American Catholic Church. Many of the movement's members nevertheless continue to be concerned and involved Catholics, and perhaps through them the fruits of the Grail's continuing "religious search" will make their way into the Catholic consciousness.

For the historian, however, the past and what may be learned from it must take the first place. The Grail's story, and that of the lay apostolate, exemplifies above all the more or less inevitable demise of the Catholic Revival's vision of Church and world. This vision had its distinct strengths: a firm Catholic identity and a distance from the secular world which allowed Catholicism to function as critic. As long as Catholics remained outside the social mainstream, all was well. But once in, as American Catholics came to be in the 1950s, the distance between the Catholic Revival's ideals and the reality of both Church and world came clear. Since then the danger has been that Catholic identity, with its critical distance, will be lost through its very dedication to the world. But this is the challenge of the time. "Christendom," though it still controls the minds of many, is gone, and a "new Christendom" in pluralistic America is a chimera. So also is a Church which cloaks itself in authority, or even holiness, to the neglect of hard questions about its discipline and teaching. American Catholicism is faced with a hard task: the forging of a vision which engages the contemporary world in all its complexity and which is at the same time self-critical in a positive way.

Notes

INTRODUCTION

1. In the published version of his 1978 presidential address to the American Catholic Historical Association, Philip Gleason noted that secondary literature concerning the lay apostolate was "virtually non-existent" ("In Search of Unity: American Catholic Thought, 1920–1960," *Catholic Historical Review* 65 [April 1979]: 191, note 11). The situation has not been much remedied since that time. See James Hennesey, S.J., *American Catholic Bibliography 1970–1982*, Cushwa Center for the Study of American Catholicism, University of Notre Dame, Working Paper Series 12, no. 1, Fall 1982, p. 22. Gleason's essay also appears in his *Keeping the Faith: American Catholicism Past and Present* (Notre Dame, Ind., 1987), pp. 136–51.

2. Brochure, "The Grail Movement in the New York State Region, 1980–81."

1. THE RICH ROMAN LIFE

1. Decree on the Apostolate of the Laity, chapter 1, in Walter M. Abbot, S.J., and Joseph Gallagher, eds., *The Documents of Vatican II* (New York, 1960), p. 491.

2. "Clericis Laicos" in Colman Barry, ed., *Readings in Church History*, vol. I (Westminster, Md., 1965), p. 464.

3. Yves Congar, *Lay People in the Church* (Westminster, Md., 1957), p. 43, note 23.

4. For the nineteenth-century background, see Roger Aubert et al., *The Church in a Secularized Society* (New York, 1978); E. E. Y. Hales, *The Catholic Church in the Modern World* (New York, 1958); H. Daniel-Rops, *A Fight for God* (New York, 1966).

5. Etienne Gilson, ed., *The Church Speaks to the Modern World: The Social Teachings of Leo XIII* (New York, 1954).

6. Daniel-Rops, *A Fight for God*, p. 292.

7. Barry, *Readings in Church History*, vol. III, pp. 119-20.

8. Michael de la Bedoyere, *The Cardijn Story* (Milwaukee, 1957).

9. Jacques van Ginneken, *Voordrachten over het Katholicisme voor niet-Katholieken* (Rotterdam, 1927), p. 201, quoted in Eleanor Walker, "The Spirit of Father van Ginneken," *Grail Review* VII, no. 2 (1965): 25.

On the citation of Grail journals in this book: The *Grail Review* was published by the Grail International Secretariate in Europe exclusively for lifetime members of the Grail beginning in November 1953. It appeared once a year until January 1958, when it became a monthly. Through December 1958 issues were numbered 1 through 16. When it became a quarterly for "all members and interested parties" in 1959, the review adopted a new system of enumeration. The first issue that year was designated "vol. I, no. 1." This and succeeding issues are therefore cited with the Roman numerals they originally carried. In 1965 the American Grail inaugurated its own journal, *Exchanging News and Views*. In 1968 this became *Reaction: Exchanging News and Views*, which is cited simply as *Reaction*. In this case enumeration was continuous.

10. "From a conference in 1918," quoted in Rachel Donders, *History of the International Grail 1921-1979* (Grailville, Loveland, Ohio, 1983), p. 3; L. J. Rogier and P. Brachin, *Histoire du Catholicisme Hollandais Depuis le XVI Siècle* (Paris, 1974), p. 201.

11. On the history of Catholicism in Holland, see L. J. Rogier and N. De Rooy, *In Vrijheid Herboren: Katholiek Nederland 1853-1953* ('s-Gravenhage, 1953); Rogier and Brachin, *Histoire*; John A. Coleman, *The Evolution of Dutch Catholicism 1958-1974* (Berkeley, 1978).

12. Van Ginneken, "Movement for Conversion in Holland," *Stimmen der Zeit* 106 (1923-24): 3; Rogier and De Rooy, *In Vrijheid Herboren*, p. 584, quoted in "Some Traits of the Times," *Grail Review* V, no. 4 (1963): 2.

13. Van Ginneken, *Voordrachten*, p. 6, quoted in Walker, "The Spirit of Father van Ginneken," p. 27.

14. Rogier and Brachin, *Histoire*, pp. 170-72.

15. Van Ginneken also continued to pursue his intellectual interests. Achieving a considerable reputation in the field of philology, he was later elected to membership in the Dutch Royal Academy of Sciences, the Royal Flemish Academy, and other learned societies in Germany and France. His contention that Gert Groote, founder of the Brethren of the Common Life, and not Thomas à Kempis, was the

author of *The Imitation of Christ* was not widely accepted. Van Ginneken is remembered in Holland today chiefly as a pioneer in the application of linguistics to early childhood education.

Biographical details on van Ginneken are found in Rachel Donders, *History of the International Grail 1921–1979* and Lydwine van Kersbergen, "Life of Father van Ginneken and Principles of the Grail," no date, Archives of the American Grail, Loveland, Ohio (hereafter cited as AAG).

16. The account given here of the Grail's early years is based primarily on Gerti Lauscher, "The Grain of Wheat in the Soil," an unpublished manuscript which draws on the few remaining archival sources at de Tiltenberg, Vogelensang, Holland, and interviews with many long-time Dutch Grail members. The author read and discussed this article with Ms. Lauscher and Emma Verwey on August 8, 1980, in The Hague. See also "The Grail begins to be," *Grail Review* V, no. 4 (1963): 6–9; interview with Lydwine van Kersbergen, August 5, 1980; John G. Vance, *The Ladies of the Grail* (London, 1933), pp. 11–21.

17. The principal source for the following account is Frederica C. Bulte, "The Grail Youth Movement in the Netherlands," unpublished M.A. dissertation, Catholic University of America, 1957. See also Herbert Antcliffe, "A Dutch Catholic Pageant," *Ave Maria* 36 (July 9, 1932): 49–52; E. Boland, "The Grail Movement," *Catholic Mind* 31 (August 8, 1933): 289–98; John G. Rowe, "The Grail: The Modern Movement for Catholic Girls," *Ave Maria* 39 (April 7, 1934): 424–27; H. van Meer, "The Grail in Holland," *Homiletic and Pastoral Review* 36 (May 1936): 838–40; J. B. McAllister, "The Ladies of Nazareth," *Catholic World* 146 (February 1938): 602–5; Eva Ross, "Successful Youth," *Commonweal* 25 (November 1936): 40–42; J. B. McAllister, "Grail Movement," *Sign* 18 (March 1939): 474–76; Donders, *History of the International Grail*, pp. 9–23. A recent study is Els Naayer, "En onderzock naar de Katholieke vrouwelijke jeugbeweging 'de Graal' in het bisdom Haarlen 1929–1940," unpublished doctoral dissertation, Groningen, 1980.

18. The statutes were published in *St. Bavo*, the official organ of the diocese of Haarlem. Quoted in Donders, *History of the International Grail*, p. 10.

19. Decree quoted in "The Grail begins to be," p. 8.

20. Bulte, "The Grail Youth Movement," p. 45.

21. Michel van der Plas, *Uit het rijke Roomsche Leven, een documentaire over de jaren 1925–1935* (Utrecht, no date), passim.

22. L. J. Rogier in Hella Haase, ed., *Beatrix 18 Jaar* (Amsterdam, 1945), p. 120, quoted in "Some Traits of the Times," p. 3.

23. For the texts of *Ubi Arcano, Non Abbiamo Bisogno* (On the

Apostolate of the Laity), and other encyclicals of Pius XI, see Terence P. McLaughlin, ed., *The Church and the Reconstruction of the Modern World* (Garden City, N.Y., 1957). See also Daniel-Rops, *A Fight for God*, pp. 285-95.

24. On the political dimensions of Catholic Action in Italy, see Jean Guy Vaillancourt, *Papal Power, a Study of Vatican Control over Lay Elites* (Berkeley, 1980), especially pp. 45-50.

25. "Catholic Action in 1936," *Commonweal* 23 (January 3, 1936): 253-54.

26. Donders, *History of the International Grail*, pp. 20-22.

27. "The Grail as a Young Woman's Movement: Aims, Methods, and Basic Ideas," given at de Tiltenberg, August 1932; "Retreat by Father van Ginneken," given at de Tiltenberg, August 10-19, 1932. Both series were taken down and transcribed unedited. Copies of English translations in AAG. They are cited hereafter as "Grail Movement" and "Retreat," respectively, followed by a lecture or conference number.

Two other important statements of van Ginneken are "Reisbriefen," a series of sixteen letters sent to the Women of Nazareth as van Ginneken toured Europe in August-September 1931, and *Litanie van Jesus' Volkomenden* (Lier, no date). English translations, AAG.

28. "Grail Movement," 22, p. 6.

29. Ibid., 19, p. 4; 18, p. 1.

30. Ibid., 18, p. 11.

31. "Retreat," 25, pp. 1, 2, 3.

32. Ibid., p. 3.

33. "Grail Movement," 24, p. 23.

34. Ibid., 14, pp. 4, 5, 6, 8. On Mary Ward, see *The New Catholic Encyclopedia* (New York, 1967), s.v. "Mary Ward," by M. P. Trauth; and Mary Oliver, *Mary Ward* (New York, 1959).

35. "Grail Movement," 20, p. 2.

36. Ibid.

37. On the canonical distinctions see T. Lincoln Bouscaren, Adam C. Ellis, and Francis N. Korth, *Canon Law, a Text and Commentary* (Milwaukee, 1966), pp. 345-46 and 379-80. For the present organization of the Grail in England and a brief comment on its history see *A Society of Lay People: Way of Life of the Grail Society* (Middlesex, 1974).

After Vatican II the Grail filed, without difficulty, the set of guidelines approved by its 1967 international general assembly with the newly established council on the laity in Rome.

38. "Grail Movement," 24.

39. "Retreat," 5, p. 3.

40. Ibid.

41. Ibid., 11, p. 2.
42. Ibid., 11, p. 4; 15, p. 3.
43. Van Ginneken, *Voordrachten*, pp. 91–96, passim, quoted in Walker, "The Spirit of Father van Ginneken," p. 21. The same theme is pursued in "Retreat," 26.
44. "Retreat," 15, p. 3.
45. Donders, *History of the International Grail*, pp. 27–30.
46. "Grail Movement," 24, p. 4; 25, p. 6.

2. IN THE HEARTLAND OF CATHOLIC ACTION

1. *Souvenir Volume of the Centennial Celebration and Catholic Congress* (Chicago, 1883), p. 18, quoted in Daniel Callahan, *The Mind of the Catholic Layman* (New York, 1963), p. 69. See also Callahan, pp. 72–76.
2. Martin H. Work and Daniel Kane, "The American Catholic Layman and His Organizations," in Philip Gleason, ed., *Contemporary Catholicism in the United States* (Notre Dame, Ind., 1969), pp. 352–53.
3. Charles E. Curran, *American Catholic Social Ethics: Twentieth-Century Approaches* (Notre Dame, Ind., 1982), pp. 84–87.
4. Peter Maurin, "The Dynamite of the Church," *Easy Essays* (West Hamlin, Va., 1974), p. 15.
5. David J. O'Brien, *American Catholics and Social Reform: The New Deal Years* (New York, 1968), p. 211. See also Mel Piehl, *Breaking Bread: The Catholic Worker and the Origin of Catholic Radicalism in America* (Philadelphia, 1982); William D. Miller, *Dorothy Day: A Biography* (San Francisco, 1982); Marc H. Ellis, *Peter Maurin: Prophet in the Twentieth Century* (New York, 1981).
6. Paul Marx, *Virgil Michel and the Liturgical Movement* (Collegeville, Minn., 1957); Curran, *American Catholic Social Ethics*, chap. 4.
7. Frank Sheed, "Catholic England: A Quarter Century Chronicle," *Thought* 26 (1951): 271.
It should be pointed out that the literature of the Catholic Revival did not go unnoticed in America before the 1930s. The Jesuits Francis X. Talbot and Daniel A. Lord, among others, promoted it vigorously in the previous decade. But their goals were primarily apologetic: to prod Catholics to higher literary achievement and thus enhance the esteem of Catholicism in America. It was only in the Depression decade that the link was forged between the Catholic Revival and social renewal. See Arnold Sparr, "The Catholic Literary Revival in America, 1920–1960," unpublished Ph.D. dissertation, University of Wisconsin, 1985.

Also on the Catholic Revival, see Frank Sheed, *Sidelights on the Catholic Revival* (New York, 1940) and *The Church and I* (Garden City, N.Y., 1974); Calvert Alexander, *The Catholic Literary Revival* (Milwaukee, 1935); Francis B. Thornton, ed., *Return to Tradition* (1948); James Hitchcock, "Postmortem on a Rebirth, the Catholic Intellectual Renaissance," *American Scholar* 49 (Spring 1980): 211–25; Dolores Elise Brien, "The Catholic Revival Revisited," *Commonweal* 106 (December 21, 1979): 714–16.

8. Dennis Michael Robb, "Specialized Catholic Action in the United States, 1936–1949: Ideology, Leadership, and Organization," unpublished Ph.D. dissertation, University of Minnesota, 1972; Edward R. Kantowicz, *Corporation Sole: Cardinal Mundelein and Chicago Catholicism* (Notre Dame, Ind., 1983), pp. 197–202.

9. See above, chap. 1, note 17.

10. Van Kersbergen to Day, February 21, 1936, Dorothy Day–Catholic Worker Collection, the Marquette Archives, Milwaukee, Wisconsin.

11. Interview with Msgr. James Coffey, May 20, 1980.

12. Taped interview with Mary Louise Tully by Sharon Thomson, July 1979, AAG (Grail Oral History Project). Tully's father was a businessman whose interest turned to disseminating and publishing Catholic literature. See Floyd Anderson, "John C. Tully, Founder of the Thomas More Association," *Catholic Press Annual*, 1963, pp. 26, 37–39.

13. Interview with Lydwine van Kersbergen, August 5, 1980.

14. Norman McKenna, "Pax Romana in America," *Columbia* 19 (October 1939): 12, 17.

15. Van Kersbergen to "Your Excellency" [Bernard Sheil], December 12, 1939, AAG (copy signed by van Kersbergen).

16. Statement of authorization signed by Margaret van Gilse, February 12, 1940, AAG.

17. Van Kersbergen to Sheil, December 12, 1939. As mentioned earlier, the Grail continued until after World War II to use such terms as "novitiate," ostensibly to assure Church leaders of the seriousness of its commitment. The movement's leaders in America were disturbed, however, when this usage was misunderstood.

18. Sheil to van Kersbergen, December 30, 1939, telegram "Hollandradio, AAG.

19. Interviews with van Kersbergen, August 5–7, 1980, Maria J. A. Groothuizen, August 8, 1980.

20. William Larkin to Lydwine van Kersbergen, April 9, 1940, AAG.

21. Interview with van Kersbergen, August 5, 1980.

22. Interviews with Coffey, May 20, 1980; Catherine Leahy, April 18, 1980.

23. Interview with van Kersbergen, August 5, 1980.

24. Dennis Geaney, "The Chicago Story," *Chicago Studies* 2 (Winter 1963): 291.

Bernard Sheil (1886–1969) was consecrated an auxiliary bishop of Chicago by Cardinal Mundelein in 1928. He founded the Catholic Youth Organization in 1930 and the Sheil School of Social Studies in 1943. Among the other groups encouraged and supported by Sheil were Catherine de Hueck's Friendship House and the Thomas More Associates. See Andrew Greeley, *The Catholic Experience* (Garden City, N.Y., 1967), p. 252, note 4 (where Greeley declares that Sheil "Was not in any real sense part of the ferment" of Catholic Action); Robert E. Burns, "CYO and the Christian Revolution," in Leo R. Ward, ed., *The American Apostolate* (Westminster, Md., 1952), pp. 204–16; Kantowicz, *Corporation Sole*, chaps. 12 and 13.

25. *Catholic Herald*, September 13, 1940, *Waukegan Sun-News*, December 19, 1940, clippings, AAG; "1942 Report to Archbishop Stritch," p. 6, AAG.

26. Robb, "Specialized Catholic Action," p. 170.

27. "Doddridge Farm—A Challenge," *Action* 1 (August 5, 1940): 1–2, quoted in Robb, "Specialized Catholic Action," p. 107.

28. "Grail Report 1940–41," p. 15, AAG.

29. John C. Rawe and Luigi G. Ligutti, *Rural Roads to Security: America's Third Struggle for Freedom* (Milwaukee, 1940), p. 303. See also Ligutti, "Cities Kill," *Commonweal* 32 (August 2, 1940): 300–301.

Luigi Ligutti (1895–1984) was born in Italy. He migrated to the United States in 1912 and was ordained a priest in 1917. Having served as a pastor in Woodbine and Granger, Iowa, he was elected president of the National Catholic Rural Life Conference in 1937 and appointed its executive secretary in 1940. Besides his position at the United Nations, Ligutti also served on the Pontifical Commission for Justice and Peace. See Vincent A. Yzermans, *The People I Love: A Biography of Luigi G. Ligutti* (Collegeville, Minn., 1976); Raymond W. Miller, *Monsignor Ligutti: The Pope's County Agent* (Washington, D.C., 1981).

30. Yzermans, *The People I Love*, p. 74.

31. Janet Kalven, "The Grail Spirit in America," *Orate Fratres* 15 (June 1941): 382–83.

32. "Grail Report 1940–41."

33. Ibid. The above quotations are from pp. 3, 5, 8, 9, 11, 12, 25–34.

There never was a Grail air force, but Mary Louise Tully, "out of holy obedience," actually earned a pilot's license in November 1943. After her qualifying solo flight Tully never again operated a plane. (Interview with Mary Louise Tully by Sharon Thomson.)

Neither was there to be a Grail studio in Hollywood. But the movement did produce one filmmaker. Maclovia Rodriguez won the Golden Eagle Award of the Council on Non-Theatrical Events in 1966 for her thirty-minute work "New Born Again."

34. Ibid., p. 26.

35. "Summer Camp at the Grail," no date, AAG.

36. Ibid.

37. "Nuns in Mufti," *Time*, July 24, 1941, p. 50; "The Situation at Doddridge," handwritten notes, no date, AAG. The *Time* article did attract the attention of a young woman who later became a prominent journalist and author and the wife of United States Senator Eugene McCarthy. In her autobiography, *Private Faces, Public Places* (Garden City, N.Y., 1972), p. 98, Abigail McCarthy recalled that she had "read in *Time* of the coming to America of a new kind of nun, Dutch women who were the dedicated core of a women's movement. . . . They did not wear habits, did not necessarily live in community, moved freely about, and were not interested in the traditional women's roles of teaching and nursing." A few years later the McCarthys became more closely acquainted with the Grail (*Private Faces*, pp. 122–23).

38. *National Liturgical Week* (Newark, N.J., 1942), pp. 201–2.

39. Janet Kalven, "The Spirit of the Grail," *Orate Fratres* 16 (February 1942): 185–86. See also Dorothy Dorszyski, "Training Course at the Grail, Christmas 1941," no date, AAG.

40. Stritch to van Kersbergen, May 24, 1942, AAG.

41. Typewritten notes on meeting of July 9, 1942, AAG.

42. Ibid.

43. "The Vineyard," mimeographed, AAG. This unpaginated booklet, which was circulated privately, contains an introduction and the texts of the major addresses given during the course.

The Baroness Catherine de Hueck's apostolic concern was interracial harmony. See de Hueck, *Friendship House* (New York, 1947) and Ann Harrigan, "Friendship House, U.S.A.," in Leo R. Ward, *The American Apostolate*, pp. 94–108.

44. Draft of press release for "The Vineyard," p. 2, AAG.

45. Ibid., p. 4.

46. Grace Elizabeth Gallagher, "Rural Life School," *Catholic Worker* 9 (November 1942): 8. See also "1942 Report."

47. "1942 Report"; Program of the 1942 NCRLC Convention, Ar-

chives of the National Catholic Rural Life Conference, the Marquette Archives.

48. *National Liturgical Week* (Newark, N.J., 1943), pp. 133, 64.

49. See *Histories of the Grail in Individual Countries* (Grail History Project, 1984), AAG. The group at Green Bay, led by George and Agnes Holmiller, was especially active. See "A Lay Leadership Course," *Orate Fratres* 23 (November 6, 1949): 560–62.

50. Barbara Ellen Wald, "Wanted: A New Type of Woman," *Torch*, April 1943, reprint, AAG.

51. Bernard McWilliams, "The Apostolate Grows in Pittsburgh," reprint, no source, AAG.

52. Patrick T. Quinlan, "Keep Them Plowing" (National Catholic Rural Life Conference Folder no. 8, 1943).

53. "1943 Report," [April 7, 1943], AAG.

54. Stritch to van Kersbergen, May 23, 1943, AAG.

55. Van Kersbergen to Stritch, May 29, and June 9, 1943, Stritch to van Kersbergen, June 10, 1943, AAG.

56. "The Valiant Woman," 1943 brochure, AAG. See also Virginia Bogdan, "The Grail Training Course," *Orate Fratres* 17 (September 1943): 465–66.

57. Dorothy Day, "The Harvest," typewritten draft, pp. 2 (emphasis added), 5, 6, AAG. Edited in the light of suggestions by Lydwine van Kersbergen, this text appeared as "Notes by the Way," *Catholic Worker* 10 (October 1943): 1, 2. See also William D. Miller, *A Harsh and Dreadful Love: Dorothy Day and the Catholic Worker Movement* (New York, 1973), pp. 190–91.

58. Grace Elizabeth Gallagher, "New Horizons for Young Women," *Wanderer*, November 25, 1943, p. 4. See also Raymond P. Witte, *Twenty-Five Years of Crusading: A History of the National Catholic Rural Life Conference* (Des Moines, Iowa, 1948), p. 126, where the author states that "the purpose of the Grail is to train Catholic young women for a role of rural leadership."

59. Day, "The Harvest," p. 6.

3. PERMANENT ROOTS: GRAILVILLE, LOVELAND, OHIO

1. Yzermans, *The People I Love*, p. 74.

2. John T. McNicholas (1877–1950) was a Dominican priest who served as bishop of Duluth, Minnesota, before being appointed archbishop of Cincinnati in 1925. See M. E. Reardon, *Mosaic of a Bishop* (Paterson, N.J., 1957). McNicholas was a leading candidate for the arch-

bishopric of New York until Francis Spellman was named to the post in 1938. On this circumstance see Robert I. Gannon, *The Cardinal Spellman Story* (Garden City, N.Y., 1962), p. 129.

3. Interview with Lydwine van Kersbergen, August 5, 1980; McNicholas to Pastors, Superintendents of Schools, Presidents of Colleges for Women, and Principals of High Schools for Girls, December 20, 1943, Archives of the Archdiocese of Cincinnati, Cincinnati, Ohio.

4. Dempsey and Dempsey, Attorneys, to Msgr. John K. Muzio (chancellor of the archdiocese of Cincinnati), March 21, 1944, Archives of the Archdiocese of Cincinnati. A tenant farmer held the remaining half interest. He was later succeeded by a farmer of the Grail's choosing, Bernard Hutzel.

5. Interview with Janet Kalven, April 19, 1980. The Grail was not responsible for "Loveland." The town, which existed for many years before the Grail's arrival, bore the name of a local landowner.

6. The name comes from Psalm 136, verse 1: "By the rivers of Babylon, there we sat and wept, remembering Zion." Details of the purchase are contained in "Loans Received by the Grail from the Archdiocese of Cincinnati," October 24, 1947, AAG.

7. "The Christian Conspiracy," 1944 Grail brochure, AAG. The text of this brochure also appeared in *Orate Fratres* 18 (June 1944): 367–70 and *Catholic Worker* 11 (May 1944): 8.

8. Rt. Rev. Ignatius Esser, O.S.B., to van Kersbergen, August 25, 1944, Archives of the Archdiocese of Cincinnati.

9. [Fargo] *Catholic Action News*, May 25, 1945, clipping, AAG.

10. Edward Skillin, "Why Rural Life?" *Commonweal* 41 (December 1, 1944): 166.

11. Janet Kalven, "Woman and the Post-War Reconstruction," in *Catholic Rural Life Objectives* (Des Moines, Iowa, no date), pp. 25, 26, 27; *Catholic Mind* 43 (February 1945): 78–82; *Catholic Worker* 12 (April 1945): 4, 8. For the ideas of Vincent McNabb, see his *Old Principles and the New Order* (New York, 1942).

12. Skillin, "Why Rural Life?" p. 167.

13. Interview with Mary Louise Tully by Sharon Thomson; Janet Kalven to Benedicta, October 11, 1944, Dorothy Day–Catholic Worker Collection.

14. Stanley Hamilton, "Something's Happening at Grailville," *Town and Country Church*, 1945: 3–4; James M. Shea, "To Be Saints and Apostles," *Land and Home*, June 1947: 46–49.

15. Alonso Rodriguez, *The Practice of Christian and Religious Perfection* (Chicago, 1929).

16. Grail Membership List, 1944–1950, AAG.

17. Barbara Ellen Wald, "Grail Adventure," *The Living Parish*, 10 (April 1943): 10.

18. Interview with Janet Kalven.

19. Interview with Mary Imelda Buckley, October 8, 1980.

20. Catherine E. Dorff, "Home Making," reprint from *Land and Home*, March 1945, AAG. Dorff's article also appeared in *Catholic Worker* 13 (June 1946): 8.

21. Josephine Drabek, "Love Made Visible," *Land and Home*, June 1945: 53. This article also appeared in *Catholic Worker* 12 (November 1945): 7, 11.

22. See Ed Willock, "Toward Peace in the Lay Apostolate," *Integrity* 3 (December 1948): 16–23.

23. Mary Caplice to John Fitzsimons, August 5, 1946, YCW Papers, University of Notre Dame Archives, Notre Dame, Indiana, quoted in Robb, "Specialized Catholic Action," p. 244.

24. "Discussion with Father John Fitzsimons on Lay Apostolate," typewritten notes, March 9, 1947, AAG. Fitzsimons was co-author with Paul McGuire of *Restoring All Things: A Guide to Catholic Action* (New York, 1938).

25. Dorothy Day, "The Church and Work," *Catholic Worker* 13 (September 1946): 1, 3, 7, 8. See Robb, "Specialized Catholic Action, p. 246, note 55.

26. "Discussion with Father Fitzsimons."

27. Ibid.

28. Ibid.

29. Interview with Lydwine van Kersbergen, August 6, 1980. According to van Kersbergen, Hillenbrand came to the point where he "resisted" the Grail's approach, but there were no open quarrels between them. Nevertheless, the YCW remained quite wary of accepting any young woman who had been trained by the Grail into its ranks. See Robb, "Specialized Catholic Action," pp. 281–82.

On Hillenbrand's mentality and accomplishments, see Robert McClory, "Hillenbrand: U.S. Moses," *National Catholic Reporter*, September 7, 1979; Andrew Greeley, *The Catholic Experience*, pp. 249–56.

Another priest who became interested in Jocism and with whom the Grail experienced difficulty was the Dominican Francis Wendell of St. Vincent's Priory in New York. From his circle of aspiring lay apostles at Hunter College, several young women went to the Grail, and another, Carol Jackson, founded (with Ed Willock) *Integrity* magazine. See Wendell, "Spiritual Direction of Lay Apostles," *Integrity* 2 (September 1948): 29–34; Patricia McGowan, "Priest for Apostles," *Today*, January 1957: 3–7.

30. 1945 Grail brochure, AAG; Joan Overboss, "Grail Offers Courses in Lived Christianity," *Orate Fratres* 19 (May 1945): 325–26.

31. See Callahan, *The Mind of the Catholic Layman*, pp. 91–94; Philip Gleason, "The Crisis of Americanization," in Gleason, ed., *Contemporary Catholicism in the United States*, pp. 8–11, and in Gleason, *Keeping the Faith*, pp. 58–81.

32. Canon Paul Sobry, "The Notion of Renascence," in Norman Weyand, ed., *The Catholic Renascence in a Disintegrating World* (Chicago, 1951), p. 14.

33. Joan Overboss, "Talk on the Grail," Libertyville, Illinois, 1942, typescript, AAG; Janet Kalven, "The Crisis of Our Times," 1943, typescript, AAG; Mariette Wickes, "The Vision of the Lay Apostolate," July 1945, typescript, AAG.

34. *Program of Action: A Suggested Outline for the Lay Apostolate of Young Women* (Grailville, 1946), pp. 20, 18, 10, 25, 29, 32, 38, 40.

35. Ibid., pp. 91, 94. O'Malley's essay was entitled "The Restlessness of Our Times." On O'Malley, see Sparr, "The Catholic Literary Revival," chap. 7.

Carl F. Bauer was much influenced by the Grail and his Center for Men of Christ the King in some ways imitated the style of Grailville. See Ned O'Gorman, "An Education for a Poet," in Daniel Callahan, ed., *Generation of the Third Eye* (New York, 1965), p. 183.

36. Janet Kalven, *The Task of Woman in the Modern World* (Des Moines, Iowa, 1946), pp. 15, 2, 16, 17, 4, 6, 8, 11, 12, 13.

The Baroness Gertrud von Le Fort was a convert to Roman Catholicism in 1925 and the author of *The Eternal Woman* (Milwaukee, 1954) and *The Song of the Scaffold* (New York, 1933), among many other works. The latter, scenes from which were frequently presented as dramatic readings at Grailville, inspired George Bernanos' play, *Dialogues des Carmelites*, which in turn served as the basis of the libretto of an opera of the same title by Francis Poulenc (1957). See Doris Grumbach, "Eternal Woman," *Today* 13 (March 1948): 34–35.

The main source for Chesterton's antifeminist views is his early work (antedating his conversion to Catholicism by some years), *What's Wrong with the World* (London, 1910). An abridged version, with a "tutorial introduction" by Frank Sheed, appeared later (New York, 1942) as No. 6 of the "Catholic Masterpiece Series." See Alzina Stone Dale, *The Outline of Sanity: A Life of G. K. Chesterton* (Grand Rapids, Mich., 1982), pp. 143–52, 171–72, 194.

37. Interview with Lydwine van Kersbergen, August 6, 1980.

38. Ibid.; "Report to International," Spring 1948, p. 6, AAG.

39. Grace Elizabeth (Gallagher) Rogan, "A Red Brick School-

house," in Maisie Ward, ed., *Be Not Solicitous* (New York, 1953), p. 148. Interviews with Daniel and Mary Kane, June 19, 1980; William and Mary Schickel, May 27, 1980; Bernard and Patricia Hutzel, April 28, 1980; Grace Rogan, April 19, 1980; James and Catherine Shea, April 16, 1980.

40. *National Liturgical Week* (Conception, Missouri, 1949), p. 65.

41. On van Gilse's visit and changing attitudes within the Grail following World War II, see Donders, *History of the International Grail*, pp. 33–34.

42. Adolph Schalk, "Lay Apostles in China," *Torch*, January 1952: p. 18. See also Nicholas Maestrini, "Lay Missionaries," *Missionary Union of the Clergy Bulletin* 13 (March 1949): 61–67, and "Invitation to the Lay Missionary," *Shield*, April 1949: 17–19.

43. Mary Louise Tully, "I'm a Lay Missionary Overseas," *Shield*, January 1950, reprint, AAG; Elizabeth Reid, *I Belong Where I'm Needed* (Westminster, Md., 1962), pp. 12, 23–25.

44. "Report to International," Spring 1948, pp. 4–5.

45. Shea, "To Be Saints and Apostles," p. 48.

46. "Report to International," Spring 1948, p. 5.

47. Elsa Chaney, "Writing and Being," a brochure for a course of the same name given July 12–17, 1949, AAG.

48. *Integrity* 1 (October 1946): 1, 2. See above, note 29.

49. Gustave Weigel, in his Introduction to Thomas O'Dea's *American Catholic Dilemma* (New York, 1962), p. 12, describes the Catholic Commission on Intellectual Affairs (CCICA) as the product of "a certain amount of pressure brought to bear on American Catholics by the work of the Pax Romana association of Europe, which was a Catholic organization for all Catholic intellectuals." With a membership of fewer than three hundred college and university professors in 1958, CCICA was "ever gentle and harmless enough," according to Weigel. Nevertheless, its meetings gave rise to three important contributions to American Catholic self-awareness: John Tracy Ellis' *American Catholics and the Intellectual Life* (Chicago, 1956); Weigel's "American Catholic Intellectualism—A Theologian's Reflections," *Review of Politics* 19 (1957): 275–307; and O'Dea's *American Catholic Dilemma*.

The Catholic Renascence Society held its first symposium at the Convent of the Sacred Heart in Chicago in 1940. Succeeding meetings and *Renascence*, begun at St. Mary's College in Milwaukee in 1948 and later published at Marquette University, gave much of their attention to French Catholic literature.

50. "On Secularism," November 14, 1947, and "On the Christian in Action," November 21, 1948, statements of the National Catholic

Welfare Conference Administrative Board, in Raphael M. Huber, ed., *Our Bishops Speak* (Milwaukee, 1952), pp. 137, 147.

51. "The Restoration of the Sunday, Goal of the Modern Lay Apostolate," in *National Liturgical Week* (Conception, Missouri, 1949), p. 41.

52. "Youth Day Program," Silver Jubilee Convention of the National Catholic Rural Life Conference. See Leonard Austin, "A Catholic Culture for America," *Integrity* 1 (July 1947): 19–23, and "Modern Dancing and Christianity," *Integrity* 2 (July 1948): 5–9. In Austin's view, the "waltz mania" and its successor, "the current fad of 'sweet' music," were signs of cultural decline which could lead America in the direction of "militarism, regimentation, and cruelty."

53. 1948 Grail brochure, AAG.

54. "Report to International," Spring 1948, p. 4.

55. Jop Pollman, ed., *Laughing Meadows: A Collection of Folk Melodies Drawn from Traditional Sources* (Grailville, 1947); *This Is Marriage: A Simplified Version of the Encyclical "Casti Connubii" (On Christian Marriage) by Pope Pius XI*, Introduction by Emerson Hynes (Grailville, 1946); *This Is Social Justice: A Simplified Version of the Encyclical "Quadragesimo Anno" (On the Reconstruction of the Social Order) by Pope Pius XI*, Introduction by Carl F. Bauer (Grailville, 1946); *A Hymn to Work*, photographs by Abbé Albert Tessier, text by Josephine Drabek (Grailville, no date); *Families for Christ* (Grailville, 1949).

56. *Grail National Newsletter*, Lent 1949, AAG.

57. Ibid.; *The Christian Observance of Candelmas* (Grailville, 1950). Other pamphlets were: *Holy Spring* (Grailville, no date); *The Christian Observance of Thanksgiving* (Grailville, 1949); and *New Life for New Year's Eve* [by Anne M. Mulkeen] (Grailville, 1951).

58. *Restore the Sunday*, compiled and edited by Janet Kalven, Mariette Wickes, and Barbara Ellen Wald, in close cooperation with Mr. James M. Shea (Grailville, 1949), pp. 141–53; *Toward a Christian Sunday, an Apostolic Program Based on the Volume, Restore the Sunday* (Grailville, 1949).

59. *Grail National Newsletter*, Autumn 1949, AAG.

60. Lydwine van Kersbergen, *The Normal School of Sanctity for the Laity* (Grailville, 1949), pp. 15, 19, 21.

61. Ibid., p. 14.

62. "The Restoration of the Sunday, Goal of the Modern Lay Apostolate," pp. 34, 35, 36. "One wild divorce court" is another echo of G. K. Chesterton.

63. "Report to International," Spring 1948, p. 5.

64. James Shea, "School for Apostles," *St. Joseph Magazine*, May 1949: 9–11.

65. Press release, typewritten, AAG. See also Maestrini, "Lay Missionaries"; Edward Freking, "Lay Apostles for the Overseas Missions," *Shield*, November 1949: 21–23.

66. The Mission Secretariate was affiliated with the National Catholic Welfare Conference but was responsible to the national director of the Pontifical Society for the Propagation of the Faith. Its executive secretary was Frederick McGuire, C.M. The Grail participated in the meetings of the secretariate from its beginnings.

On the prevailing attitude toward laypersons as missionaries see *The New Catholic Encyclopedia*, s.v. "Lay Missionaries," by F. A. McGuire; James Rogan, "The Lay Apostolate in the Missions," *Torch*, March 1951: 16–18. The tide began to turn when Pope Pius XII included a section entitled "Cooperation of the Laity" in his encyclical *Evangelii Praecones* (On Promoting Catholic Missions) of June 2, 1951 (Washington, D.C., no date).

67. Joseph T. Nolan, "Grailville's Valiant Women," *America* 78 (October 1947): 9.

68. H. A. R. [Reinhold], "Grailville," *Orate Fratres* 23 (November 1949): 544, 545, 547.

69. [Godfrey Diekmann], "The Apostolate," *Orate Fratres* 23 (October 1949): 524.

70. Ibid.

71. Interview with James and Catherine Shea.

72. Evelyn Waugh, "The American Epoch in the Catholic Church," *Life*, September 19, 1949: 152.

73. A speaker at a 1966 Grail meeting recalled that when she returned home after just a few months at Grailville her father asked her, "What are you talking like that for?" (Alice McCarthy, "The Grail is an Existential Movement," typewritten manuscript, p. 10, AAG).

74. "Report to International," Spring 1948, p. 3.

4. "CANNOT AMERICA GIVE MORE?"

1. Frank O'Malley, "The Culture of the Church," *Review of Politics* 16 (April 1954): 133; Romano Guardini, *The Church and the Catholic and the Spirit of the Liturgy* (New York, 1953), p. 51, quoted in O'Malley, ibid., p. 134.

2. James Hennesey, S.J., *American Catholics: A History of the Roman Catholic Community in the United States* (New York, 1981), pp. 283–84.

3. William Clancy, "Catholicism in America," in *Catholicism in America* (New York, 1954), pp. 11, 18; on Cogley, see Sparr, "The Catholic Literary Revival," pp. 364–65.

4. Jean Daniélou, *La Maison Dieu* (Première trimestre, 1951), quoted in English translation in "Report on the Relations between the Grailville Institute and St. Columban's Parish," p. 3, attached to Lydwine van Kersbergen to Karl Alter, July 12, 1951, Archives of the Archdiocese of Cincinnati.

5. Clarence C. Issenman to Lydwine van Kersbergen, May 17, 1951, AAG.

6. Karl Alter to Lydwine van Kersbergen, July 9, 1951, Archives of the Archdiocese of Cincinnati.

7. "Comments on the Various Charges Made at the Meeting at St. Columban's Rectory, July 13, 1951," attached to Lydwine van Kersbergen to Monsignor Wagner, July 14, 1951, Archives of the Archdiocese of Cincinnati.

8. "Report on the Relations between the Grailville Institute and St. Columban's Parish," p. 1.

9. Lydwine van Kersbergen to Rachel Donders, July 14 and July 21, 1951, AAG; van Kersbergen to Karl Alter, July 24, 1951, Archives of the Archdiocese of Cincinnati.

10. Karl Alter, "Statement Made at Loveland Parish," July 20, 1951, pp. 2, 6, Archives of the Archdiocese of Cincinnati.

11. Rachel Donders, "Impressions of Grailville and Super Flumina," October 2, 1951, pp. 1, 2, AAG.

12. Ibid., p. 9.

13. "Grail Movement," 23, quoted in Donders, *History of the International Grail*, p. 41.

14. "Impressions of Grailville and Super Flumina," pp. 7, 8. Donders also took this occasion to explain the Grail's view of its autonomous role within the Church. "Our idea," she said, "is to be lay apostles who work independently, in cooperation with priests, but not as their helpers" (pp. 8–9).

15. "Dedication Dates" [1951–1962], AAG.

16. Grail brochure, Summer 1951, AAG; Elsa Chaney, "Mission Ventures of the Grail," *Catholic World* 173 (August 1951): 157.

17. Oriental Institute brochure, 1951–52, AAG.

18. Chaney, "Mission Ventures."

19. Maurice E. Reardon to Lydwine van Kersbergen, February 22, 1951, AAG; van Kersbergen to Karl Alter, March 6, 1951, AAG; Roy J. Ferrari to Janet Klaven [*sic*], November 7, 1951, Grailville Institute file, Archives of the Catholic University of America, Washington, D.C.

The relationship with Catholic University enabled Grailville students to earn some college credits and visitors from overseas to obtain visas. Grail members were advised, however, that under the arrangement, "we have no obligation whatsoever to confine our curriculum to the official academic regulations" (Barbara Wald, "Grailville," *Grail Review* 1 [November 1953]: 4).

20. "Voyagers for the World," *Shield*, April 1952: 11–12; [Brooklyn] *Tablet*, February 16, 1952.

21. Lydwine van Kersbergen, "African Journey," *Commonweal* 59 (November 20, 1953): 159, 160; *Grail National Newsletter*, Summer 1953.

22. Therese McDermit and Lorraine Machan, "Assignment in Uganda," *Catholic Nurse*, September 1954: 19–21; Mary I. Buckley, "The Grail," in *Union Catholique de Cooperation Interraciale, Annuaire 1955*, pp. 155–60.

The lay mission vocation was also taken up at this early date by one of the Loveland families. James and Grace Rogan, with their two young children, journeyed to South Africa in 1952, where for the next four years they worked closely with Archbishop Denis Hurley of Durban. (Interview with Grace Rogan, April 19, 1980; James Rogan, "We Served in South Africa," *Ave Maria* 90 [July 11, 1959]: 20–23.)

23. Josephine Drabek, "Can Women Remake Latin America?" *Maryknoll* 48 (January 1954): 23.

24. Raymond A. Lane, "The General's Corner," *Maryknoll* 47 (September 1953): 13.

25. Staff of the Grail Institute for Overseas Service to Rachel Donders and Mary Louise Tully, December 10, 1956, AAG.

26. "The Grail Institute for Overseas Service, Confidential Report," August 1960, p. 3, AAG.

27. Dolores Brien, "Departure Ceremony," *Grail Review* 11 (July 1958): 17–18.

28. "The Grail Institute for Overseas Service: Confidential Report," August 1960, pp. 1, 2.

29. Staff of the Grail Institute for Overseas Service to Rachel Donders and Mary Louise Tully, December 10, 1956, AAG.

One woman who passed through the Grail's program without joining the movement, Patricia Smith, nevertheless gained international attention for her work in Southeast Asia. See Patricia Smith, "Doctor Smith and her 300,000 Tribesmen," *Sign* 41 (April 1962): 7–10; "The Grail Girls," *Newsweek*, May 7, 1962, p. 82.

30. "The Grail Institute for Overseas Service: Confidential Report," August 1960, p. 4. See also *Lay Missionaries: New Horizons for the Laity* (Washington, D.C., 1957).

31. Douglas Roche, "The New Boom in Lay Missionaries," *Sign* 38 (April 1959): 36–38.

32. Barbara Wald, "Brief Report on Visit of Rev. Robert Leonard —PAVLA Director [St. Cloud, Minnesota]," August 1962, AAG.

33. "Application to the Archdiocese of New York for Permission for the Grail to Work among the Young Women Foreign Students in the Greater New York Area," 1952, p. 1, AAG; Lydwine van Kersbergen, "Foreign Mission at Home," *Commonweal* 63 (April 10, 1953): 14, 15, 17.

34. "Application to the Archdiocese of New York," p. 3.

35. Raskob Foundation for Catholic Activities, Inc., to Barbara Ellen Wald, October 24, 1952, AAG. The midtown apartment was later retained for the use of Lydwine van Kersbergen, who served as a consultant at the United Nations for the Union Fraternelle entre les Races et les Peuples, an international organization of lay mission movements.

36. Dolores Brien, "The Grail Program for International Students," *Catholic Charities Review* 38 (January 1954): 7–10, and "Foreign Students," *Integrity* 10 (January 1956): 30–35; Silvester Alvarez, "The Grail International Center," *Lamp*, August 1960: 12–13, 28, 30, 31; "International Party," *Jubilee* 6 (July 1958): 14–15.

37. Brien, "The Grail Program," p. 10.

38. Alvarez, "The Grail International Student Center," p. 13.

39. Dolores Brien, Janet Kalven, and Barbara Wald, "Some Observations on the Training of Latin American Girls," August 23, 1955, AAG.

40. Barbara E. Wald, "The Problems of Duplicated Action in Foreign Student Work in New York," March 12, 1953, AAG.

41. Brien, "Foreign Students," p. 32.

42. Therese Martin and Kay Walsh, "Reflections on Work with Latin American Women in New York," no date, AAG.

5. RADIATING FROM THE CENTER

1. Barbara Ellen Wald, "Grailville," p. 2.

2. "History of Monica House," no date, AAG.

3. Coffey to Molloy, April 12, 1948; Molloy to Coffey, April 14, 1948, Coffey Papers, Bay Shore, New York. It was Coffey, for example, who requested permission for Molloy "to arrange and direct in cooperation with the Grail's leaders" a training week called "The Christian Woman" held in June 1948 in Syosset, on Long Island. The program, which attracted an audience of two hundred, including twenty-five priests, is described in Coffey to Molloy, May 1, 1948, Coffey Papers.

4. Coffey, handwritten notes, no date, Coffey Papers; "A Summary of the Program of Monica House During October 1949–Tuesday Evenings," AAG.

5. "A Report on the Program of Monica House, July 1949–June 1950," p. 4, AAG; *Love the Chief Instrument: An Apostolic Program*, prepared by the Writing Group at Monica House, Brooklyn, New York (Barbara Ellen Wald and Elsa Chaney), 1950; "Report of Monica House," October 1950–1951, AAG.

6. "A Summary of the Program at Monica House During October 1949"; "A Report on the Program of Monica House, July 1949–June 1950," pp. 2, 6.

7. Ibid., pp. 2–3.

8. "Request to the Diocese of Brooklyn," 1953, AAG; Molloy to Lydwine van Kersbergen, April 9, 1955, Coffey Papers; Staff of the Grail Institute for Overseas Service to Rachel Donders and Mary Louise Tully, December 10, 1956, AAG.

9. "Evaluation and Future Plans, Brooklyn Center," April 1960, AAG.

10. Dolores Brien to Lydwine van Kersbergen and Janet Kalven, May 28, 1956, AAG; "Evaluation and Future Plans."

11. See Mariette Wickes, "Joan Overboss," *Reaction* 33 (September 1970): 18.

12. [Joan Overboss], "Plans for the Growth of the Lay Apostolate in the Detroit Area," [1950], pp. 1, 2, AAG.

13. Hubert Roberge, "Integration–It's Here," *Integrity* 8 (April 1954): 11.

14. Eileen Schaeffler, "The Apostolate in Detroit," manuscript for a talk given at Grailville on July 24, 1953, AAG.

15. Joan Overboss, "The Gateway, Detroit," *Grail Review* 1 (November 1953): 20.

16. Walter J. Schoenherr, "How Participation Grew in a City Mission Parish in a Changing Neighborhood," in *National Liturgical Week* (Washington, D.C., 1960), p. 181.

17. Ibid., p. 182; Joan Overboss and Mariette Wickes, "Report to Cardinal Mooney," August 4, 1955, AAG. *The Church in a City Parish* was distributed in mimeographed form. Much of the response to it resulted from a review by John Buchanan in *Orate Fratres* 30 (September 1956): 525–36.

18. "Report of Programs of the Gateway Grail Center 1955–1956," October 1956, p. 5, AAG; Betty Ford, "Motor City Gateway," *Today* 12 (November 1956): 29.

19. Mariette Wickes, "Joan Overboss," pp. 13–16.

20. Mariette Wickes to Edward Mooney, April 10, 1957, AAG. In 1964 Overboss began working with an information agency serving missionary orders in the third world and took up residence in Rome. She died there on September 17, 1969.

21. Elaine Jones, "New Born Again," *Grail Review* 7 (March 1958): 22–24.

22. Mariette Wickes to Edward Mooney, April 10, 1957; Elaine Jones, "Report to Lydwine [van Kersbergen], Barbara [Wald], and Eileen [Schaeffler]," June 5, 1959, AAG.

23. "Detroit's New Outpost," *Grail Review* III, no. 1 (1961): 16–17; Brochure for Grail Expansion Fund, 1960, AAG.

24. Mary Ann Kimbell, "Family Service," *Integrity* 7 (August 1953): 38; Elsa Chaney, "This is Gabriel House," *Today* 8 (January 1953): 20.

25. News release, May 23, 1952, AAG.

26. J. O'G., "The Spirit of Personal Service," *Catholic Charities Review* 38 (April 1954): 81.

27. *Grail Review* 4 (May 1956): 43; "Report on the Activities of the Grail Center Gabriel House, October–December 31, 1958," AAG; Mary Anne Kimbell, "Comments," *National Liturgical Week* (Washington, D.C., 1960), p. 135; [?] to Lydwine van Kersbergen, Barbara Wald, Eileen Schaeffler, and Dolores Brien (Outline and Evaluation of Past Year's Work in Cincinnati), May 27, 1960, pp. 1, 9, AAG.

28. "Gabriel Miner about the Center for Negro Young Women in Philadelphia," *Grail Review* 1 (November 1953): 15.

29. "Request to Purchase Property for Grail Work in Archdiocese of Philadelphia," 1953, pp. 3, 6, AAG.

30. Barbara Ellen Wald (concerning the Philadelphia Grail Center), *Grail Review* 2 (May 1954): 1, 2.

31. Anne Mulkeen to Lydwine van Kersbergen, December 2, 1954, AAG.

32. "[Philadelphia] Resident Program – 1958," AAG; Barbara Wald to Lydwine van Kersbergen, November 4, 1960, AAG; "V." to Lydwine van Kersbergen and Eileen Schaeffler, November 16, 1960, AAG.

33. Marvin Bordelon to Bishop Charles Greco, August 13, 1952, AAG; "Summary of Grail Work in the Lafayette Diocese," 1960, AAG.

34. "Summary of Grail Work in the Lafayette Diocese."

35. J. B. Gremillion, *The Journal of a Southern Pastor* (Chicago, 1957), p. 91. Gremillion's observations on the Grail originally appeared in his "Notes on a Journey in the South," *Social Order* (October 1956): 386–91.

36. Barbara Wald and Eileen Schaeffler, "Report on Situation in Louisiana," December 1959, AAG.

37. Jeanne Plante, "Louisiana Report—A Summary of Discussions with Father Marvin Bordelon, December 30, 1956–January 1, 1957," p. 4, AAG.

38. "Visit from the Fathers Bordelon and Gremillion to Holland, June 1954," August 6 and 10, 1954, Part II, p. 3, AAG. The Louisiana priests went on to achieve prominence outside their local confines, Sigur in the Newman movement, M. Bordelon at the United States Catholic Conference, and Gremillion at the United Nations and the Vatican (where he was the first secretary of the Pontifical Justice and Peace Commission).

39. Ibid.

40. [?] to Kathleen Price, August 5, 1959, AAG.

41. Maurice Schexnayder to Katherine Price, May 16, 1960, AAG; "1961 Lafayette Grail Center Report, September–October," "The Grail in Louisiana," 1961 brochure, AAG.

42. See Donna Myers, "Our Father Abraham," in Daniel Callahan, ed., *Generation of the Third Eye* (New York, 1965), pp. 157–59.

6. THE HEART OF THE MOVEMENT

1. Sally Collett, "I Live in an International Family," *St. Joseph's Lilies*, 1953: 41.

2. Lydwine van Kersbergen, "A Program for Youth," *Catholic World* 50 (February 1952): 98.

3. Collett, "I Live in an International Family," pp. 41, 42, 43–44.

4. Mary McGuigan, "The Women of Grailville, Loveland, Ohio," *Ave Maria* 8 (May 14, 1955): 8–9.

5. Wynni Kelly, "Grailville, An Apostolic Adventure," *Christian Family* (January 1957): 22.

6. "Report on 1953–54 Year's School," p. 5, AAG; *Grail National Newsletter*, Fall 1953, p. 1.

7. *Towards a World Vision—An Apostolic Program*, written and compiled by Elsa Chaney and Donna Myers, with illustrations by Jeanne Heiberg (Grailville, 1954), p. 5.

8. Ibid., pp. 51, 16, 19.

9. Ibid., p. 50.

10. Lydwine van Kersbergen, *The Normal School of Sanctity for the Laity*, pp. 37–38.

11. Typewritten announcement, November 13, 1953, AAG; *Times*

review quoted in brochure advertising the record, AAG; *Caecilia* 84 (December 1957): 367 (review by Sister M. Casimir); *New York Times,* March 22, 1959 (review by Ross Parmenter).

12. Review quoted in Grail Art Productions Catalogue, 1960, AAG.

13. Eleanor Walker, "Music in the Grailville Program," *Musart* (February–March 1956): 25. See also Walker, "Music at Grailville," *Caecilia* 84 (February 1957): 51–53. Walker was a convert to Catholicism. Her godfather was the philosopher Jacques Maritain.

14. Art catalogues, AAG. See also Maurice Lavanoux, "Gather Them All Together," *Liturgical Arts* 22 (May 1954): 73–74.

15. Jeanne Heiberg, "Art at Grailville," Supplement to *Catholic Arts Quarterly* (October 1957): 4, 5, 6.

16. Ibid., p. 6.

17. Elsa Chaney, "The New Eve," *Ave Maria* 83 (March 1956): 16; "A Cultural Calendar," *Grail Newsletter,* 1957, pp. 11–12, AAG.

18. Chaney, "The New Eve," p. 6.

19. "A Cultural Calendar" and various brochures, AAG.

20. Eleanor Walker, "Shapers of Culture," *Our Sunday Visitor,* April 13, 1958; Walker, "The Cooperative Community Year at Grailville, *Grail Review* I, no. 1 (1959): 5–7; Grailville Programs file, 1960, AAG.

21. Trina Paulus, "Report to the National Committee," September–October–November 1960, pp. 3, 4, AAG. Paulus later produced *Hope for the Flowers* (New York, 1972), which she described as "a tale partly about life, partly about revolution, and lots about hope." Illustrated by the author, this book achieved enormous popularity. One million copies were in print by 1985.

22. Barbara Wald, "Grailville," p. 8.

23. Brochure, "The American Woman – 1954," AAG.

24. Lydwine van Kersbergen, *Woman, Some Aspects of Her Role in the Modern World* (Grailville, 1956), p. 8. "The Role of Woman in Motherhood" (pp. 43–54) appeared here for the first time. The other chapters originally appeared as: "Woman's Role in the Vocation of Virginity," *Worship* 29 (April 1955): 240–53; "The Search for Woman's Role," *Catholic World* 181 (September 1955): 431–66; "Toward a Christian Concept of Woman," *Catholic World* 182 (October 1955): 6–11.

25. *Woman,* p. 14.

26. Ibid., pp. 15, 16.

27. Ibid., pp. 16, 17.

28. Ibid., pp. 22–23.

29. Ibid., pp. 23, 24, 25, 26.

30. Ibid., p. 24.

31. Ibid., p. 28.

32. Wald, "Grailville," p. 9; Pius XII, "On Holy Virginity," March 25, 1954, in *Selected Documents of His Holiness Pope Pius XII* (Washington, D.C., no date).

33. *Woman*, pp. 30, 33.

34. Ibid., pp. 34, 35, 38.

35. Ibid., pp. 30, 31.

36. Ibid., pp. 43, 50.

37. See William B. Faherty, *The Destiny of Modern Woman in the Light of Papal Teaching* (Westminster, Md., 1950); John Fitzsimons, *Woman Today* (New York, 1952); Gerald Vann, *The Water and the Fire* (New York, 1954).

38. Wald, "Grailville," p. 10; Joan Overboss, "Dear Everybody," *Grail Review* 2 (May 1954): 6, 7.

39. "Growth of the Movement in the U.S.," March 11, 1957, AAG.

40. "Outline of Janet's Talk on the Grail, Saturday, May 31, 1958, Grail Reunion Weekend," no date, AAG.

41. Eva Fleischner, "Grail Program of Catechetics in the United States," *Grail Review* II, no. 4 (1960): 14.

42. Grailville Program files, AAG.

43. *Bulletin of Religious Education* 30 (October 24, 1964): 1. The *Bulletin* continued in publication until 1965. At that time the Grail believed it could "peacefully vanish," since in the meanwhile a host of catechetical journals had appeared in the United States, "most recently and impressively *The Living Light*." (*Bulletin* 34 [June 1963]: 1.)

44. Fleischner, "Grail Program of Catechetics," p. 18.

45. *Histories of the Grail in Individual Countries*, p. 83. Lydwine van Kersbergen gave a series of prayer hours based on the work of Teilhard de Chardin at Grailville in 1959. (Dorothy Rasenberger, conversation with the author, October 24, 1981.)

46. Eleanor Walker, "The Cooperative Community Year," p. 5.

47. "Scheduled Events for the Cooperative Community Year at Grailville," typewritten calendar, AAG.

48. Henry J. Imbus to Edward A. McCarthy (Secretary to Archbishop Alter), May 16, 1957; Joseph Urbain to Karl Alter, May 22, 1957, Archives of the Archdiocese of Cincinnati.

49. Eileen Schaeffler, "Introduction to North America," *Grail Review* I, no. 1 (1959): 4.

7. "WHICH ONLY WOMEN CAN ACHIEVE"

1. John Sheerin, "The Coming Era of the Layman," *Catholic World* 184 (October 1956): 1.
2. Barbara Wald, "Grailville," pp. 7, 10. The meeting place in Burlington was a house belonging to the wealthy Philadelphia physician Sidney Newcomer. The Grail purchased the house from Newcomer in 1957 and retained it until 1964.
3. "Summary of Round Table Meeting of November 6, 1953," pp. 4, 5, AAG.
4. "Summary of the Round Table Meeting of December 3, 1953," p. 11, AAG.
5. Ibid., pp. 5, 6.
6. "Summary of the Round Table Meeting of March 21–26, 1955," pp. 1, 2, AAG; "The Grail Movement: U.S.A. – 1955," p. 1, AAG.
7. "The Grail Movement: U.S.A. – 1955," p. 8.
8. Ibid., p. 1.
9. Janet Kalven, "The Grail in the United States," *Grail Review* 4 (May 1956): 29. The text quoted was used in Brooklyn.
10. "Decisions made by Lydwine van Kersbergen and the Round Table concerning the spirit of prayer in our apostolate," September 1956, pp. 1–2, AAG.
11. "Summary of the Round Table Meeting of March 21–26, 1955," p. 1.
12. "National Structure of the Grail," March 10, 1957, p. 3, AAG. The Round Table's discussions of March 9–14, 1957, were summarized in this and five other booklets: "What Is the Grail Movement?"; "Growth of the Movement in the U.S."; "The Council Programs"; "The International Unity of the Grail"; "Round Table Discussion," AAG.
13. "Growth of the Movement in the U.S.," March 11, 1957, p. 15.
14. "The Grail Movement: U.S.A. – 1955," pp. 4–5. A Council on Religious Education, headquartered at Grailville, was added to this list in 1959. The names of the councils varied in time: the Council on the Integration of Life, for example, became the Council on Family and Community Life, and the Council on Work for Women became the Council on Career Services.
15. "National Structure of the Grail," p. 4.
16. "Constitution of the National Committee in the U.S.A.," no date, AAG.
17. "Dedication Dates" [1951–1962], AAG.
18. Rachel Donders to the National Committee, November 2, 1960, AAG. Donders in fact stated here that from the unity she envi-

sioned would come "much more authority . . . which is very precious and needed."

19. *Guiding Principles of the Lay Apostolate, Address of His Holiness Pope Pius XII to the Second World Congress of the Lay Apostolate, October 5, 1957* (Washington, D.C., 1957), pp. 6, 8, 11.

20. Figures given here are taken from the *1959 National Catholic Almanac* (Paterson, N.J., 1959) pp. 546–49. On the national councils see Leo R. Ward, *Catholic Life, U.S.A.: Contemporary Lay Movements* (St. Louis, 1959), pp. 121–37, and Martin H. Work and Daniel J. Kane, "The American Catholic Layman and His Organizations," pp. 359–63.

21. Vincent Giese, *The Apostolic Itch* (Chicago, 1954), p. 2; Sheerin, "The Coming Era of the Layman," p. 2; Greeley, *The Catholic Experience*, p. 261; Ward, *Catholic Life, U.S.A.*, p. 4.

22. Dolores Brien, "A Catholic Approach to World Patterns," in *The Laity and the International Scene* (Grailville, 1957), p. 10.

23. Lydwine van Kersbergen, "Growth of the Lay Apostolate," *Commonweal* 67 (January 10, 1958): 381.

24. "What is the Grail Movement?" pp. 9, 10.

25. Ellis, *American Catholics and the Intellectual Life* (see above chap. 3, note 49). Among the responses to Ellis' essay was Frank L. Christ and Gerard Sherry, eds., *American Catholicism and the Intellectual Ideal* (New York, 1961).

26. John Courtney Murray, "Special Catholic Challenges," *Life*, December 26, 1956, pp. 144–47; Dolores Brien, "The Catholic Church in America," *Grail Review* 4 (May 1956): 12, 13.

27. Brien, "A Catholic Approach," pp. 10, 13, 12.

28. O'Dea, *American Catholic Dilemma* (see above chap. 3, note 49), pp. 127–37.

29. Ward, *Catholic Life, U.S.A.*, p. 120.

8. FROM ORGANIZATION TO MEETING PLACE

1. See Greeley, *The Catholic Experience*, chap. 9.

2. For the texts of John XXIII's *Mater et Magistra* and *Pacem in Terris* (1963), see David J. O'Brien and Thomas A. Shannon, eds., *Renewing the Earth* (New York, 1977); John XXIII, Opening Speech to the Council, October 11, 1962, in Abbott, *Documents of Vatican II*, p. 712.

3. Robert Graham, "The Laity, the Council and the New Apostolate," *America* 105 (May 6, 1961): 246.

4. Donald J. Thorman, "Free Speech and the Laity" (editorial), *Ave Maria* 91 (April 2, 1960): 18.

5. Michael Novak, *The Open Church* (New York, 1964), chap. 1; Xavier Rynne, *Vatican Council II* (New York, 1968); Robert B. Kaiser, *Pope, Council, and World* (New York, 1963).

6. Lydwine van Kersbergen, "Lay Women Rejoice," *America* 106 (February 3, 1962): 580.

7. The Oratory received some admiring notices. See [Maurice Lavanoux], *Liturgical Arts* 30 (May 1962): 97-101; "Old Barn Becomes a Handsome Chapel," *Architectural Forum* (October 1962): 138D-39.

8. "Summary of the National Advisory Board Meeting of January 4-7, 1961," pp. 1-2, AAG.

9. Jeanne Plante to National Board members, November 24, 1961, AAG.

10. Handwritten and typewritten letters of various members of the National Board, AAG.

11. Mary Imelda Buckley ["Report on the Future Development of Grailville"], presented to the National Advisory Board, January 8, 1961, pp. 14, 33, 35, AAG.

12. Ibid., pp. 29, 25, 11.

13. Ibid., pp. 17, 5, 16.

14. "Statement of the Married Grail Members on their Role in the Movement," no date, pp. 1, 2, AAG.

15. Memorandum: Married Women's Meeting in Burlington, April 28, 29, 30, 1961 [Dolores Brien to Rachel Donders, Lydwine van Kersbergen, Eileen Schaeffler, Jeanne Plante, and Barbara Wald], no date, pp. 1, 2, AAG.

16. *Married Woman's Newsletter*, August 1961, p. 1, AAG.

17. *Married Woman's Newsletter*, February 1962, pp. 1, 2, 4, AAG.

18. "The Grail National Conference," *Grail Review* V, no. 1 (1963): 10.

19. Eileen Schaeffler, "Through Us—to the World," ibid., p. 6.

20. This title appeared on the conference program. In its published form the address was entitled "Inner Space in the Grail," ibid., pp. 17-21.

21. Brien, "Inner Space," pp. 17, 18, 19, 21.

22. "These Were the Decisions," *Grail Review* V, no. 1 (1963): 16.

23. "Summary of the National Advisory Board Meeting of March 16-18, 1963," AAG.

24. Novak, *The Open Church*, p. 132.

25. Vincent A. Yzermans, *American Participation in the Second Vatican Council* (New York, 1968), pp. 449-50; Vaillancourt, *Papal Power*, pp. 84-91.

26. Novak, *The Open Church*, p. 14-15.

27. Ibid., p. 202-3.

28. This publication continued on until August 1966 when its editors judged that it too, like the *Bulletin of Religious Education*, could "disappear peacefully" from a then crowded scene. (*Ecumenical Notes* 5 [June 1966]: 10.)

29. Various brochures and flyers, 1960–1963, AAG; Anne Mulkeen, "Crossroads at Grailville," *Worship* 37 (November 1963): 650–55.

30. Grailville Program file, AAG.

31. Ibid.

32. Eileen Schaeffler to Lydwine van Kersbergen, June 30, 1961, AAG.

33. Dolores Brien, "The Grail Movement: 1963," *Grail Review* V, no. 4 (1963): 33.

34. "Report to International," February 21, 1962, AAG.

35. Brien, "The Catholic Revival Revisited," p. 716.

36. "Report to International," November 13, 1963, pp. 2, 3, AAG.

37. Therese Martin to Lydwine van Kersbergen, June 6, 1961; Kay Walsh to Eileen Schaeffler, March 31, 1962, AAG.

38. "Possibilities for Developing the Movement through a Pilot Project in Brooklyn," November 1962, p. 1, AAG.

39. Jacqueline Kemp to Eileen Schaeffler, June 16, 1962; "Report to the National Committee from the Philadelphia Region" (Ann Burke to Eileen Schaeffler), October 1963; General Letter to Friends from the Philadelphia Grail Members, August 5, 1966, AAG.

40. Dorothy Rasenberger to Eileen Schaeffler, April 19, 1968; Rasenberger to Walter Schoenherr, May 14, 1968, AAG.

41. Various Grailville brochures, AAG; Mary Lou Suhor, "Sodalists at Grailville," *Queen's Work* 55 (March 1963): 6–8.

42. "Brainstorming," typewritten notes, April 1964, AAG. In 1964 Catholic University, aware of changing ideas at Grailville, recommended that the Grail undertake a self-study of its program. This was carried out by Audrey Sorrento and Ruth Gallant and submitted in June 1966. (Roy J. Ferrari to Janet Kalven, September 2, 1964; Evaluation Document HD4: 57, June 1966, "Grailville Institute" file, Archives of the Catholic University of America.) A new arrangement was put in place in 1967.

43. "Report of the Working Team on Grailville," January 13, 14, 15, 1965, pp. 1, 3, 4, AAG.

44. "The Aggiornamento Process in North America from May 1964 to February 1965," p. 5; Deborah Schak, typewritten notes [August 1965], AAG.

45. Dorothy Rasenberger to "Dear Everyone," May 24, 1965, AAG.

46. Ibid.

47. "The Aggiornamento Process in North America from May 1964 to February 1965."

48. Eleanor Walker and Janet Kalven, "Grail Guidelines," *Grail Review* VIII, no. 4 (1965): 4, 5.

49. Ibid., pp. 6, 7.

50. Ibid., pp. 8, 9, 10.

51. Ibid., p. 11.

52. Typewritten manuscript of Schaeffler's address, AAG.

9. THE AGONIES OF OPENNESS

1. Donald Thorman, "Today's Layman, an Uncertain Catholic," *America* 116 (January 14, 1967): 39–41; Andrew Greeley, *The Hesitant Pilgrim: American Catholicism after the Council* (New York, 1966), pp. 5–7.

2. See Vaillancourt, *Papal Power*, pp. 91, 95–170; Daniel Callahan, *Honesty in the Church* (New York, 1965).

3. Thorman, "Today's Layman," p. 40. On the NAL, see Doris Grumbach, "Laymen Meet in Chicago: Last Look or First Hope?" *Commonweal* 88 (July 26, 1968): 487–89, and Douglas Roche, *The Catholic Revolution* (New York, 1968), pp. 161–65. On the impact of *Humanae Vitae*, see Andrew Greeley, "Going Their Own Way," *New York Times Sunday Magazine*, October 10, 1982.

4. Grailville Program File, AAG; "Building the City of Man," *Word*, February 1967: 5–6, 17.

5. "First Quarterly Report of the Grail in North America (Late September to Late December 1965)," AAG. Mary Imelda Buckley obtained her doctorate at the University of Münster, Westphalen, and Eva Fleischner hers at Marquette University.

6. Grailville Program file.

7. Alice McCarthy, "The Grail as an Existential Movement," typewritten manuscript, pp. 9, 8, 10, 11, 15, 16, AAG.

8. Grailville Program file. The Peace Corps program was based at Antioch College in Yellow Springs, Ohio.

9. Eva Fleischner to Peg Siegmund, September 18, 1967, AAG.

10. Abigail McCarthy, *Private Faces, Public Places*, p. 123.

11. "Quarterly Report of the Grail in North America to the International Presidency and Board, February 1968," p. 3, AAG.

12. "Round Table Discussion," March 1957, p. 15, AAG.

13. Wynni Kelly, "The Three Paradoxes," typewritten manuscript, August 23, 1966, pp. 1, 2, AAG.

14. Mary Brigid Niland, "Conference Summary," typewritten text, August 23, 1966, p. 3, AAG.
15. Anne Mulkeen to the Members of the National Board, January 1967, AAG.
16. Anne Mulkeen to Fellow Grail Members, April 1967, AAG; Charles Davis, *A Question of Conscience* (New York, 1967).
17. Ann Burke, "About the Nucleus," *Reaction* 32 (May 1970): 2, 3; "A Summary of Responses to the Draft Statement," January 1967, p. 4, AAG.
18. Eileen Schaeffler to "Dear Everybody," November 16, 1966, AAG.
19. Grailville Self-Evaluation file, AAG.
20. "Working Paper" (from the National Board meeting of September 16–17, 1967), p. 1, AAG (emphasis added).
21. Ibid.
22. Ibid., p. 2; "Quarterly Report of the Grail in North America to the International Presidency and Board, October 1967," p. 2, AAG.
23. Carol White, "Task Force Beginnings . . . The Job Ahead . . . ," *Reaction* 15 (February 1968): 2, 3, 4.
24. Dorothy Rasenberger, "Reflections on the Year '67–'68," *Reaction* 21 (November 1968): 4 (emphasis added).
25. See Lillian Johnson, "Lay Women Make Discoveries of Faith," *Methodist Woman*, September 1967: 29–31.
26. "General Assembly 1969," p. 6, AAG.
27. Ibid., p. 4.
28. Ibid., p. 6; Eleanor Walker, "A Contextual Commentary on the Paper presented by the Religious Search Task Force to the General Assembly, August 1978," AAG.
29. "Grail Assembly 1969," p. 6.
30. Barbara Ellen Wald, letter (excerpts), *Reaction* 30 (January 1970): 2.
31. "Responses . . . on Prayer . . ." *Reaction* 30 (March 1970): 8, 9.
32. Ibid., pp. 11, 12, 13.
33. Ibid., p. 13; "Joyful General Assembly, 1975," pp. 21–22, AAG; Walker, "A Contextual Commentary."
34. SAG reports, AAG.
35. "SAG Report, 1973," pp. 38–39, AAG.
36. Ibid., p. 1; "Report on the Council Weekend," March 5–7, 1971, p. 4, AAG.
37. "General Assembly 1969," p. 4.
38. "Quarterly Report of the Grail in North America to the International Presidency and Board, June 1969," p. 2, AAG.

39. Ibid., pp. 6, 7.

40. The Cornwall-on-Hudson site, which included a sizeable property and several houses, was received by the Grail from the estate of Chauncey Stillman in the 1960s. A small Grail community makes its home there at present and makes its main building available to other groups for retreats and conferences.

41. Quoted in "Outline for Grail History Teach-In" (November 26, 1971), p. 5, AAG.

42. Lynn Malley to "Dear All" (Report on Planning Meeting of January 24–25, 1971), February 5, 1971, p. 2, AAG.

43. "Draft of Structure Amendment Proposal in Preparation for Election of February, 1972," no date, pp. 3, 4, AAG.

44. Peg Siegmund, "Plotting Strategy—New Teams Swing into Action," *Reaction* 37 (March 1972): 12.

45. "Joyful General Assembly, 1975," p. 21.

46. "Working Paper: Outline of Structure Proposal" (August 1971), p. 1. The international presidency was eventually transformed into a presidency team of three members, with the requirement that one of the three be a member of the nucleus. (Donders, *A History of the International Grail*, p. 86.)

47. Mary Kay Louchart, "Proposal Re: Grail Activities in Saginaw, Michigan," December 1970, pp. 1, 2, AAG.

48. Ceci Figueroa, Duane Welsch, and Ann Bohlen to Mary Kay Louchart, Dorothy Rasenberger, and Cay Charles, February 2, 1971, AAG; "Report on the Council Weekend," March 5–7, 1971, pp. 3–4.

49. Dorothy Rasenberger, in *International General Assembly Bulletin No. 1*, 1970, quoted in "Outline for Grail History Teach-In."

50. "General Assembly 1978," p. 3, AAG.

51. Grailville Newsletter, Spring 1985, AAG.

52. Joan E. Lark to Publication Editor, National Catholic Rural Life Conference, February 24, 1966, Archives of the National Catholic Rural Life Conference.

53. NOW's stated aim quoted in Deane William Ferm, *Contemporary American Theologies, A Critical Survey* (New York, 1981), p. 77.

54. Janet Kalven, "Grailville Experience," *Woman* 4 (Winter 1974): 50. See also Kalven, "Women's Voices Began to Challenge," *National Catholic Reporter*, April 13, 1984, pp. 10–11, 20.

55. Mary Buckley, "True to Our History and Purpose: The Grail and Feminism," p. 3, AAG.

56. Sally Bentley and Claire Randall, "The Spirit Moving: A New Approach to Theologizing," *Christianity and Crisis* 34 (February 4, 1972): 4.

57. *Your Daughters Shall Prophecy: Feminist Alternatives in Theo-*

logical Education (New York, 1980), pp. 136–37. This volume is a product of the Cornwall Collective, a consultation on women's programs in theological education which emanated from SQAG.

The Grail also turned its attention to the matter of non-sexist language in worship in *The Grail Prayer Book* (1975) and *Supplement to the Grail Prayer Book* (1976), which were not intended for general circulation. In a preface to the former, Grail member Marian Ronan said that the task was "not a simple one, with literary, aesthetic, historical and theological as well as feminist considerations influencing the work."

Later Grail conferences gave rise to Linda Clark, Marian Ronan, and Eleanor Walker, *Image-Breaking, Image-Building: A Handbook for Creative Worship with Women of Christian Tradition* (New York, 1981) and Janet Kalven and Mary I. Buckley, eds., *Womanspirit Bonding* (New York, 1984).

58. Grailville Programs, 1982, 1984, 1985, AAG.

59. *New York Times*, March 2, 1987. Janet Kalven and Mary Imelda Buckley were members of a coordinating committee. A previous ad (*New York Times*, October 7, 1984) had argued for recognition and open discussion of a *de facto* diversity among Catholics on the morality of abortion. The burden of the second ad was a call for dialogue on sanctions invoked against signers of the first one. Both ads were criticized as ambiguous, the second as disingenuous.

60. Mary Jo Weaver, *New Catholic Women: A Contemporary Challenge to Traditional Religious Authority* (San Francisco, 1985), p. 126.

61. Donna Steichen, "Embracing the New Age Asp: The Suicide of the Grail," *Fidelity*, May 1987, p. 31.

62. Grailville Calendar, 1987, AAG.

AFTERWORD

1. Gleason, "In Search of Unity," p. 185, and his *Keeping the Faith*, chap. 7.

2. It may be worth pointing out that as far as the lay apostolate was concerned unity within Catholicism was not governed by Neo-Scholastic philosophy, as it may have been in seminaries and colleges, but by the theological symbol of the Mystical Body.

3. "Mobilization" is a term introduced by Philip Gleason in his essay "A Browser's Guide to American Catholicism," *Theology Today* 38 (October 1981): 373–88, reprinted in his *Keeping the Faith*, pp. 181–201.

4. See above, chap. 7.

Selected Bibliography

GENERAL

Books

Abbott, Walter M., and Gallagher, Joseph, eds., *The Documents of Vatican II.* New York, 1966.
Alexander, Calvert. *The Catholic Literary Revival.* Milwaukee, 1935.
Bedoyere, Michael de la. *The Layman in the Church.* Chicago, 1955.
_____. *The Cardijn Story.* Milwaukee, 1959.
Belloc, Hilaire. *Survivals and New Arrivals.* New York, 1930.
Berdyaev, Nicholas. *The End of Our Time.* London, 1933.
Blanshard, Paul. *American Freedom and Catholic Power.* Boston, 1949.
Callahan, Daniel. *The Mind of the Catholic Layman.* New York, 1963.
_____, ed. *Generation of the Third Eye.* New York, 1965.
Carter, Paul A. *Another Part of the Fifties.* New York, 1983.
Catholicism in America (a series of articles from the *Commonweal*). New York, 1953.
Catholicism in American Culture. The College of New Rochelle, New Rochelle, N.Y., 1955.
Chesterton, Gilbert Keith. *What's Wrong with the World.* Abridged version with a "tutorial introduction" by F.J. Sheed (No. 6 of the Catholic Masterpieces Series). New York, 1942.
Christ, Frank L., and Sherry, Gerard E., eds. *American Catholicism and the Intellectual Ideal.* New York, 1961.
Civardi, Luigi. *A Manual of Catholic Action.* New York, 1935.
Cogley, John, ed. *Religion in America.* Cleveland and New York, 1958.
Coleman, John A. *The Evolution of Dutch Catholicism, 1958–1974.* Berkeley, 1978.
Corwin, Jay P. *G. K. Chesterton and Hilaire Belloc: The Battle against Modernity.* Athens, Ohio, 1981.
Crosby, Donald F. *God, Church, and Flag: Senator Joseph R. McCarthy and the Catholic Church, 1950–1957.* Chapel Hill, N.C., 1978.

Dawson, Christopher. *The Historic Reality of Christian Culture*. New York, 1960.

_____; Wust, Peter; and Maritain, Jacques. *Essays in Order*. New York, 1931.

Dohen, Dorothy. *Women in Wonderland*. New York, 1960.

Dolan, Jay P. *The American Catholic Experience*. New York, 1985.

Doohan, Leonard. *The Lay-Centered Church*. Minneapolis, 1984.

Faherty, William B. *The Destiny of Modern Woman in the Light of Papal Teaching*. Westminster, Md., 1950.

Fitzsimons, John. *Woman Today*. New York, 1952.

_____, and McGuire, Paul. *Restoring All Things: A Guide to Catholic Action*. New York, 1952.

Gannon, Robert I. *The Cardinal Spellman Story*. Garden City, N.Y., 1962.

Geise, Vincent. *The Apostolic Itch*. Chicago, 1954.

Gleason, Philip. *Keeping the Faith: American Catholicism Past and Present*. Notre Dame, Ind., 1987.

_____, ed. *Contemporary Catholicism in the United States*. Notre Dame, Ind., 1969.

Goldman, Eric. *The Crucial Decade—and After: America, 1945–1960*. New York, 1960.

Greeley, Andrew M. *The Hesitant Pilgrim: American Catholicism after the Council*. New York, 1966.

_____. *The Catholic Experience*. Garden City, N.Y., 1967.

Greene, Michael J., ed. *The Layman and the Council*. Springfield, Ill., 1964.

Gremillion, J.B. *The Journal of a Southern Pastor*. Chicago, 1957.

Halsey, William M. *The Survival of American Innocence: Catholicism in an Era of Disillusionment, 1920–1940*. Notre Dame, Ind., 1980.

Handy, Robert T. *A History of the Churches in the United States and Canada*. Oxford, 1976.

Hennesey, James. *American Catholics: A History of the Roman Catholic Community in the United States*. New York, 1981.

Herberg, Will. *Protestant-Catholic-Jew*. Garden City, N.Y., 1955.

Hesburgh, Theodore M. *The Theology of Catholic Action*. Notre Dame, Ind., 1946.

Hitchcock, James. *The Decline and Fall of Radical Catholicism*. New York, 1971.

Huber, Raphael M., ed. *Our Bishops Speak*. Milwaukee, 1952.

Kane, George L. *Lay Workers for Christ*. Westminster, Md., 1957.

Lay Missionaries: New Horizons for the Laity. Washington, D.C., 1957.

McCarthy, Abigail. *Private Faces, Public Places*. Garden City, N.Y., 1972.

McMahon, Francis B. *A Catholic Looks at the World*. New York, 1945.
McNabb, Vincent. *Old Principles and the New Order*. New York, 1942.
Maritain, Jacques. *Reflections on America*. New York, 1958.
_____. *Integral Humanism*. Notre Dame, Ind., 1973.
Merton, Thomas. *The Seven Storey Mountain*. New York, 1948.
Michaels, Peter (Jackson, Carol). *Designs for Christian Living*. New York, 1947.
Miller, Raymond W. *Monsignor Ligutti: The Pope's County Agent*. Washington, D.C., 1981.
Miller, William D. *A Harsh and Dreadful Love: Dorothy Day and the Catholic Worker Movement*. New York, 1973.
The Mind of Christ: An Annotated Bibliography for Catholic Action. Chicago, 1953.
Murphy, J. Stanley, ed. *Christianity and Culture*. Baltimore, Md., 1960.
Newman, Jeremiah. *What Is Catholic Action?* Westminster, Md., 1958.
Novak, Michael. *The Open Church*. New York, 1964.
_____, ed. *A New Generation—American and Catholic*. New York, 1964.
O'Brien, David J. *American Catholics and Social Reform: The New Deal Years*. New York, 1968.
_____. *The Renewal of American Catholicism*. New York, 1972.
O'Dea, Thomas F. *American Catholic Dilemma*. New York, 1958.
O'Gara, James, ed. *The Layman in the Church*. New York, 1962.
Ong, Walter J. *Frontiers in American Catholicism: Essays in Ideology and Culture*. New York, 1957.
_____. *American Catholic Crossroads*. New York, 1959.
Putz, Louis. *The Modern Apostle*. Chicago, 1957.
_____, ed. *The Catholic Church, U.S.A.* Chicago, 1956.
Rawe, John C., and Ligutti, Luigi G. *Rural Roads to Security: America's Third Struggle for Freedom*. Milwaukee, 1940.
Reid, Elizabeth. *I Belong Where I'm Needed*. Westminster, Md., 1962.
Riga, Peter. *Catholic Thought in Crisis*. Milwaukee, 1963.
Roche, Douglas L. *The Catholic Revolution*. New York, 1969.
Rodriguez, Alonso. *The Practice of Christian and Religious Perfection*. Chicago, 1929.
Sheed, Frank J. *Sidelights on the Catholic Revival*. New York, 1940.
_____. *The Church and I*. Garden City, N.Y., 1974.
Sorokin, Pitrim A. *The Crisis of Our Age*. New York, 1941.
Tavard, George. *The Church, the Layman, and the Modern World*. New York, 1959.
Thorman, Donald J. *The Emerging Layman*. Garden City, N.Y., 1962.
Thornton, Francis B., ed. *Return to Tradition*. Milwaukee, 1948.
Todd, John. *Problems of Authority*. Baltimore, Md., 1962.

Vaillancourt, Jean Guy. *Papal Power, A Study of Vatican Control over Lay Elites*. Berkeley, 1980
Van der Plas, Michel, comp. *Uit het Rijke Roomsche Leven: en Documentaire over de Jaren 1925–1935*. Utrecht, no date.
_____ and Suer, Henk, eds. *Those Dutch Catholics*. London, 1967.
Vann, Gerald. *The Water and the Fire*. New York, 1954.
Von Le Fort, Gertrud. *The Eternal Woman*. Milwaukee, 1954.
Wakin, Edward, and Scheuer, Joseph. *The De-Romanization of the American Catholic Church*. New York, 1970.
Ward, Leo R. *Catholic Life, U.S.A.: Contemporary Lay Movements*. St. Louis, 1959.
_____, ed. *The American Apostolate*. Westminster, Md., 1952.
Ward, Maisie. *Be Not Solicitous*. New York, 1953.
Weaver, Mary Jo. *The Catholic Women: A Contemporary Challenge to Traditional Religious Authority*. San Francisco, 1985.
Weyand, Norman, ed. *The Catholic Renascence in a Disintegrating World*. Chicago, 1951.
Wills, Gary. *Bare Ruined Choirs*. Garden City, N.Y., 1972.
Witte, Raymond P. *Twenty-Five Years of Crusading: A History of the National Catholic Rural Life Conference*. Des Moines, Iowa, 1948.
World Crisis and the Catholic: Studies Published on the Occasion of the Second World Congress for the Lay Apostolate, Rome. New York, 1958.
Yzermans, Vincent A. *American Participation in Vatican II*. New York, 1967.
_____. *The People I Love: A Biography of Luigi G. Ligutti*. Collegeville, Minn., 1976.

Articles

Austin, Leonard. "A Catholic Culture for America." *Integrity* 1 (July 1947): 12–23.
Bentley, Sally, and Randall, Claire. "The Spirit Moving: A New Approach to Theologizing." *Christianity and Crisis* 34 (February 4, 1974): 3–7.
Blomjous, Joseph J. "The Lay Apostolate." *Catholic Mind* 53 (April 1955): 193–98.
Brien, Dolores Elise. "Advertising and the American Woman." *Integrity* 1 (July 1947): 34–37.
_____. "The Catholic Revival Revisited." *Commonweal* 106 (December 21, 1979): 714–16.
Cogley, John. "Missionaries in Mufti." *Commonweal* 53 (March 23, 1951): 582.

Connolly, Francis X. "1950 – Crisis and Challenge." *Thought* 25 (March 1950): 8–20.

Dawson, Christopher. "Education and Christian Culture." *Commonweal* 59 (December 4, 1953): 216–20, and 59 (February 26, 1954): 526–27.

_____. "Future of Christian Culture." *Commonweal* 59 (March 19, 1954): 595–98.

_____. "Catholic Culture in America." *Critic* 17 (June-July 1959): 7–9, 58.

Dwyer, Robert J. "The American Laity." *Commonweal* 60 (August 27, 1954): 503–6.

Geaney, Dennis J. "New Frontiers for the Layman." *America* 105 (June 10, 1961): 423–25.

_____. "The Chicago Story." *Chicago Studies* 2 (Winter 1963): 287–300.

Gleason, Philip. "In Search of Unity: American Catholic Thought, 1920–1960." *Catholic Historical Review* 65 (April 1979): 185–205.

_____. "A Browser's Guide to American Catholicism, 1950–1980." *Theology Today* 38 (October 1981): 373–88.

Graham, Robert A. "The Laity, the Council, and the New Apostolate." *America* 105 (May 6, 1961): 246–49.

Grumbach, Doris. "Laymen Meet in Chicago: Last Look or First Hope?" *Commonweal* 88 (July 26, 1968): 487–89.

Hitchcock, James. "Postmortem on a Rebirth, the Catholic Intellectual Renaissance." *American Scholar* 49 (Spring 1980): 211–25.

Jung, Eva-Marie. "Laymen on the March." *Catholic World* 186 (January 1958): 259–65.

Lauer, W. G. "Christian Integralism." *Catholic Mind* 39 (June 8, 1941): 17–23.

McClory, Robert. "Hillenbrand, U.S. Moses." *National Catholic Reporter*, September 7, 1979, pp. 3, 38–39.

McKenna, Norman. "Pax Romana in America." *Columbia* 19 (October 1939): 12, 17.

Maestrini, Nicholas. "Lay Missionaries: Their Role and Goal." *America* 80 (April 2, 1949): 715–16.

_____. "The Laity, the Missions, and the Liturgy." *Orate Fratres* 23 (May 1949): 300–308.

Murray, John Courtney. "Special Catholic Challenges." *Life*, December 26, 1956, pp. 144–47.

Niebuhr, Reinhold. "The Catholic Hierarchy's Diagnosis of Our Ills." *Christianity and Crisis* 14 (December 27, 1954): 171–73.

O'Malley, Frank. "The Culture of the Church." *Review of Politics* 16 (April 1954): 131–54.

Putz, Louis J. "An Emerging Theology." *Commonweal* 66 (August 23, 1957): 510–12.

———. "Reflections on the Role of the Laity." *Perspectives* 5 (July-August 1960): 13–16.

Reid, Elizabeth. "Challenge to the Laity." *Perspectives* 5 (March-April 1960): 7–19.

Reinhold, H. A. "Secular and Liturgical Civilization." *Orate Fratres* 14 (October 27, 1940): 558-60.

———. "True Humanism: Liturgical Movement and the New Christendom." *Orate Fratres* 17 (April 18, 1943): 272-75.

Roche, Douglas L. "The New Boom in Lay Missionaries." *Sign* 38 (April 1959): 36–38.

Sheed, Frank J. "Catholic England: A Quarter Century Chronicle." *Thought* (June 1951): 267–78.

Sheerin, John B. "The Coming Era of the Layman." *Catholic World* 184 (October 1956): 1–5.

Skillin, Edward. "Why Rural Life?" *Commonweal* 41 (December 1, 1944): 166–69.

Stone, Geoffrey. "American Life and Catholic Culture." *Thought* 22 (December 1947): 679–87.

Thorman, Donald J. "Today's Layman, an Uncertain Catholic." *America* 116 (January 14, 1967): 39–41.

Waugh, Evelyn. "The American Epoch in the Catholic Church." *Life*, September 19, 1949, pp. 134–55. (Reprinted in Herr, Dan, and Wells, Joel, eds. *Through Other Eyes*. Westminster, Md., 1965.)

THE GRAIL MOVEMENT

Articles on the Grail

Alvarez, Silvester. "The Grail International Student Center." *Lamp*, August 1960: 12–13, 28, 30, 31.

"American Nurses Trained at Grailville Lay Mission School Leave for Africa." *Missionary Laity*, September 1952: 9–11, 23.

Antcliffe, Herbert. "A Dutch Catholic Pageant." *Ave Maria* 36 (July 9, 1932): 49–52.

Benziger, Marieli. "The Ladies of the Grail." *Grail* 24 (February 1942): 36–40.

Bogdan, Virginia. "The Grail Training Course." *Orate Fratres* 17 (September 5, 1943): 465–66.

Boland, E. "The Grail Movement." *Catholic Mind* 31 (August 8, 1933): 289–98.

Brien, Dolores, Elise. "The Grail Program for International Students." *Catholic Charities Review* 38 (January 1954): 7–10.

_____. "Foreign Students." *Integrity* 10 (January 1956): 30–35.

Brna, Vera. "Grailville School of the Apostolate." *Catholic Miss,* April 1951.

Buckley, Mary Imelda. "The Grail." *Union Catholique de Cooperation Interraciale, Annuaire 1955,* pp. 156–60.

"Building the City of Man." *Word* 4 (February 1967): 5–7, 17.

Byrne, Francis. "Revolution at Bristow." *Catholic Virginian* 20 (August 1945): 5, 31–33.

Chaney, Elsa. "Mission Ventures of the Grail." *Catholic World* 173 (August 1951): 152–57.

_____. "The Girl Next Door." *Sign* 31 (April 1952): 31–33.

_____. "This is Gabriel House." *Today* 8 (January 1953): 20–22.

_____. "Assignment in Hong Kong." *Sign* 33 (September 1953): 52–54.

_____. "Woman's Apostolate." *Ave Maria* 80 (July 17, 1954): 8–10.

_____. "The New Eve." *Ave Maria* 83 (March 1956): 16–17.

_____. "From All Walks." *Voice of St. Jude,* April 1957: 18–21.

"The Christian Conspiracy." *Orate Fratres* 18 (June 11, 1944): 367–70.

Collett, Sally. "I Live in an International Family." *St. Joseph Lilies,* 1953: 40–46.

Cunningham, Sarah. "The Grail is a Movement." *Church Woman* 31 (November 1965): 8–11.

Day, Dorothy. "Notes on the Way." *Catholic Worker* 9 (October 1943): 1, 2.

Dehner, Anthony (pseud.). "Grailville Lends a Hand." *Ave Maria* 83 (June 1956): 8–11, 30.

[Diekmann, Godfrey]. "The Apostolate." *Orate Fratres* 23 (October 2, 1949): 523–25.

Donoghue, Mary Kay. "The Woman in the Coffee Shop." *Way of St. Francis* 12 (October 1956): 49–55.

Dorff, Catherine E. "Home Making." *Land and Home* 9 (March 1946): 10–12.

Drabek, Josephine. "Rogations at Maranatha." *Land and Home* 9 (June 1946): 39–40.

_____. "Love Made Visible." *Land and Home* 8 (June 1945): 52–54.

_____. "Can Women Remake Latin America?" *Maryknoll* 48 (January 1954): 23–27.

Duddy, Mary Alice. "The Parable of the Bread." *Catholic Worker* 12 (July–August 1945): 4, 8.

Ford, Betty. "Motor-City Gateway." *Today* 12 (November 1956): 20–31.

Freking, Edward A. "Lay Apostles for the Overseas Missions." *Shield*, November 1949: 21–23.

Gallagher, Grace Elizabeth. "The Idea Behind the Grail." *Torch*, 1940.

———. "Rural Life School." *Catholic Worker* 9 (November 1942): 8.

———. "New Horizons." *Catholic Worker* 11 (December 1944): 8.

Geiger, Annette. "Grailville . . . In Loveland . . . In Ohio." *Christian Family*, September 1952: 9–11, 23.

[Grail 50th Anniversary]. *National Catholic Reporter*, July 7, 1971, p. 16.

"The Grail Girls." *Newsweek*, May 7, 1962, p. 82.

"Grail's Gail on the Nile." *Sign* 38 (April 1959): 38–42.

"Grailville Catholic Action Extraordinary." *Oblate World* 13 (April 1951): 14–17.

Hamilton, Stanley. "Something's Growing at Grailville." *Town and Country Church*, November 1945: 3–4.

Headapol, Marjean. "The Grailville School Story." *Organic Farming*, November 1953: 29–31.

Heiberg, Jeanne. "Art at Grailville." Supplement to *Catholic Arts Quarterly*, October 1957: 4–6.

Heywood, Robert B. "Spirit of the Grail." *Orate Fratres* 15 (June 15, 1941): 360–67.

Horst, Bernard. "Ladies of the Grail." *The Apostle of Mary* 34 (March 1943): 106–10.

International Party." *Jubilee* 6 (July 1958): 14–15.

Kalven, Janet. "Grail Spirit in Action." *Orate Fratres* 15 (June 15, 1941): 382–83.

———. "Grail Spirit: Christmastide at Doddridge Farm." *Orate Fratres* 16 (February 22, 1942): 185–86.

Kelly, Wynni. "Grailville, an Apostolic Adventure." *Christian Family*, January 1957.

Kimbell, Mary Anne. "Family Service." *Integrity* 7 (August 1953): 38–46.

"The Kind of Help Latin American Wants." *Shield* 35 (May 1956): 34–35.

Lane, Raymond A. "The General's Corner." *Maryknoll* 48 (January 1953): 13.

Lavanoux, Maurice. "Gather Them All Together." *Liturgical Arts* 22 (May 1954): 74–75.

———. [Photo Essay.] *Liturgical Arts* 30 (May 1962): 95–101.

"A Lay Leadership Course." *Orate Fratres* 23 (November 6, 1949): 544–48.

"Laywomen Rejoice." *America* 106 (February 3, 1962): 580.

McAllister, Joseph B. "The Ladies of Nazareth." *Catholic World* 146 (February 1938): 602–5.

_____. "Grail Movement." *Sign* 18 (March 1939): 474–76.

McCafferty, J. J. "Ladies of the Grail." *Catholic Charities Review* 24 (January 1940): 12–18.

McDermit, Marie Therese. "The Story of Grailville." *Catholic Nurse*, June 1954: 51–53.

_____ and Machan, Lorraine. "Assignment in Uganda." *Catholic Nurse*, September 1954: 12–21.

McGuigan, Mary. "The Women of Grailville." *Ave Maria* 81 (May 14, 1955): 8–11.

Machan, Lorraine. "Our Student Visitors from Asia and Africa." *Shield* 39 (May 1960): 2–3.

Maestrini, Nicholas. "Lay Missionaries." *Missionary Union of the Clergy Bulletin* 13 (March 1949): 61–67.

_____. "Invitation to the Lay Missionary." *Shield*, April 1949: 17–18.

_____. "Four Years with Lay Missionaries." *America* 86 (October 6, 1951): 12–14.

Morris, Gertrude. "Arabic with a New York Accent." *Catholic Miss*, June 1961: 9–14.

Mulkeen, Anne. "What to Do with Your Twenties." *Information*, December 1952: 44–48.

_____. "What Wonderful Work You're Doing." *Today* 13 (November 1957): 7–9.

_____. "Crossroads at Grailville." *Worship* 37 (November 1963): 650–55.

Myers, Donna. "The Grail Movement." *World YMCA Monthly*, April 1958: 96–98.

Nolan, Joseph T. "Grailville's Valiant Women." *America* 78 (October 4, 1947): 9–11.

"Nuns in Mufti." *Time*, July 24, 1941, p. 50.

O'G, J. "The Spirit of Personal Service." *Catholic Charities Review* 38 (January 1954): 7–10.

"Old Barn Becomes a Handsome Chapel." *Architectural Forum*, October 1962: 138D–39.

Overboss, Joan. "The Christian Conspiracy." *Torch* 28 (June-July 1944): 11–12, 31.

_____. "Grail Offers Course in Lived Christianity." *Orate Fratres* 19 (May 20, 1945): 325–26.

Rasenberger, Dorothy. "Grail Program." *Catholic School Journal* 58 (December 1958): 65–66.

Reardon, Maurice E. "Graduates Who Follow the Grail (The Story of a Miniature International Alumnae)." *Catholic Alumnae Quarterly* 36 (March 1953): 5–12.

Reinhold, H. A. "Grailville." *Orate Fratres* 23 (November 6, 1949): 544–48.

Rogan, James. "Assignment to Africa." *Ave Maria* 89 (March 7, 1959): 21–23.

Ross, Eva. "Successful Youth." *Commonweal* 25 (November 6, 1936): 40–42.

_____. "Building for Useful Womanhood." *Catholic Women's World* 2 (September 1940): 15, 30.

_____. "The Leakage and a Dutch Experience." *Catholic Education Review* 39 (February 1941): 84–88.

Rowe, John G. "The Grail: The Modern Movement for Catholic Girls." *Ave Maria* 39 (April 7, 1934): 424–27.

Schaeffler, Eileen. "The Grail Movement—a Position Paper on Inter-American Collaboration." *Linacre Quarterly* 34 (November 1967): 346–47.

Shea, James M. "To Be Saints and Apostles." *Land and Home* 10 (June 1947): 46–49.

_____. "School for Apostles." *St. Joseph Magazine*, May 1949: 9–11.

_____. "Grailville." *Jubilee* 1 (September 1953): 35–41.

_____. "The Spirit of Advent." *Marianist*, December 1957: 13–21.

Sigur, Alexander O. "The Grail and the Christian Revolution." *Notre Damean*, May 1944: 23–26.

Suhor, Mary Lou. "Sodalist at Grailville." *Queen's Work* 55 (March 1963): 6–8.

_____. "Artists at Grailville." *Direction* 9 (June-July 1963): 15–19.

"The Supernatural Vocation." *Marianist* 43 (January 1952): 4, 30.

Tansey, Anne. "Horizons Unlimited." *Catholic Home Messenger*, December 1954: 16–17, 22.

Tully, Mary Louise. "I'm a Lay Apostle Overseas." *Shield*, January 1950.

Van Meer, H. "The Grail in Holland." *Homiletic and Pastoral Review* 36 (May 1936): 848–50.

Vincent, Amos. "Your Missions Are at Home." *Notre Damean*, November 1952: 15–20.

"Voyagers for Christ." *Shield*, April 1952: 11–12.

Wald, Barbara Ellen. "Wanted: a New Type of Woman." *Torch*, April 1943.

_____. "Grail Adventure." *Living Parish* 10 (April 1943): 10–13.

_____. "Today's Apostles." *Catholic Life Around the World* 1 (November 1954): 4–7.

Walker, Eleanor. "Music in the Grailville Program." *Musart*, February-March 1956: 25–26.

_____. "Music at Grailville." *Caecilia*, February 1964: 51–53.

Walsh, Kay, "Modern Women of the Grail." *Sign*, February 1964: 30–35.

"Women in the Lay Apostolate." *Franciscan Message*, October 1960: 167–70.

Grail Publications (Loveland, Ohio)

Advent Ember Days. 1948.

"*Are You Ready? A Four-Week Advent Program in Preparation for Christmas*. 1956.

The Christian Observance of Candlemas. 1950.

The Christian Witness: A Study-Action Guide for Young Women. 1955.

The Church Blesses Motherhood. 1957.

Donders, Rachel. *History of the International Grail, 1921–1979*. 1983.

Epiphany. 1945.

Families for Christ. 1949.

Hennessey, Nancy, and White, Carol. *Life in the Church, Discussion Sessions for High School CCD*. 1965.

Holy Spring (Lenten Sundays). 1949.

A Hymn to Work. Photographs by Abbé Albert Tessier; text by Josephine Drabek. 1948.

Hynes, Emerson. *Youth, You Have a Task Today*. No date.

The Laity and the International Scene. 1957.

The Laity Looks Eastward. 1950.

Let Us Baptize Thanksgiving. 1949.

Maestrini, Nicholas. *Lay Apostles in the Missions*. 1950.

———. *The Laity, Missions, and the Liturgy*. No date.

Mulkeen, Anne M. *New Life for New Year's Eve*. 1951.

Overboss, Joan. *The Church Year in a City Parish*. 1955.

The Paschal Meal: An Arrangement of the Last Supper as an Historical Drama. No date.

Pollmann, Jop, ed. *Laughing Meadows: A Collection of Folk Melodies Drawn from Traditional Sources*. 1947.

Program of Action: A Suggested Outline for the Lay Apostolate of Young Women. 1946.

Promised in Christ. 1955.

Restore the Sunday. Compiled and edited by Janet Kalven, Mariette Wickes, and Barbara Wald, in close cooperation with Mr. James M. Shea. 1949.

Songs of Unity. 1962.

This is Marriage. A Simplified Version of the Encyclical "Casti Connubii" by Pope Pius XI. Introduction by Emerson Hynes. 1946.

This is Social Justice. A Simplified Version of the Encyclical "Quadragesimo Anno" by Pope Pius XII. Introduction by Carl L. Bauer. 1946.

Towards a Christian Sunday: An Apostolic Program Based on the Volume, Restore the Sunday. 1949.

Towards a World Vision: An Apostolic Program. Written and compiled by Elsa Chaney and Donna Myers. Illustrated by Jeanne Heiberg. 1954.

Van Kersbergen, Lydwine. *The Normal School of Sanctity for the Laity.* 1949. Also published as *Living with the Church,* 1950.

———. *Woman, Some Aspects of Her Role in the Modern World.* 1956. Revised Edition, 1960.

Van Straelen, H. *Through Eastern Eyes.* Conferences given at the Lay Mission School, Grailville, Loveland, Ohio. Introduction by Rev. Msgr. Fulton J. Sheen. 1951.

Published Material by Members of the Grail

A. Books, Parts of Books, and Pamphlets

Buckley, Mary Imelda. "Christian Culture and Rural Life." In *Land and Life for Women,* pp. 4–8. Des Moines, Iowa, 1947.

Clark, Linda; Ronan, Marian; and Walker, Eleanor. *Image Breaking, Image Building: A Handbook for Creative Worship with Women of Christian Tradition.* New York, 1981.

Cooney, Nancy Hennessey, with Bingham, Anne. *Sex, Sexuality, and You.* Dubuque, Iowa, 1979.

Feast Day Melodies. Cincinnati, Ohio, 1957.

Fleischner, Eva. "The Religious Formation of Children in the Second, Third, and Fourth Grades." In *Modern Catechetics,* ed. Gerard Sloyan, pp. 125–53. New York, 1960.

———. *Auschwitz: Beginning of a New Era? Reflections on the Holocaust.* New York, 1974.

———. *Judaism in German Christian Theology since 1945: Christianity and Israel Considered in Terms of Mission.* Metuchen, N.J., 1975.

The Good News in Pictures. Twelve Prints of the Mysteries of the Redemption by Jeanne Heiberg, with commentary by Eva Fleischner. Introduction by Daniel Berrigan, S.J. Collegeville, Minn., 1962.

Gratton, Carolyn. *Trusting, Theory and Practice.* New York, 1982.

Hennessey, Nancy; Lark, Joan; and White, Carol. *Friendship.* New York, 1982.

Kalven, Janet. *The Task of Women in the Modern World*. Des Moines, Iowa, 1946.
_____. "Woman and Post-War Reconstruction." In *Catholic Rural Life Objectives*, pp. 1–4. Des Moines, Iowa, 1947.
_____. "Women in Rural Life." In *Rural America*, ed. Joseph V. Urbain and Raymond J. Wilson. Cincinnati, 1948.
_____ and Buckley, Mary I., eds. *Womanspirit Bonding*. New York, 1984.
Myers, Donna. "Our Father, Abraham." In *Generation of the Third Eye*, ed. Daniel Callahan, pp. 149–61. New York, 1965.
_____, comp. *Prayers for Christian Unity*. Introduction by Gregory Baum. New York, 1962.
Paulus, Trina. *Hope for the Flowers*. New York, 1972.
The Twelve Days of Christmas. Texts and photographs by Elsa Chaney; Layout and designs by Jeanne Heiberg. Collegeville, Minn., 1955.

B. Articles

Chaney, Elsa, "They Go Prepared to Foreign Lands." *Catholic World* 189 (June 1959): 11–14.
Fleischner, Eva. "The Formation of the Catechist." *Perspectives* 8 (September–October 1963): 146–50.
Hennessey, Nancy. "Customed-Tailored Teacher Training." *Living Light* 4 (Summer 1967): 6–11.
Malley, Gail. "Kom Kharib and the Magic Lantern." *Ave Maria* 90 (October 3, 1959): 11–14.
Siegmund, Peggy. "Is the Church Speaking Out in the South?" *Ave Maria* 104 (October 8, 1966): 14–16.
_____. "The New Breed of Catholic Editor." *U.S. Catholic* 32 (February 1967): 47–51.
_____. "Poverty from Behind the Plow: The Rural Generation and Spread of American Poverty." *Journal of Human Relations* 15 Second Quarter, 1967): 158–68.
Van Kersbergen, Lydwine. "A Program for Youth." *Catholic Mind* 50 (February 1952): 97–101.
_____. "Foreign Mission at Home." *Commonweal* 58 (April 10, 1953): 14–17.
_____. "African Journey." *Commonweal* 59 (November 20, 1953): 159–61.
_____. "African Notebook." *Voice of St. Jude* (March 1955): 13–16.

_____. "Woman's Role in the Vocation of Virginity." *Worship* 29 (April 1955): 240–53. (This and the following two articles were included in van Kersbergen's *Woman, Some Aspects of Her Role in the Modern World*.)

_____. "The Search for Woman's Role." *Catholic World* 181 (September 1955): 431–36.

_____. "Toward a Christian Concept of Woman." *Catholic World* 182 (October 1955): 6–11.

_____. "New Frontiers." *Commonweal* 66 (August 23, 1957): 516–19.

_____. "Growth of the Lay Apostolate." *Commonweal* 67 (January 10, 1958): 381–83.

_____. "The Netherlands Have a New Catechism." *Living Light* 4 (Summer 1967): 100–103.

Wald, Barbara Ellen. "Brazil's New Women." *America* 98 (February 8, 1959): 537–39.

Unpublished Material

A. Archives

Archives of the Grail in America, Grailville, Loveland, Ohio
Archives of the Archdiocese of Cincinnati, Cincinnati, Ohio
    Grail Files
The Marquette Archives, Marquette University, Milwaukee, Wisconsin
    The Dorothy Day-Catholic Worker Collection
    National Catholic Rural Life Conference Archives
Archives of the Catholic University of America, Washington, D.C.
    Grailville Institute File

B. Dissertations

Bulte, Frederica C. "The Grail Youth Movement in the Netherlands." (M.A.) Catholic University of America, 1957.
Robb, Dennis Michael. "Specialized Catholic Action in the United States, 1936–1949: Ideology, Leadership, and Organization." (Ph.D.) University of Minnesota, 1972.
Sparr, Arnold. "The Catholic Literary Revival in America, 1920–1960." University of Wisconsin-Madison, 1985.

C. Manuscript

Lauscher, Gerti. "The Grail of Wheat in the Soil." [The Hague, 1980].

D. Personal Papers

Monsignor James P. Coffey, Bay Shore, New York
Daniel and Mary Cecilia Kane, Loveland, Ohio

E. Interviews

   Author with:

Dolores Elise Brien, October 16, 1981
Mary Imelda Buckley, October 8, 1980
James F. Coffey, May 20, 1980
George V. Fogarty, April 7, 1981
Maria J. A. Groothuizen, August 8, 1980
Bernhard and Patricia Hutzel, April 28, 1980
Janet Kalven, April 19, 1980
Daniel and Mary Cecilia Kane, June 19, 1980
Mary Catherine Leahy, April 18, 1980
Grace Elizabeth Rogan, April 19, 1980
Eileen Schaeffler, June 19, 1980
William and Mary Schickel, May 27, 1980
James and Catherine Shea, April 16, 1980
Lydwine van Kersbergen, August 5–7, 1980

   Sharon Thomson (tape recording, Grail Oral History Project) with:
Mary Louise Tully, July 1979.

Index

225